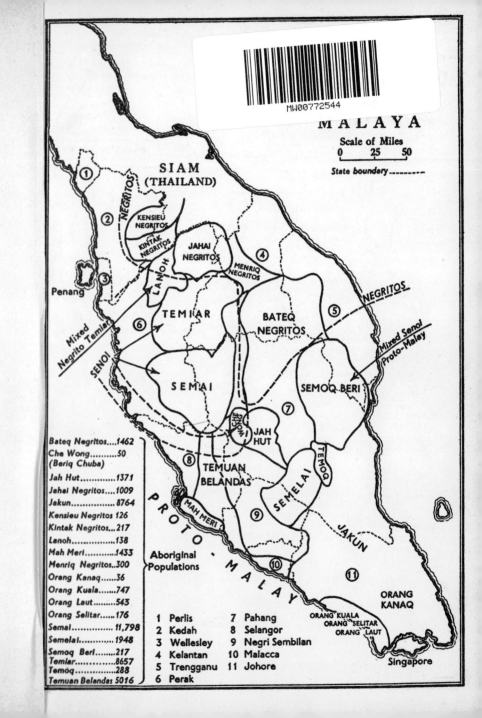

MALAYA

Scale of Miles

0   25   50

State boundary ----------

SIAM
(THAILAND)

NEGRITOS

KENSIEU
NEGRITOS

KINTAK
NEGRITOS

JAHAI
NEGRITOS

MENRIQ
NEGRITOS

Penang

LANOH

Mixed
Negrito Temiar

SENOI

TEMIAR

BATEQ
NEGRITOS

NEGRITOS

Mixed Senoi
Proto-Malay

SEMAI

SEMOQ BERI

JAH
HUT

TEMUAN
BELANDAS

SEMELAI

TEMOQ

PROTO - MALAY

MAH MERI

JAKUN

ORANG
KANAQ

ORANG KUALA
ORANG SELITAR
ORANG LAUT

Singapore

Bateq Negritos....1462
Che Wong...........50
(Beriq Chuba)
Jah Hut.............1371
Jahai Negritos....1009
Jakun...............8764
Kensieu Negritos 126
Kintak Negritos...217
Lanoh...............138
Mah Meri...........1433
Menriq Negritos..300
Orang Kanaq.......36
Orang Kuala.......747
Orang Laut.........543
Orang Selitar......176
Semai...............11,798
Semelai.............1948
Semoq Beri........217
Temiar.............8657
Temoq..............288
Temuan Belandas 5016

Aboriginal
Populations

1 Perlis   7 Pahang
2 Kedah   8 Selangor
3 Wellesley   9 Negri Sembilan
4 Kelantan   10 Malacca
5 Trengganu   11 Johore
6 Perak

£10-95

PAT NOONE

DENNIS HOLMAN

NOONE OF THE ULU

With a Foreword by

Field-Marshal Sir Gerald Templer,

G.C.B., G.C.M.G., K.B.E., D.S.O.

SINGAPORE
OXFORD UNIVERSITY PRESS
OXFORD NEW YORK
1984

Oxford University Press

Oxford London New York Toronto
Kuala Lumpur Singapore Hong Kong Tokyo
Delhi Bombay Calcutta Madras Karachi
Nairobi Dar es Salaam Cape Town
Melbourne Auckland

and associates in
Beirut Berlin Ibadan Mexico City

OXFORD is a trademark of Oxford University Press

First published by William Heinemann 1958
First issued in Oxford in Asia Paperbacks in 1984

ISBN 0 19 582610 8

PUBLISHER'S NOTE

We have been informed by both William Heinemann Ltd., the original publishers, and by the
author's former agent, Curtis Brown, that rights in
this book reverted to the author several years ago.
We have been unable to contact the author. If he or
his Estate would get in touch with Oxford University Press at the address given on the title verso, an
agreement can be drawn up

Printed in Malaysia by Peter Chong Printers Sdn. Bhd., Ipoh
Published by Oxford University Press,
10, New Industrial Road, Singapore 1953

CONTENTS

v

CONTENTS

ILLUSTRATIONS

AUTHOR'S NOTE

This book could not have been written without the assistance of a large number of people, and I would like to express my gratitude to:

The Federal Government of Malaya for facilities; the Air Ministry for facilities; the War Office for information and advice; Field-Marshal Sir Gerald Templer for kindly writing the fore-word; Mr. Richard Noone and personnel of the Department of Aborigines for their help and co-operation; R.A.F. air-crews in Malaya for flying me to deep jungle forts and on operational missions; personnel of the Department of Information, Federation of Malaya; personnel of the Malayan Police; Colonel George Lea, Major John Slim and Major John Cooper of 22 S.A.S. Regiment; the Hon. To' Pangku Pandak Hamid bin Puteh Jali of Lasah; Dr. Kilton Stewart; Mrs. Norah Noone; Mr. and Mrs. Dennis Trumble; Mr. John Davis; Mr. Robert Chrystal; Mr. John Creer; Mr. Michael Tweedie; Mr. Peter White; Mr. Harry Miller; K. C. Arun; Mr. Richard Corfield; Ché Puteh bin Awang; the shaman Angah Sideh; Penghulu Toris; Penghulu Pangoi; Penghulu Asoh; Penghulu Ngah; and Akob.

It has been necessary to disguise the names of certain people in this story. This is for reasons of security, and also to safeguard them and their relatives from the vengeance of the Communist terrorists.

Field-Marshal Sir Gerald Templer

Let me be quite frank. The only reason why I directed that something must be done about the aborigines of Malaya was that they had become a vital factor in the Emergency.

Our job at the time was to destroy the terrorists, and this was absorbing all our available resources. We certainly had too much on our hands to think of the welfare of primitive tribes, however desirable it might be from an administrative point of view. In fact, nobody had ever bothered much about them, that is except for one man, a young anthropologist named Pat Noone. He had discovered a tribe inhabiting the deep jungle of the main range, which is some of the most difficult and inaccessible jungle in the world. He had lived among them, and he had disappeared mysteriously.

I had naturally heard of Pat Noone—he had created an extraordinary legend in Malaya—but I only became aware of his tribe when large numbers of the terrorists withdrew into their Shangri-La. The terrorists then dominated the aborigines, and made vital tactical use of their wonderful skill and jungle craft. At the best of times it had been difficult for our patrols to make contact with the enemy, who kept out of fights unless they had superiority in numbers and the advantage of surprise; but now contact became virtually impossible. The terrorists' aborigine allies would not only warn them of the approach of a patrol, but lead them away to safety by secret paths known only to the guides. Moreover, the terrain was unsuited for the deployment of troops in large numbers.

The obvious solution was to deny the aborigines of the deep jungle to the terrorists. But how was this to be done, and who was going to do it? Luckily, Pat Noone's younger brother Richard was on my staff in Kuala Lumpur at the time: he was an anthropologist himself, with some experience of Malayan aborigines before the war, and I put him in charge of the whole campaign to win over these people to our side. How he succeeded and what he uncovered about Pat is the substance of this story.

It is an inspiring story, for its heroes, first Pat, then Richard, were dedicated men. Their combined work has been of inestimable value, because the terrorists had got themselves into a position they could have held indefinitely at a relatively low cost to themselves, while at the same time draining the country's resources and perpetuating a state of affairs almost intolerable to most people. The terrorists would still be cocking a snook at the Security Forces, if Pat Noone had not provided the clue to the tribal personality of the remarkable people who inhabit the main range, and if Richard Noone had not been available to interpret his brother's work: for Pat left little that was published, and Richard had to depend largely on letters and other private documents in his possession. There are still terrorists in the jungle, and their destruction will involve a lot of hard work and sacrifice. Yet with all but a few of the aborigines now working for us, the deep jungle is no longer the secure haven it used to be for the hunted. Indeed, a high percentage of the eliminations over the last four years have resulted from information supplied by the aborigines.

This is a book about a primitive jungle people whose timeless, idyllic pattern of life was suddenly and brutally violated by politics and killing. Dennis Holman, the author, has written of them with real sympathy. He has filled a wide canvas with the fruits of his diligent research, and his narrative is intensely readable. One is seldom out of the jungle reading this book, but it is not so much the dank, steamy low-lying type, as the higher-level jungle with its delightful valleys, waterfalls and chattering streams, and, higher still, its cold, wet moss forests.

In order to observe the hill stock aborigines at first hand, and to help investigate Pat's disappearance, Dennis Holman and Richard Noone went up into the headwaters of one of the main rivers of the range, and they came out by rafting from the level where the river is navigable—a dangerous journey in view of the terrorists, as indeed it proved.

It is of course arguable whether the aborigines have gained from the welfare benefits they have received since they came over to Government. The big monetary rewards some of them earned for assisting the Security Forces must have affected their primitive sense of values. A number have had glimpses of town life, and the outcome has not always been to the credit of civilisation. The policy is to try wherever possible to restore the groups to their tribal life; when times are happier, the intention is to leave them undisturbed. Yet they should never again be forgotten as they have been in the past. It is fitting that they should continue to enjoy at least the medical advantages which they would not have known if their welfare had not suddenly become a matter of expediency.

The aborigines of Malaya have demonstrated their military value. They could be integrated into the defence plans of the country, for in the event of an invasion a most effective resistance could be continued with their goodwill and co-operation.

There is another lesson to be learnt from the last few years. We have seen how the aborigines of Malaya became dominated by the Communists and exploited to the detriment of the country. What has happened in Malaya could happen elsewhere in South-East Asia, because there are over five million primitive peoples of one sort or another inhabiting the jungles that cover most of the land in that part of the world. A large proportion of these ethnic minorities have been of little interest to anybody except the anthropologist. It would seem there is a need now of extending to them a wise and sympathetic administration.

Since August 1957 the Federation of Malaya has been an independent country. I know very well that its new government will continue to have the interests of these simple people at heart.

30th December 1957.

PROLOGUE . THE ASSIGNMENT

For nine months in 1953 Richard Noone had been Secretary to the Federal Intelligence Committee in Kuala Lumpur, Malaya. One morning early in October the telephone rang on his desk and he picked it up.

"Noone speaking."

"Chief Secretary here," a voice said. "General Templer has asked me to inform you of your new appointment. You are to take over the Department of Aborigines."

This was good news for Richard, though not entirely unexpected. The post had been vacant for four months, since the death of the previous head of the department. Richard knew that Templer particularly wanted him for the job, as he was a qualified anthropologist and had worked with his brother among Malayan aborigines before the war. There had, however, been a stumbling block—the Director of Intelligence, who had strenuously resisted the idea of losing one of his key men. But now he was away on tour, and it looked as though Templer had made swift tactical use of the opportunity.

"I hesitate to congratulate you," the Chief Secretary went on. "The General has decided that the Department of Aborigines is to play a vital new rôle in his future operations against the terrorists. He has a special assignment for you. I'll wish you luck. You'll need all you can get."

Later that day Richard was summoned to King's House, which Templer occupied in his dual rôle of High Commissioner and Director of Operations. He was at his desk in the long room that served both as an office and a top-level conference chamber. On the walls were operational maps stuck thickly with coloured pins.

"Noone," the General said, after he had asked his visitor to sit down, "the Chief Secretary has told you of your appointment."

"Yes, sir."

"Are you entirely happy about taking it on?"

"There's nothing I'd like better, sir."

Templer looked at him searchingly. The man he wanted had to combine scientific knowledge and experience of aborigines with administrative ability. Templer particularly did not want a desk man, and he had said so. However, he seemed satisfied with his choice, because he went over to one of the wall maps and swept his hand up the mountainous spine of Malaya. He slapped the upper vertebræ of Perak, Kelantan and Pahang, the area known as the deep jungle.

"The aborigines in there have become the most serious problem of the Emergency," he said. "They have been dominated by the Communists, and are helping them, in some cases fighting for them." Templer came back to his desk. He went on: "It's going to be your job, Noone, to win those aborigines in the deep jungle over to our side."

Richard was a little bewildered when eventually he left King's House and drove back to his office. He spent the rest of the day conscientiously preparing to hand over to his successor, so that it was nearly eight o'clock before he went home to his flat in a rambling, wooden-slatted house in Bellamy Road.

Richard had a shower. He changed into a clean cotton vest and checked sarong, then went bare-footed into his large, high-ceilinged living-room furnished in light, honey-coloured *rotan*. In the jungle *rotan* is a feathery palm that coils for hundreds of feet through tangled undergrowth and up the giant trees in search of sunlight, but in Richard's living-room the tough, rope-like stem formed the basis of a suite of tropical furniture. On the walls were Bugis spears and round shields, Malayan *kris*, aborigine blow-pipes and poisoned dart quivers, primitive musical instruments, paddles, axes, ornaments, fetishes. In a glass cabinet were *objets d'art* his father had collected in India and the Far East, and a monkey-tooth necklace Richard himself had acquired on his first trip into the jungle when he was eighteen. A crowded book-case reflected his scientific interests. It was a man's room in which the only feminine touch, a bunch of zinnias in a brass vase on the writing-desk, had been added by the cook's wife, who cleaned the flat and washed Richard's clothes. Presently the cook came in, a kindly old Javanese.

"Ali, get me a *stengah*," Richard said in Malay.

He was sitting near one of the barred windows, smoking a cigarette, when Ali returned with a whisky in a tumbler full of soda, and placed it on a table near the window. He padded softly out of the room.

Richard sipped his whisky. He was thinking of the assignment General Templer had given him, and wondering how he should start to tackle it. His brother Pat would have known exactly what to do, for he had understood the aborigines better than any man. But Pat had disappeared mysteriously in the jungle, and for years a number of people had been trying to find out what had happened to him. Richard had always wanted to investigate the matter himself. His new job, which would take him back into the jungle a great deal, would provide him with an ideal opportunity.

He stubbed out his cigarette in an ash-tray, and went to the writing-desk, where he unlocked one of the drawers and took from it a thick file in a pink folder with the inscription 'H. D. Noone' in neat block capitals. The initials were those of his brother, whose names, Herbert Deane, bestowed at his christening in Madras, had never been used by the family or friends and acquaintances as far back as Richard could remember. For some unknown reason Herbert Deane Noone had acquired the name Pat. Possibly it was more descriptive of the personality that emerged from the christening robes. Whatever it was, 'Pat' had stuck.

The file contained newspaper articles describing his brilliant study of the Temiar, a light-skinned, wavy-haired race of aborigines inhabiting the deep jungles of the Main Range of the Peninsula.

Before Pat had penetrated to their remote settlements the Temiar were unknown. He had revealed them as an anthropological phenomenon—primitives whose material culture had not progressed for thousands of years, yet who lived in perfect harmony with themselves and their environment. They were so wise and well-adjusted that violence and crime were practically unknown among them. Pat had called them the Happy People. He had studied their customs, their beliefs and their psychology, and learned their language, which had never previously been recorded. He had become their friend and champion, and had married a beautiful Temiar girl, the ward of a powerful shaman or medicine man.

A Singapore newspaper had first referred to him as Noone of the Ulu—*ulu* being the Malay word for the upper reaches of a river and used generally to mean the interior jungle. It was apt, and Pat, who was always prepared to live the part, had become a legend in Malaya before he was twenty-five.

In the file were papers Pat had read to learned societies, copies of reports he had submitted to Government, letters he had written, documents relating to his mysterious disappearance in the jungle. There were a few photographs. Richard glanced through them, stopping at a portrait of a girl with bared breasts and lustrous, wavy hair falling about her shoulders. On the back of the picture was a single word—'Anjang'.

Anjang! The girl's name evoked the sound of her laughter ringing through Pat's house in Taiping, and the jungle songs with which she beguiled the "whisky hour", as he called it, when the sun set behind the tall trees and bamboo clumps at the lake's edge in that beautiful old town.

Richard remembered how her dark eyes shone and how graceful her movements were when she waited on Pat: it had seemed as if she was putting all she had into such simple gestures as striking a match and holding out the flame for him to light his pipe. Pat would be reclining in a long, low *rotan* chair, with his bare feet up on its extended arms, while the soft evening faded and darkness blurred the scene around them on the lawn. A few yards away an aborigine brave named Uda would be twanging softly on a *rangoin*, a Jew's harp made from the midrib of a langkap palm.

The memory of it suddenly brought the sound vividly back to Richard. There had always seemed a touch of mockery in Uda's playing of the *rangoin*, but then the *rangoin* is a mocking instrument.

The file never failed to conjure up the past, and the aborigines who had been Pat's life. But in it too was all the basic information Richard required to enable him to produce a satisfactory plan for General Templer. These were the very aborigines who had to be won over, and here was a record of how Pat had approached them and gained their confidence twenty years before.

The only difference was that Pat's Happy People were now dominated by the Communists. Some were armed and had been known to shoot at police or military patrols on sight. But fundamentally they were the same Happy People. Their character and reactions would not have changed.

Richard replaced the photographs and took the file back to his chair. He gulped down the remainder of his whisky, opened the folder again, and began reading the first letter Pat had written to his parents from Taiping, telling them of his new job and plans for his first expedition into the jungle.

Richard was going back to the source. He felt Pat would not let him down.

PART ONE . THE LEGEND

*

1 . The Wooing

Pat was the eldest of four children of Herbert Vander Vord Noone and his wife Norah: then came two girls, Sheelah and Doreen, and finally Richard, ten years younger than his brother. H.V., as the head of the family was known to the others, had made a fortune trading in India as a member of the firm of Shaw Wallace & Company, East India merchants, but had been forced through ill-health to retire at the age of forty-four.

In 1919 he had bought a house in Dymchurch, between Folkestone and Dungeness, and settled down to a life of study. However, the Kentish coast proved too cold and windy for him, and the Noones moved to France in search of warmth and sunshine. For a while they lived on the Brittany coast, then they moved down to the Pays Basque, to St. Jean de Luz.

At that time H.V. was immersed in a study of Buddhism, though his interest was steadily being diverted to prehistory. He began visiting various archæological sites, excavating in a small way, and was fascinated by what he found. One day his wife picked up a flat piece of schist and passed it to him, thinking it might be of interest. He was about to throw it away, when he turned it over and saw on the back a wonderful engraving of a reindeer. It turned out to be a palæolithic relic of the Magdelenian Period, and is now in the museum at Les Eyzies in the Dordogne Department in central France.

Later H.V. took his family to stay at Les Eyzies, which is regarded as the capital of the prehistoric world, where habitation layers have been exposed that go back to the dawn of human history. Here the Noone children spent most of their school holidays. H.V. would hire a car and the family would set out for a cave site with a picnic hamper and picks and shovels, and spend the day digging for flint and bone tools, while H.V. directed the excavation, telling them where to look and how to recognise specimens.

When the Noones went to London or Paris, H.V. always insisted that the museums should come first. They did not merely visit a museum, they had to 'acquire an intimacy' with it. The result was that although the girls were put off museums for life, both boys became absorbed.

The boys were educated in England, at Aldenham and Cambridge, and Richard, following his brother after an interval of ten years, found himself expected to live up to Pat's extraordinary athletic and academic record.

In 1931, Pat came down from Cambridge with a First in anthropology and was offered the post of field ethnographer to the Perak Museum in Taiping. As it was an opportunity to do original field-work in Malaya, he jumped at it.

Pat arrived in Malaya in January 1931, and spent the first few months learning Malay and reading all the available literature on the aborigines of the Peninsula. He described them in a letter to his parents:

"Ethnically these Sakai[1] can be divided into three main groups," he wrote. "In the north, north-east, and north-west are the Negritos, a race of negroid pygmies. In the south are the

[1] A general term for Malayan aborigines no longer in administrative or ethnographic use. The word *sakai* in Malay means 'dependant', a most unfair description of the jungle folk.

Proto-Malays—a racial hotch-potch who generally resemble the Malays and speak an archaic form of their language. But my interests lie in between, in the people inhabiting the vast block of mountainous jungle in the centre of the Peninsula. These are the Senoi, composed of two sub-groups—the Temiar in the north and the Semai in the south. My boss, Ivor Evans, has done some work on the Semai and he has visited some of the fringe Temiar groups in Perak. But the Senoi pie-crust has barely been broken, and of the Temiar virtually nothing is known."

It had been proposed that Pat should undertake a study of the Temiar, and apart from equipping himself academically for his first expedition into the *ulu* he was getting himself physically fit. "I'm attacking that layer of tissue acquired at Cambridge with fifteen minutes of Müller's exercises each day, and diet and vegetable laxative to keep me regular. There is a veritable cage of muscle round the insides now, which has formed from the fat that used to be there. I always do my exercises in front of a mirror, and you can imagine the joy to see the old lines coming back."

In May he went up to the Cameron Highlands to prepare for his first trip into the jungle. Tanah Rata, where he stayed at the rest house, was then only the site of the projected hill station of Malaya. Some of the jungle had been cleared, and the road was through, but there were no shops except for a few Chinese shanties. He was enthusiastic about the place.

"During the day it is beautifully cool and the nights are really cold: I cannot believe I am still in the tropics. But it is not only the climate that makes the Cameron Highlands such a wonderful spot. The soil produces the best quality tea with an astonishing display of orange tips, the coffee is of a very high grade, while the quinine plant matures bigger and two years in advance of that in the Dutch East Indies. Lemons and cabbages grow to a prodigious

3

size, and I have also seen excellent rhubarb and beetroot. Several Europeans here have chosen this area to settle in permanently after retirement, in preference to India, Burma or Ceylon. Land is only $4.70[1] an acre."

At Tanah Rata Pat arranged for the local aborigine chief, Dato Muda, to bring up a number of his men to meet him. They were engaged to carry his baggage, which he arranged in forty-pound loads, with the food packed for protection against the rain in tin-plate boxes he had had made in Taiping.

"I am steeled for a high purpose," he wrote to his parents the day before he left Tanah Rata. "I carry that pistol H.V. gave me, and a *parang* at my belt. I am taking a mandolin and a 'self-tutor' so as to while away a few hours if need be, and of course a few books, including the *Complete Works of Shakespeare* and Arnold's *Light of Asia*. So I shall be well accompanied."

Pat's first expedition was down the Bertam river from Lubok Tamang on the Cameron Highlands road. The Bertam is Semai country, but part of it touches the Temiar on its south side, and the border groups of the two are mixed. He hoped to make friends with these border Semai, who had been contacted previously, and through them to meet the Temiar on the upper slopes of the Kelantan Divide.

"I should explain that the only means of travelling through the deep jungle is by following the rivers," he wrote describing the expedition. "The path down the Bertam river began as a single foothold that mounted precipitous spurs and descended ravines made by fresh-water streams that rushed into the river. At first these streams were spanned by a slender bridge consisting of a sapling or tree trunk, which the barefooted Sakai streaked across, and I followed performing a circus feat of balancing in these

[1] One Malayan dollar = 2s. 4d.

4

confounded European shoes. But after a few miles the path petered out altogether, and we had to hack our way through the undergrowth and ford the ice-cold torrents. It was hard going, and we reached a tributary called the Lemoi after four days."

He had hoped to make his initial approach to a friendly group who lived at Kuala Lemoi, but the settlement there was deserted, so they made their way back up the Bertam river to another tributary, the Relong, where they camped for four days. Here various headmen and their retinues from the surrounding Semai groups came to pay their respects to Dato Muda, and Pat was able to meet them and offer *tembakau Jawa* (Javanese tobacco), which the Semai of this area smoked. But though he tried hard to make friends he got little response.

"I came up against that amazing sullen reserve which Evans and Schebesta[1] have deplored about the Semai. It makes me despair of ever making any headway. The most distressing thing about them is their appalling bad manners, accentuated perhaps by contrast with the Malays, who are gentlemen to the last degree in their kampongs, where their hospitality is magnificent. The only answers I could get from these Semai to my questions were '*Ta tahu*' ('I don't know') or '*Entah*' ('I am not sure').

They went farther up the Relong, and camped on a spur jutting out from Gunong Bujang, the dominant peak of the area. It was a beautiful site, overlooking the river, with an aborigine settlement on the opposite bank. But the group became particularly suspicious of this move, and overnight all the women and children disappeared. After a couple of days they returned. But the moment they saw Pat crossing the river to pay a visit, the alarm was given and they took to the jungle again with their babies and their back-baskets.

[1] Pater Paul Schebesta, the German anthropologist who was sponsored by the Vatican to do a study of Negritos in 1923.

Meanwhile he persevered with his courteous advances, and eventually the headman invited him into the long-house. Only one wizened old woman was there, and Pat made her a present of some tobacco. It was a start. After a day or so he noticed from across the river that some of the women were back. He sent further gifts of tobacco, and finally he was rewarded with another invitation. This time the entire group was in the long-house, and he counted eight families numbering some fifty adults and children.

A week later he emerged from the jungle with anthropometric measurements and notes on Semai customs, medicine and economic life, as well as a number of objects of their material culture for the Perak Museum.

Early in July Pat went back into the jungle. He again went down the Bertam river where he camped on a lip of sand at Kuala Cherkok. Here, for some reason he never discovered, he was snubbed outright.

There was a settlement on the opposite bank of the Telom, which at that point is about 250 feet wide and flowing over a sand and gravel bed. The moment Pat was seen coming across the river on a bamboo raft, the women and children took to the jungle, and the men met the visitors with sullen expressions. Pat went back to his camp and waited, hoping that the headman would sooner or later invite him to the long-house, or come over to the camp to smoke his tobacco. But over a week passed and still nobody came.

Then one day Puteh, Pat's young cook, came across a small hut in the jungle about half a mile from the settlement. He went in and was startled to find what he thought at first was a dead body. He was about to run out, when a slight movement stopped him, and he went closer. It was a young girl, her body covered with sores, and so emaciated that her ribs and the bones of her limbs stuck out. In a faint voice she asked for water.

Puteh brought her some, then he went to the long-house to find out who the girl was, and why she had been left in the hut without food or water. The headman replied that she was dying and that it was taboo for any of the tribe to go near her until she was dead.

When Pat heard what had happened, he went immediately to the girl, examined her, then sent a letter by runner to the medical officer in Tapah, describing her condition and asking for medicine. He and Puteh gave her food and nursed her, and when the runner returned with the medicine they began treatment for what was diagnosed as tertiary yaws. The girl got better. After a week she was so much improved Pat was able to get the taboo lifted so that she could be taken back to the long-house.

"She continues to make excellent progress," he wrote a few weeks later. "She now has a fine healthy skin, is well and plump, and can walk about. But I am giving her more treatment during convalescence to prevent a relapse and effect a complete cure. You can imagine how much this has enhanced my prestige."

The girl happened to be the daughter of the headman, Batu, who was so grateful to Pat for saving her that he personally introduced him to all the other headmen in the area. The result was that Pat was now accepted wherever he went, and the major obstacle to his research work, the difficulty he had encountered in making contact, was dramatically removed.

"I cannot describe the difference it makes to have the complete co-operation of these delightful people, and I am working in a high state of elation. I have been able to investigate both from inter-rogation and direct observation the grand plan of Sakai economics, magic, medicine and religion. I have made extensive notes on beliefs and ritual with regard to birth, marriage and death, and I have recorded some myths in the actual phrases of the natives, which I set down in phonetic transcription. I have charts of genealogy and the relationship system, and I am also working on a scheme provisioned by Thurnwald and the Dutch psychologist, Van Loon, who has worked in Java, for the collection of data on individual psychology, in order to work out racial psychology. My last fortnight here will be devoted to gathering the anthropometric data."

Meanwhile Pat had been making changes within his domestic staff, as he informed his parents: "I have had to dismiss my cook-boy Mat, but the vacancy has been filled admirably by Puteh bin Awang, who is a *kampong* Malay and only fifteen. The *kampong* Malay, unspoiled by the town, has all the instincts of a gentleman, and an amazing delicacy of manner. Add to this a presentable appearance, real charm, and the best Malay infatuation for cleanliness, and you will realise why I am content. His elder brother, in the Forestry Department, has one of the most magnificent figures of any Malay I have seen, and Puteh shows every sign of developing as powerfully. *Puteh* means white and indeed his complexion is honey-coloured, like most northern Malays nearly white under the arms."

Puteh had been quick to learn how to cook. "His gastronomic triumph is bread. Mrs. Drewett in Tanah Rata had given us a demonstration. She said that after three failures we ought to learn the pitfalls, but it was at Kuala Lemoi, at the second attempt, that he turned out crisp, golden-brown loaves of wholemeal bread, using one of my *barang*[1] tins as an oven. He has also made excellent cakes and a currant loaf. By the addition of an egg, and the use of milk, necessarily tinned, which has been allowed to stand a little in an open jug, he gets scones to rise to about an inch

[1] Baggage.

8

at the sides and more in the middle, beautifully soft and flaky."

Puteh worked for Pat for the next eleven years, sharing his adventures and often his confidence. Later he joined the Department of Aborigines where his special experience and contacts proved invaluable.

Another Malay in Pat's entourage on his early trips was a hunter named Pandak Ishmael. "Pandak is rather medieval in that he wears lustrous tapestries woven out of skins and feathers, the trophies of his berserking," Pat wrote. "His function is to keep me supplied with game and fish. The other evening he shot a young deer, and we had venison for dinner. Next morning the meat was smoked in bamboo into a pemmican, which preserved it. I left off after four days, though the Malays ate the meat safely for a week longer. The udder was delicious, and so was the brain.

"Actually I am cutting down my meat intake. Life becomes much simpler on the sexual and emotional side if one avoids too much meat in the jungle. I relish a large plate of hill rice, and now maize is ripening so I can add that to my diet. There are two or three native vegetables which are delightful. Tapioca, which tastes like potato, is excellent, and there is also the pith of the sago palm that can be made into a substitute for suet pudding with Lyle's Golden Syrup. Thus I am practically living on the jungle and eating the food of my savages. I have a bottle of whisky with me, but have not opened it as yet, which shows that I have not developed the prevailing habit for *stengahs* out here. However, I confess I have begun to smoke a pipe. In the evenings when the moon (now a silver crescent) shows up over the Telom, I light my pipe and we talk the talk of the camp-fire. I took to a pipe not without some deliberation, and use it for 'impressement' or demonstration during a chat. But when I put it back in my mouth the dash thing has gone out!

"Please excuse me if this letter seems a trifle disjointed, but the fact is that fellow Pandak, who is a splendid fellow and all that in his lucid moments, has been chanting one of those turpitudinously monotonous and nasally melancholy Malay songs. The darned thing never seems to vary more than a sixteenth of a tone all the way along, and it sounds as if some other Malay were titillating his liver with a red-hot needle. I hope to heaven my songs don't strike the Malays like the Malay songs strike me!"

Towards the end of his third month in the jungle Pat passed through a phase of depressions which settled on him in the afternoons. He had lost a lot of weight, and when at last he set out to return, the march back to Tanah Rata proved too much for him.

The day after he reached Tanah Rata he ran a temperature of 105°, with severe pains in his limbs and lower backbone. It was dengue, or 'break-bone' fever, and he was laid up in Batu Gagah Hospital for three weeks. However, he was fit enough early in December to motor to Penang to meet his mother and Sheelah, who had come out to spend the winter in Malaya.

---

2 . Along's Letter

In March 1932 Mrs. Noone and Sheelah returned to the South of France and Pat went back into the jungle down the Bertam river. He was accompanied by a young planter on leave named Bellamy-Brown.

The rains had been prolonged unaccountably that year, and the first night they had to change their camping site at midnight in drenching rain, as the river was rising so swiftly there was danger of their being flooded. They reached Kuala Relong, but the downpour persisted, holding them up for three days. They got tired of waiting for the weather to change, and continued the march in the rain to Kuala Bertam where they crossed from the north to the south bank of the Bertam, jumping from rock to rock with the foaming river in spate. They camped in the rain, and it went on raining for another three days, until they could stand it no longer and moved on to Batu's settlement at Kuala Cherkok. They camped on their old site, opposite the settlement.

Just as they were beginning their evening meal bees swarmed round the tents, and they quickly had to put out into midstream on a raft, leaving behind all they possessed. However, Batu offered them shelter in his long-house, where they spent three nights before the bees left the camp and it was safe to return.

They went on down to Kuala Misong, and camped on a pleasant sandy site. There was a settlement about a mile up the Misong, which they visited by a track leading past a salt lick. It was here one evening that they had a strange and rather terrifying experience.

"On our way up to the settlement that afternoon we had heard and smelt enough to realise that several elephants were in the neighbourhood. Returning to camp at dusk, we found a tree lying uprooted across our path, which had not been there before, and, thinking we had taken the wrong turning, we went off in search of the right way. The jungle round the salt lick was very much thinner than elsewhere: there were countless animal tracks, those of elephant and rhinoceros literally making avenues through the scrub. But again and again we found our progress blocked. Wisely we kept our heads and returned each time to a point on the route of which we were certain. Then to add to our difficulties it got dark. We had torches, but their light had the effect of distorting the pattern of the jungle, and we eventually ran up against the side of a hill, suddenly coming upon a great muddy pool still bubbling after the elephants had wallowed in it. The next moment we heard them, no more than a few yards away. We put out our torches and waited, scarcely daring to breathe. After some time they moved off and we tumbled to what had caused our predicament. The elephants had been responsible, because they had pushed over the tree that had made us go astray in the first place. What we had to do now was find it and continue over the other side. This was not easy, but it was not impossible, and we finally got back to camp, only to be greeted with warnings by the Malays that the elephants had been trumpeting on the ridge above the site.

"We had dinner and turned in, with our shot-guns ready, loaded with ball, but we had scarcely lain down when a tree fell with a crash not far from us. Then another crashed, and later yet another. It is not unusual to hear sounds of falling timber in primary jungle, but not so frequently. So when a few minutes later there were two more loud crashes in rapid succession, I quickly decided to move down to an aborigine shelter a little farther upstream, where our two rafts were moored; in an emergency we would be able to board the rafts and push off. However, we were not molested, and just as well, since the Telom was swollen with rain and moving very swiftly, and it would have been no easy matter negotiating the rapids that began just below the *kuala*."

They returned to Kuala Cherkok, and Batu took them up the Telom river to Kuala Rening, where they stayed with a border group, that of a wily old headman named Hondai. Batu said Hondai had influence with the Temiar chiefs up to and over the

Kelantan Divide, and that if he wished he could induce them to come down and meet the *tuans*.

Hondai was a chocolate-coloured little man with protruding teeth and thick woolly hair that clung close to his scalp: there was Negrito and probably even more primitive blood in his veins, resulting from intermarriage with Older Strata[1] groups. But his expression was almost a personification of cunning. He assumed wise attitudes, which certainly impressed most of the aborigines of the area, for they addressed him respectfully as 'Krani' which is the Malay word for 'clerk'.

Krani Hondai would not be rushed. For three days he smoked Pat's *tembakau Jawa* before he announced dramatically that he had had an auspicious dream and would send word for the Temiar to come down from the *ulu*.

Pat waited with mounting excitement. At last he was going to see representatives of this hidden race, whose existence had barely been recorded in anthropological literature. The current opinion was that the Semai were the purer stock. Evans had been impressed by the contrast between the slim, pale-brown Semai and some short, dark-skinned Temiar whom he encountered in Perak, and Pater Schebesta, the only anthropologist to have crossed the Temiar territory, had described them as "a large mixed tribe". But Pat had a hunch both were wrong.

He had traced Pater Schebesta's route and found that it lay mainly through areas bordering the Negrito country where it was very likely that Negrito admixture was strong; and Evans's observations in Perak had been confined only to the more accessible lower-level Temiar groups.

[1] The term Older Strata was used by Pat to distinguish the border lowland Senoi from what he called the Hill Stock. The Older Strata are representatives of the early types of man.

Many of the hill Semai were fine types and Pat felt that through natural selective processes the even more inaccessible Temiar of the higher interior would be finer still.

He was not disappointed by his first impression of the Temiar "as they stepped out of the gloom of the jungle into the sunlit *ladang*,[1] a line of braves led by an Adonis wearing a leafy head-dress and carrying his long blow-pipe lightly against his shoulder. He was Along, chief of the Ulu Rening, with Andor, his son-in-law, and some of their kinsmen. They were magnificent specimens, tall for Sakai (Along was five feet eight inches), slim-hipped, and a light fawn or pale cinnamon in colour. There was a refinement in their features that I had not seen in Sakai before, their faces being lozenge-shaped, with no marked depression at the root of the nasal bridge; the eyes were a deep brown, and the lips only of medium thickness."

Along later took Pat and his companion up into the *ulu* of the Rening river, and what they saw far exceeded Pat's expectations. "We went right up to the Divide and camped on the very border of Pahang and Kelantan—the first men other than Sakai to do this. We met Temiar still wearing bark cloth, who could not speak a word of Malay, and we sat at their evening dances, which were most spectacular. I was not able to make any anthropometric measurements, but my observations seem to bear out my contention that the Temiar are the purest Senoi stock racially and culturally. Their economy, ritual and beliefs open many fascinating courses of research for me to follow. The *ulu* itself was gloomy and strangely forbidding. We found the skeletons of dead elephants complete with gleaming ivory tusks, where they had died by the side of a rushing torrent. The ascent was not without its thrills. Twice we surprised a herd of elephants crossing the river. One night we were suddenly roused by the

[1] Jungle clearing.

14

A Temiar fishing in an upper valley of the River Plus. Picture taken by Pat on one of his earliest expeditions into unexplored territory

Pat (standing) with John Davis shortly after their arrival in Malaya 1931. Later Davis joined Force 136. One of his tasks was to find Pat

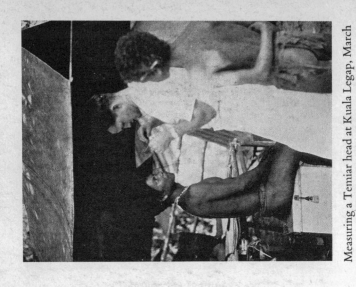

Measuring a Temiar head at Kuala Legap, March 1933. Pat sent this snap to his parents

Anjang, niece of the shaman Dato Bintang, on the day of her marriage to Pat in 1935

roaring and grunting of a large animal as it rushed past our camp:
it was a seladang, or Asiatic bison, that stampeded on smelling the
smoke of our fire. On another occasion I saw a tiger on the other
side of a stream, as he came down to drink the moment I also
descended to bathe. He bounded away, then a little later returned.
I thought he was going to cross on the stones, so I ran back and
fetched my gun but he sheered off.

"Like the Semai the Temiar live in groups of forty to a hundred
individuals, who occupy a large communal long-house constructed mainly of bamboo and leaf thatch. They practise a
shifting cultivation: every year they clear an area of jungle by
felling the trees and burning off the leaves and undergrowth, and
plant crops of tapioca, maize and hill rice between the fallen tree-
trunks.

"They hunt with the blow-pipe and poisoned dart. Along and
some of his relations took me hunting on one occasion, and I was
particularly impressed with their skill. They were moving
through the jungle like wraiths when suddenly Along stopped
and held up his hand. A small berry had dropped, indicating the
presence of a monkey in the branches high above. Slowly he
lifted the blow-pipe and put the ball-like mouth-piece into his
mouth, and with both hands cupped round his lips raised the long,
light barrel between his fingers till it was pointing almost
vertically upwards. There was a sudden contraction of his
stomach muscles which expelled the air from his lungs, and a dart
shot out faster than the eye could see. A few moments later there
was the sound of something falling through the branches,
followed by a thud as a furry body hit the ground. We ate it that
night for supper.

"Wild boar are hunted in a dangerous and exciting way. The
plantation had been fenced off, but on certain nights a gap would
be left in the fence for pig to come in and scratch up the large,

tuber-like tapioca roots. Men would sit up near the gap, and as soon as a pig or two had entered they would close the gap and go to bed. Next morning the young men would enter the plantation with spears and indulge in a wild game of pig-sticking on foot.

"In their social intercourse these people are extremely formal. No greeting passes between visitors and hosts. The visitors enter the long-house and sit down quietly near the doorway. For a while they are practically ignored. Then the headman asks casually if the rains of a few days before have made the paths slippery. That is the opening gambit and now the newcomers may explain why they have come. There are no hearty greetings, and news, good or bad, has to be broken gently."

Pat went on to tell his parents how the Senoi, in common with the other ethnic minorities in Malaya, had not discovered alcohol, but that they had however acquired the means of attaining a self-induced trance which not only provided a release of tension but played a profound part in the social and spiritual life of the group. Rhythm, he said, had a particular significance in their lives, and he speculated on the possibility of some relationship between this and the metronomic texture of many sounds in the jungle. He explained that when a child was born a rhythm was drummed close to its ear, softly at first, then progressively louder until it breathed.

"As you see, there are many interesting avenues of research for me to pursue, particularly those concerning their psychological and sociological development. Here I have come across evidence which suggests that I am on the verge of discovery. I have a hunch, dear parents, that I am about to make anthropological history. Although these primitives still practise a form of agriculture which is probably the earliest known in human history, they have an emotional maturity that is quite phenomenal. As far as I have been able to ascertain acts of violence and crime are unknown, and there is no memory of inter-tribal warfare.

"There is very little to choose between these Temiar and the Semai as far as their material culture is concerned. Ethnically they are linked. Many of their customs, dances and beliefs are identical. Yet there is no doubt which is the finer type. I have many friends among the Semai, but these Temiar are exceptional."

Bellamy-Brown had to get back and Pat decided to accompany him to the Cameron Highlands for a short break.

"Instead of returning by the Bertam, we went up the Telom to the Cameron Highlands road. No white man had previously seen those reaches of the Telom, and we found some glorious flat land full in the shine of the morning sun, with the Telom flowing softly over it like an English river, and no boulders or rapids (as elsewhere there are) to disturb the peace. Brilliantly plumaged birds, the like of which I have not seen in any book or museum, were abundant. We passed up granite gorges where the Telom descends in a series of giant steps in one waterfall after another, eighty or ninety feet in height, with crystal pools hollowed out of the rock between. There is a stupendous and violent beauty about these falls. At one of them the whole river crashes over in a single pouring, so that the spray rises up to the crest again. As we came up from below we could feel a rush of cool air being blown through the jungle a good hundred yards from the fall, while all the trees were weeping with ferns festooned from their branches. People in Tanah Rata were very interested when we told them what we had seen, and the find was reported in the *Straits Times*."

After a few days in Tanah Rata Pat returned to the Ulu Rening, where Along built him a stout bamboo cabin, to protect him at night from a man-eating tiger which had become a serious menace, and Pat continued his study of the Temiar. He emerged again about the middle of June, to find that Evans had applied to retire on pension. Soon Pat was able to inform his parents that his application had been accepted, and that he would succeed as officer-in-charge of the Perak Museum.

In August 1932 Pat began a series of expeditions into Kelantan, the true out-of-contact Temiar country. Between trips he re-provisioned in Tanah Rata, where in September he happened to meet the District Officer of Kuala Lipis, whose orbit of administration then included the Cameron Highlands and the valleys of the Bertam and the Telom. For some months Pat had been campaigning for recognition of the aborigines' inherent right to the jungles they inhabited. He had submitted a number of reports to Government on the distress caused to the jungle folk by the clearing and development of the Cameron Highlands, as the tea and market-garden estates were encroaching on hereditary tribal territories of groups whose ancestors had been there for centuries. Now he was able to plead the aborigines' cause in person.

"The D.O. was sympathetic, and asked what could be done in the circumstances. I said the Sakai simply wanted security, and suggested he demarcate an area beyond which Europeans in the hill station would not spread, and make this a properly constituted Sakai Reserve. He thought this was a good idea, and when I spread my map out before him he suggested the River Wi as the boundary, as far as the Misong, and stretching up from the Telom to the Kelantan border. I agreed right away, and thus a Sakai Reserve was created in this part of Pahang. The D.O. then said he felt it would be a good thing to make somebody chief over the reserve. I recommended Along from the Ulu Rening, and the D.O. made a note of his name, promising that he would have an appropriate letter of appointment signed by the Resident in about a month's time. That was a good morning's work."

But good not only for the aborigines. Fate was to use Along's letter of appointment as an instrument of poetic justice to save Pat's life.

He had gone up again into Kelantan, and was camped at the side of the Brok, the name for the Kelantan river at its source. One night torrential rain caused the river to rise some twenty feet while the camp slept. Pat was roused by the sound of water rushing against his tent, and shone his torch to find a number of his possessions floating beside his camp-bed. He gave the alarm. They just managed to save the tents and most of the food and baggage. But the medicine box was swept away irretrievably.

Later he wrote to his parents from Taiping: "When next we meet I will recount the incident and its sequel. How I went down with malaria and was racked with fever every other day, temperature 106° and no quinine; how I was unfortunately among a strange tribe who were afraid I was going to die, and having a dread of a dead man's ghost would not carry my things back to civilisation from Ulu Kelantan; how my Malays also went down and everything seemed hopeless; and how by the mercy of Heaven my friendly chief Along came over to greet me with his letter of appointment from the British Resident of Pahang, which guaranteed all the Temiar territory in Pahang as a reserve for the Senoi, Along himself being appointed chief by the Pahang Government. As this was entirely due to my proposals, and my work and reports, it was divine justice if you like. In two days he had organised the savages, and we were on our way to the Pahang border, Along hacking a path for us through the thick jungle. So I was carried on the shoulders of four Sakai, every jolt sending an arrow of pain from spleen to stomach.

"How we got to the Telom I do not know. But we travelled thus for seven days, and on the border at 5,000 feet I got a chill on my stomach through drinking cold water and was tortured by agonising stomach pains. These pains, which never left me for three days and nights, were nearly enough in my exhausted condition to drive me out of my mind, and I had not eaten solid food for ten days.

"When we were two days away from Tanah Rata I scribbled off a note to Hannyington[1] asking for quinine and telling him where I hoped to reach. Andor, the Rening chief's son-in-law, ran to Tanah Rata in *one* day, and brought back the medicines and a letter from Hannyington saying he would send a stretcher and some coolies down to the end of the mule track at Kuala Kial (below Drewett's place, and a half day's journey through jungle).

"Meanwhile I had been left near the Wi river with a day's journey to Lubok Nanga on the Telom river, our rendezvous for the medicines. Curiously enough, the only thing that worried me as I lay near a warming fire, trying to ease my pain, was the grief and trouble I would cause the family if anything happened; then my work—unfinished, the goal not yet reached; and lastly the untidiness of passing away like that. I thought of those lines of Kipling:

> If you can force your heart and nerve and sinew,
> To serve your turn long after they are gone,
> And so hold on, when there is nothing in you
> Except the Will which says to them: 'Hold on! . . .'

Bless Kipling. He knew the wilderness that surrounds a man away from his people when the grim tests of life arrive, and his words helped me, not only to support my own determination to survive, but to contend with the fatalism of my Malays. True

[1] J. F. Hannyington, the Assistant District Officer at Tanah Rata in 1932. He retired as British Adviser, Trengganu, in 1956.

Moslems, they lay inert under kismet, bemoaning the accumulation of ill-luck which had dogged us this month of November.

"Next morning I woke feeling less pain. The journey to Lubok Nanga took all day, and by evening the pain had gone completely. Lubok Nanga (The Dragon's Lair) is a great open space with tapering trees and shrubs growing on sandy soil, where the Telom in a big flood has deviated and left a lake. In this delectable flat spot we camped, and the next day Andor returned with the medicines and letters. I slept that night, the first for close on a fortnight, the sleep of the gods. I awoke very early, my whole body invigorated by the cool, fresh air of dawn. I walked out into the gathering light; to the east a soft pink glow heralded the rising sun. I saw my Sakai huddled round the flames of their fires in the leaf shelters. I heard them say, '*Tohat na med: saka senoi selamat!*' ('Our master is well: the Senoi land is safe!'). I wanted to pray, and I poured out thanksgiving: a solitary confession of my own humility, and joy at finding that my spirit was not to be easily broken.

"Later that morning I played the Interlude from Noël Coward's *Cavalcade*. The music of Elgar seemed to suit the jungle just then, and Coward's own spoken dedication at the end of the record struck a strangely apt note. Speaking of England he says: 'Let us drink to her sons, who made part of the pattern, and to the heart that died with them. Let us drink to the spirit of gallantry and courage which made strange heaven out of unbelievable hell.' With me it was perhaps not so much a case of 'gallantry and courage', but I had surely passed through 'unbelievable hell'.

"Andor had brought back some letters from Mummy, Sheelah and Doreen, wishing me many happy returns of my birthday. Here was a happy return indeed. A return from the darkness of the pit to a bravery of earth. I was overcome as I read of the

21

light-hearted hopes that I was well. How splendid to be able to read them."

Pat had discovered gold in the Ulu Kelantan—pieces of quartz he brought back were analysed by an engineer friend of his and found to possess a high content of the mineral. But he omitted to mention this in his report to the British Adviser, Kelantan.

"I am loath to say anything, as I don't want the Temiar to lose their territory," was the explanation he gave his parents. "These people look on me as a messiah, and I feel that my duty is towards them. . . . My love for them grows, and in this respect I feel I am fulfilling my obligation to anthropology."

It is likely that Pat first thought of marrying a Temiar girl as he lay resting in Tanah Rata for a few days after coming out of the jungle, because he spoke about it to Puteh, adding that it was the only way he could possibly get into the heart and mind of the Temiar.

"I know they like me and look up to me, but they still hold back," he said. "Now if I became a Temiar by marriage there would be no barriers. I would be party then to their most intimate secrets."

"*Tuan*, you honour me with this confidence," Puteh replied. "But surely a European girl would make you a more suitable wife?"

"Puteh, my work would not make me a suitable husband for a European girl."

"Yet to marry a European would be more suitable in outward form. *Tuan*, it might cause amazement and disapproval if you took an aborigine wife into the New Club."

"I would keep her in the jungle. I would live with her in a communal long-house, as one of the group. It would not be otherwise," Pat assured him.

Still Puteh shook his head. Although the discussion was purely academic, and Pat had not yet seen a Temiar girl he particularly fancied, Puteh did not like the idea of his *tuan* marrying into a race that the Malays considered beneath them.

Pat returned to Taiping about the middle of December, expecting a letter that would inform him of the date of his father's arrival in Penang: for months H.V. had been planning to winter in Malaya, and Pat had kept on his house, paying rent for it while he was in the jungle, so that they could live together comfortably. There was a letter from his mother waiting for him at the Museum, but the only news of his father was a postscript just briefly stating that the trip was postponed.

Pat was disappointed. However, an invitation to stay in Singapore came from an accountant named Oppenheim whom he had met in Tanah Rata, and Pat accepted. He had received a lot of newspaper publicity since his last expedition. One writer had suggested that "Noone of the Ulu" should be made Protector of Aborigines. Another had credited him with a beard and "colossal eccentricity". A third had qualified an otherwise glowing account of Pat's activities with the caution: "But is the sum of $1,000 a month, which represents the cost of Mr. Noone's expeditions in the jungle, warrantable during the present slump?"[1] So Pat was lionised when he was introduced to the social life of Singapore, and the holiday landed him in financial difficulties, regarding which an appeal went to H.V. for help.

Soon after Pat's return from Singapore he visited a Temiar group at a place called Jalong on the River Korbu in Perak. The group had a particular significance for Pat as it had recently been made accessible by a road cut from Sungei Siput, and several

---

[1] Actually Pat's salary and expenses averaged $560 per month.

estates had been opened up where previously there had been only primary jungle. Malays and Chinese were working on the estates, which meant that for the first time in their history the Temiar there had come into contact with cultures alien to their own. It was a similar situation to that to which the Semai groups in the Cameron Highlands had been exposed, and Pat wanted to see the effect of this culture contact on the Temiar.

He found a large, hybrid middle-level community, with Older Strata and Hill Stock in equal proportions. They were already comparatively sophisticated, the men wearing sarongs when not working, and the women well groomed, although their breasts were still uncovered. They grew a large variety of crops, including 'vegetables and fruit, and some of the men were *gembalas* (elephant-drivers): they had been formed into a unit known as the Elephant Patrol, the purpose of which was to use well-trained elephants to prevent wild herds from damaging the estates.

The group was prosperous. The headman, Dato Bintang, who was also chief of the area, was the most powerful and spiritually fearless shaman of all the Temiar. Yet somehow, Pat felt, something was wrong with the group. He sensed there was some element lacking, but only tumbled to it when he returned to record their statistics. There were very few babies under about one year: the group apparently had ceased to breed.

Later he discovered the reason. It was that the couples had come to believe they were being haunted by a strange evil, over which their great shaman had no control, and they were afraid either of producing deformed children or of those they had growing up to be imbeciles.

Materially, these people had never been better off, but civilisation had brought problems and uncertainties they did not understand. They had begun to feel themselves inferior to the Chinese and Malays, who looked down on them. For some reason, it seemed, nature was withholding its blessings.

On that first visit, as Pat was speaking to the headman, a girl came and sat on a log in the long-house a few feet from them. The headman addressed her as his daughter,[1] and told her to bring food for their guest. Her name was Anjang. She was about fourteen, and, as Pat observed to Puteh on their way back to Sungei Siput, she was the most beautiful Temiar he had ever set eyes on.

---

3 . A Map is Made

For his next series of expeditions Pat turned his attention farther north, to the Perak-Kelantan watershed, where the bulk of the Temiar population were believed to live. This was the impenetrable *ulu* of Malaya, in which it was thought nobody but an aborigine could survive for more than a few weeks.

A few explorers had reached the Main Range. In 1888 the Collector of the District of Upper Perak, C. F. Bozzolo, had gone up the Plus river and some way up one of its upper tributaries, the Menlik. In 1905 a surveyor, J. N. Sheffield, had taken a survey party to the headwaters of the Piah river and after a great deal of difficulty had succeeded in erecting a survey beacon on Gunong Grah. Later another surveyor, Major W. A. D. Edwards, had reached Gunong Noring, a northern peak on the boundary between the Temiar and Negrito country, to be attacked by Temiar with bows and arrows on his way down the mountain.

[1] Actually she was his niece.

Captain Hubert Berkeley, a memorable District Officer of Upper Perak, had visited the Ulu Temengor. Sir Hugh Clifford, the great pioneer in Malaya, who was British Resident of Pahang at the age of twenty-one, and a few others, had penetrated some way up the Plus river and other tributaries on the western side. Pater Schebesta had crossed the watershed from Upper Perak to reach Kuala Perias in Kelantan.

Otherwise this area of mountainous jungle nearly the size of Selangor State was unknown. The only maps were based on the observations made by Sheffield and Major Edwards, and readings taken from outlying ranges. They merely indicated the direction of a vast expanse of sustained heights, with at least sixteen peaks of over 6,000 feet.

In three years Pat explored and mapped this area in considerable detail.[1] Apart from the extended periods of intensive research which he spent with various Temiar groups, he had also to plot the distribution of the population, and of physical and cultural traits, and this took him on reconnaissance surveys over the length and breadth of the land of the Temiar. Thus he was able to mark the courses of the main rivers and their larger tributaries, the line of the Divide, the elevation of peaks, jungle routes, and the location of most of the aboriginal settlements. It was the only detailed map of the deep jungle that existed until an aerial survey was completed in 1952.

Pat began by going up the Plus river from Kampong Lasah, a flotilla of sampans taking the expedition as far as Kuala Temor. Three baggage elephants had accompanied them along the river path, and these were able to continue as far as Kuala Legap, a

[1] The mapping was done with the co-operation of the Survey Department, who instructed Pat in the survey technique generally employed in unknown country. The map itself was drawn from these readings by Captain G. H. Sworder, of that department, and mounted and printed at the Map Office, Kuala Lumpur.

rendezvous where Temiar gather from the farthest sources of the Plus and its tributaries, which open up like the fingers of an outstretched hand with the tips pressed against the Kelantan Divide.

Pat stopped at Legap for a few days to meet the local headmen and engage porters. Then he continued up the Plus to Kuala Yum, where the two rivers come cascading down precipitous slopes from either side of a mountain named Gunong Lalang. Here Pat left the Plus, following a route that climbed steeply up the banks of the Yum. Torrential rain poured down, drenching them to the skin, and making the trail so slippery that the baggage-train was held up, and Pat and his Malays, who had gone on ahead, spent the night in a long-house at Kuala Menlik, huddled next to a fire, with no protection other than loin-cloths, their clothes being wet. It was bitterly cold as their elevation was 3,500 feet.

Up around Kuala Menlik the Yum glides crystal-clear over a number of alluvial flats separated from each other by waterfalls. There were several flourishing groups situated on these flats, so Pat stayed three weeks near Kuala Menlik in a bamboo and atap hut the aborigines built for him. It was here that he was able to observe a Temiar trial, when two groups involved in a blood feud submitted their case to an independent panel of judges.

The cause of the trouble was a particularly beautiful but fickle young woman. Courtship and marriage among the Temiar is a simple, uncomplicated affair. Usually at the beginning of adolescence a lad leaves his long-house and starts visiting the surrounding groups in search of a bride. When he sees a girl whom he fancies he stays with her people, striving to impress them with his diligence in the clearing and his skill as a hunter. At night he performs the dances he has learnt in his dreams, or acquired by barter with other men. If the girl has entered his dreams it augurs well. He will tell her parents, and they may

27

encourage the couple to share the same sleeping mat. Customs vary from valley to valley, but generally at this stage if the union is consummated the parents insist on a bride-price before allowing the marriage to continue. The Temiar have no marriage ceremony as such, save that on occasions there may be a feast and a dance at which the newly-weds sit together and smoke the same cigarette, a gesture of affection and intimacy which is only countenanced among married couples.

Unions are contracted young, at about fifteen, and are soon cemented by the breeding of several children who form a tie that is very rarely severed. The Senoi are no less faithful than most other peoples to the marriage pact, although their code does allow a certain laxity, under prescribed conditions. For example, a younger brother may sleep with his elder brother's wife in the absence of the latter, who may, if he is on a journey, spend the night with any female relative of his wife. Such accommodations usually come to the ears of the husband concerned, but it is bad form to show jealousy. When adultery occurs outside the family circle, the guilty parties are warned. Should misconduct continue it may lead to divorce, which consists of no more than a husband's telling his wife to leave his hearth and never return.

That is the accepted pattern. If a girl's affairs are complicated by more than one suitor, she must, after making up her mind, settle down as a good and faithful wife. But the trouble with the beautiful girl in the Menlik Valley was that she could not make up her mind. When finally she did choose a man named Long, of whom the parents approved, and he had paid the bride-price, she then ran away with Alo, a handsome young fellow whom she had met at Legap and with whom she had been carrying on from time to time.

Their happiness was short-lived. The distraught husband brewed a deadly concentration of poison from the root sap of the ipoh tree, lay in wait, and blow-piped his rival in the back of the neck. Alo fell dead in his tracks. Unfortunately Alo's relatives were not prepared to let his death go unavenged. They speared Long's younger brother, whose group immediately retaliated with another killing. That was where the Menlik people had stepped in to prevent further bloodshed.

All the headmen of the area had gathered together to hear the case. It went on for two days, argued by spokesmen representing either party, while those directly involved kept silent and appeared quite unconcerned. But there was never any doubt concerning the final decision. It was that the group which had lost the two men should be allowed to even up the score by claiming a victim from the other side. Then the bloodshed had to stop.

The debt was paid before Pat left the Menlik. Long, the man who had lost his bride, went up to his dead rival's group ostensibly to claim her back. It was virtually an act of suicide, as he knew that Alo's cousins would be waiting for him just before he entered the settlement.

After this Pat continued along the path up the Yum river. It took him to the upper slopes of the Divide, from where they began a steep climb up to the pass leading over into Kelantan. The character of the jungle began to change. Above five thousand feet the trees became misshapen and stunted, like weird spectres, draped with moss which hung in decorative festoons from tree to tree. Underfoot the moss made a thick soft carpet, through which ran numerous rivulets of brownish, icy water, and here and there were pitcher plants and clumps of white and yellow flowers. Most beautiful of all were the orchids. These were of varying shape and colour and grew in clusters on the ground or on the smaller trees. Warming sunlight leaked through the low roof of the moss forest, although wraiths of white mist added a cold, clammy touch to the scene. They passed over the boundary into Kelantan at just under 6,000 feet. Following an old Temiar trade route, they descended by a stream to the tumbling upper reaches of the Ber river, and down along its banks to its junction with the Brok.

A few days before, Pat's aborigine porters had given him a certain wild fruit. "It was delicious, except that the part next the stone was fibrous and seemed to hold a peculiar mango flavour, with a sudden, intense bitterness which somehow impelled me to suck the stone dry. The effect on me was immediate. The fibres stuck in my throat like hairs, causing me to lose my voice for two days, and I suffered with severe gastritis.

"The fruit was a wild mango called *machang*. It grows on a tree of the genus *rengas*, one of the most sinister trees of the Malayan jungle. To touch its bark or leaves will raise a rash on the skin, and its sap is poison. Some people are so allergic to *rengas* that while walking in the jungle and chancing to pass under one of these trees their skins will tingle with irritation, and they will feel uncomfortable until they have moved out of its influence. The *machang* itself is not poisonous, and had I contented myself with eating only the fruit I should have suffered no ill effects.

"However the interesting part of this incident is the remarkable way in which I was cured. When I got to Kuala Ber, I went once more to see the hot springs I had discovered there on a previous trip to Kelantan. Here is a vast stretch of rocks, open to the sun, like a scar in the dense jungle. Steam hisses as the water comes bubbling out at boiling point, and there is a strong sulphurous smell. All kinds of wild beasts visit these hot springs when the day is cool: I surprised a couple of seladang that bolted away; and I saw the tracks of barking deer, wild pig, leopard, tiger, rhino, and of course elephants.

"Now the ordinary salt lick is generally a lukewarm trickling of water, salty to the taste. But there is nothing salt about these springs. The beasts, I am convinced, drink the waters for their tonic effects, as the chemicals clear the blood and generally benefit the body, counteracting any digestive troubles. Puteh and I bathed our faces and arms, and found the water invigorating. He drank some and swore it cured his fever, which the cold of the heights had brought on. So the next day I also drank a glassful, when it had cooled down. In ten minutes I felt pleasantly drowsy. On reaching camp I slept for nearly two hours, and I woke feeling tremendously fit. No trace of my sore throat or stomach trouble remained, and that night I ate a square meal of curried chicken and felt no ill effects."

At Kuala Ber they built bamboo rafts and set out drifting down the Brok. Their comfortable journey was interrupted by a black gorge with extended rapids, known as Jeram Gajah, where the baggage had to be unloaded and the rafts pulled with lengths of *rotan* through the frothing teeth of the rapids. Below Jeram Gajah the Brok meanders peacefully between low hills, and they rafted slowly on to where the first Malay settlements appeared side by side with the border Temiar just above Kuala Betis. At Betis they abandoned the rafts and struck eastwards along an old jungle track, and reached Gua Musang on the East Coast Railway, having completed the first crossing ever from railway to railway.

There were three further expeditions in 1933 covering the Perak side of the watershed. The first of these was in the southern part of the Temiar country, in a circuit up the Korbu river to its source near the Mu river, then down that to the Plus.

Pat had noticed a curious similarity in the character and pattern of all the rivers he had so far explored. They began on or just below the ridge of the Divide as tiny trickling rivulets. These linked up to form brooks, which in turn joined other brooks to

31

form streams that fell cascading down flights of rock steps to about the 4,000-foot level. Here they slowed down, as they were now in flat, fertile valleys, each separated by a pleasant waterfall from one at a lower level. Below these flats, however, the streams again became mountain torrents rushing through deep ravines usually too precipitous to be followed, and the jungle route would by-pass these reaches to join the river bank again at about 2,000 feet. From about this level most rivers were raftable, though formidable rapids had still to be negotiated at intervals, and frequently the narrow stretches were blocked by tree-trunks washed down when the river was in spate. Dug-out boats could be brought up to about the 1,000-foot level, but even this was a good distance above the more peaceful lower reaches where the fringe Malay *kampongs* first appeared. Downwards from the raftable limit the taller jungle began, with massive white trunks of giant trees rising two hundred feet and more. Rafting down a river was always the most pleasant part of a journey, yet for Puteh it is associated with one of his most terrifying jungle experiences.

Though they had regularly come across evidence of big game in the jungle, they had seen comparatively few animals. The reason was that on the march the expedition made sufficient noise to keep animals well out of sight. But a party can drift downstream on a line of narrow rafts a hundred yards apart without making any sound at all, as voices do not carry above the rushing of water through rocks which occur every few miles. The incident occurred on the narrow reaches of the Plus.

Pat and Puteh were on the leading raft, with two raftsmen navigating with poles. A sandy island appeared in midstream, landscaped with rocks and bushes, the right-hand channel rippling over a bed of pebbles, the other sweeping round the island to a gap between two large boulders, and tumbling into a wide pool. A herd of elephants were in the pool, eight adults and two babies.

32

It was too late to steer the raft to the bank and stop, as they were actually riding through the gap when the raftsmen first spotted them. A moment later the raft was in the pool drifting nearer and nearer to a large bull elephant that turned and raised its trunk with a scream of surprise and anger. They approached it unarmed, as the only weapon Pat had was a shot-gun and that was in a canvas bag on another raft.

The big bull was twenty yards away, poised, it seemed, waiting for them and their flimsy craft to drift within reach of its fury. Pat was about to jump into the water and try to swim for it, though he knew very well he could not hope to reach the bank before the current carried him down among the rest of the herd.

Then the raftsman in front began yelling and flaying the water with his punting pole. The rear raftsman took up the shout, and Pat and Puteh joined in as well. The bull trumpeted hysterically in reply. But to the relief of the men on the raft they won the argument, for the herd began to stampede out of the pool. They crashed into the wall of the jungle and through it, leaving a gap frayed with broken saplings and creepers, and a strong, familiar smell of elephant.

In 1934 he began an expedition up the Temor river, but after three weeks he decided to return to Taiping in order that his Malays could be with their families for the Moslem festival of Hari Raya Puasa at the end of the fasting season. On the way back one of the aborigine porters slipped as they were crossing a river and his load, the medicine box, was lost. There were further delays, so Pat sent his Malays on ahead and stayed behind with his party of aborigines.

It was a risk he should not have taken because once again he was attacked by malaria, and again without his medicines he could do nothing to combat it. Then his porters, thinking he was going to die, deserted, leaving him alone in his tent with burning fever.

Meanwhile in Taiping a young American psychologist named Kilton Stewart had arrived at Pat's house with an introduction from the Dutch prehistorian Dr. P. V. van Stein Callenfels. Pat's servants had made Stewart stay at the house, promising that their *tuan* would be back next morning. As Stewart recalled, he waited ten days before Pat finally arrived looking very thin and still shaky on his feet.

He had lain alone in his tent for five days before an aborigine and his son on a hunting trip happened to pass by the camp. To Pat's good fortune he knew the man, who sent his son to their settlement for help, and himself nursed Pat. Later he and his kinsmen brought Pat out of the jungle as far as Lasah.

There was yet another expedition in 1934. This was up the Korbu from Jalong and over into Kelantan where he came down the headwaters of the Brok to a southern tributary the Blatop. After a short stay at Kuala Blatop, he came up that river and crossed the watershed again into north-west Pahang, and so reached the Cameron Highlands.

At a settlement on the Blatop river he encountered what he described to his brother as a taboo death. The victim was a boy of fourteen, whom Pat found lying listless on a sleeping mat. Pat administered quinine to the boy, but the headman shook his head sadly.

"Atau cannot live," he said. "He has eaten Bamoh."

Bamoh is the great mythical hero of the Temiar, who taught them the secrets of childbirth. He is believed to have been reincarnated as a mountain goat, and consequently few Temiar dare to eat its flesh. Only the bodily and spiritually fit, the full members of the working group, may taste it, while the youngest born of each family may not eat it on pain of death. Without knowing, Atau had eaten mountain goat. When the headman heard this he was horrified and declared that the boy's life would begin to flow away. As Pat observed, he declined steadily until a few days later he died.

In April 1935, on his return from home leave, Pat continued his explorations and surveying of hitherto uncharted areas until he had completed a detailed reconnaissance of the whole of the Temiar territory.

4 . *The Timeless Temiar*

Pat's permanent staff on the majority of his expeditions consisted solely of two Malays. They were his cook-boy Puteh, and Yeop Ahmat, the Museum collector, who, apart from acquiring objects of aboriginal material culture, helped with the survey and photography. On some of the later expeditions Pat also took a Moslemised Temiar as a messenger. He had no regular porters, all the baggage being carried by aborigines recruited from settlement to settlement. This greatly reduced expense, as these tough, tireless hill men, who had never worked before for any motive beyond their food quest, were prepared to march great distances for the price of a *parang*.

Once Pat became known to the Temiar there was never any difficulty about porters. But during the early expeditions he had been obstructed by propaganda put out against him by some of the fringe *kampong* Malays,[1] who resented the presence of a European wanting to see the aborigines at first hand. Those who came down from the hills to trade were told he was a dangerous medicine man seeking to gain a hold over the Temiar by magic The story was believed at first by groups who had never met him, and on one occasion the outcome was nearly disastrous. One morning he woke to find that his guide and porters had disappeared, leaving him and his two Malays stranded at a settlement on the Brok river. And the settlement, which had been crowded with life the night before, was now completely deserted. They searched for miles up and down the river, but found only empty long-houses which had obviously been vacated in a great hurry. They waited, hoping the aborigines would return. But after ten days there was still no sign of them. The situation looked desperate, as they were alone in the heart of the deep jungle and entirely dependent on the aborigines to get them out.

Eventually Puteh, who had managed to find his way up the Blatop river, met a headman whom Pat had once successfully treated for fever. On hearing what had happened, the headman personally went with a party to fetch Pat and take him out to the Cameron Highlands.

Later Pat heard that the groups on the Brok had been told that he could render the men of a group impotent and wither the crops of a *ladang* with a wave of his hand. However he was soon able to counter this propaganda, and within a few years he was known throughout the deep jungle as Tata, meaning 'grandfather', a term of profound respect.

Pat's success with the Temiar came from his ability to identify himself with them. He spoke their monosyllabic language[2]

[1] At Lasah, Pat found that practically every inhabitant had aborigine relatives in the *ulu*. These *kampong* folk professed to know the secrets of aborigine magic, though few of them ever ventured above the sampan limit.

[2] Derived from the languages of the old Cambodian Empire.

fluently. He was scrupulous in his observance of their customs and usage, and his knowledge of their character enabled him to react with them in such a manner that they soon forgot he was a stranger and a white man, the first most of them had ever seen. To win their respect he became proficient with a blow-pipe, learned to play their simple musical instruments, and joined in their dances. Once he leapt so high that his foot went through the split bamboo floor of the long-house as he landed, and his leg was lacerated up to the thigh.

His warm personality attracted them to him, particularly the children, whom he would amuse with stories and antics. Michael Tweedie, later Director of the Raffles Museum in Singapore, told me that he once saw Pat standing on his head to make some aborigine children laugh. Pat always took his portable gramophone on journeys, to entertain the settlements he visited. He gave medicine to the sick. He provided seeds and suggested they tried new vegetables and crops, and advised as to how much they should accept for their jungle produce at the fringe trading-posts, where Chinese dealers were exploiting them outrageously.

He had but to enter a valley and every settlement on the river would know he was on the way. News travels fast through the Main Range, but not in the haphazard way of gossip or rumour. The passing-on of important information is one of the reciprocal obligations that exists between jungle neighbours who are linked together in the fabric of their society in a special way.

According to Pat,[1] the unit of the Temiar social structure is what he termed the extended family. This is an intimate association of a number of individual families, linked by blood relationship, who live in a communal long-house and work a

[1] *Journal of the Federated Malay States Museums*, Vol. XIX, Part 1, December 1936.

plantation. Usually an extended family is composed of a head-man and some of his younger brothers and sisters, together with their families and generally an older generation of aunts and uncles and their families too. Each family consists of a man and his wife, or wives,[1] with their unmarried children, and they occupy their own compartment in the long-house, preparing their own food separately at their own hearth. Thus the extended household approximates to a small village, with the central floor as the street, and the compartments round it as the houses.

Society with the Temiar is entirely a family affair, in which everybody is addressed or referred to by his or her appropriate relationship term, the system being classificatory. Thus, although real parents and actual blood-brethren are clearly recognised, such terms as 'mother' or 'brother' refer to a wide variety of relatives, and even those too remote to be included in the Western system are specified and classed with close blood-kin. Every Temiar has a large number of 'social equivalents' or persons to whom he applies the same relationship-term.

Family ties go beyond the communal long-house, for every extended household is part of a still wider grouping composed of a number of such households, known as a kindred. The kindred owns a hereditary area of common land called the saka, on which the individual groups clear plantations and their members hunt. The limits of the saka are clearly defined and jealously guarded. Any aborigine in the jungle may pass through a saka, but he must obtain permission before he can hunt, fish or cut jungle produce in a saka not his own.

The saka is an important source of food supply. There are fish in the rivers which are hooked, speared, netted, trapped or

---

[1] Custom allows two wives, but a man must be hard-working enough to satisfy the parents of the girl whom he wishes to make his second wife. Attempts to marry more than two wives are very rare. In some areas polyandry occurs.

stupefied. In the jungle there are small animals and birds to be hunted with the blow-pipe; wild pig and deer to be trapped; as well as edible jungle flowers, leaves, shoots, tubers, roots, wild fruits, ferns, mushrooms and palms. Besides, the jungle also provides medicines in the form of sap from certain trees and the water of aerial roots; poison for blow-pipe darts; tuba fruit, the juice of which is used for stupefying fish; bark for making cloth; fibres, leaves and grasses for decoration; rushes and other plants for making baskets; and of course bamboo and *rotan* for building houses, plumbing and making cooking utensils, spears, musical instruments, fetishes, rafts and a score of other things.

The Negritos live entirely on the jungle. But the basis of the Temiar and for that matter all Senoi economy is the plantation—the *ladang*—and all the families comprising the extended household share every year in the major job of felling the jungle trees on the site selected, burning off the leaves and undergrowth when dry, and planting. The main crops are tapioca, the staple food, and at some seasons hill rice, millet and maize. Alongside these crops the individual families grow their own vegetables, fruit, sugar-cane, hill tobacco, medicinal herbs, and flax plant from which twine for fishing nets is obtained.

In some areas the Temiar practise a modified shifting cultivation, planting each successive *ladang* next to the previous one, so that they can live in the same long-house for several years. In many *sakas* the groups of the kindred will agree to plant their *ladangs* on a co-operative basis, one household planting *padi*, another maize, another millet, in addition to tapioca which they all plant; the groups go the round of the *ladangs*, helping in the work, and the produce is shared.

The Temiar have a law: "When a man has given his work he has a share in the harvest." But it is the spirit behind their notions of ownership that makes these large community undertakings possible. Centuries have taught them that they must live together in harmony in order to survive.

The child is brought up to recognise the bonds of kinship, and the duties and privileges these imply. Its environment is the closely-knit family with its doctrine of mutual responsibility and abhorrence of selfishness. It is not an environment to foster the individualist. There is no place in a group for the outsider.

Every member of the community has an equal right to everything the community owns. Yet individual ownership is not entirely absent from the scheme, for private property follows upon personal endeavour. For example a man makes or buys his own blow-pipe and quiver, loin-cloth, beads and *parang*. He can keep what money he makes out of cutting and selling jungle produce. If he goes fishing he is the owner of his catch. It is the same with an animal killed on a hunt, although if several men are out together the carcass does not belong to the individual who fires the fatal dart, but the one who first sights the animal. The surrounding jungle may belong to the kindred as a whole, but if a man discovers a fruit tree off the beaten track, he can claim it as his own.

Yet so much is the custom of sharing everything with one's fellows taken for granted, that the habit of keeping food to himself was quoted to Pat as an indication of a certain youth's insanity.

Behind this attitude is the concept that man has a great many malignant and destructive forces in nature to contend with and that anybody who thinks he can manage without the help and goodwill of his relatives must indeed be mad. "Co-operate with your fellows," is the Temiar maxim, "but if you must oppose their wishes then oppose them with good will." Other primitives are capable of equally wise sayings. But the Temiar, insulated from the world in their inaccessible Shangri-La, have discovered an educative process which has made it possible for the entire race actually to *live* their kindly philosophy.

Temiar children, like children all over the world, are naughty, selfish, greedy and aggressive. Yet they develop into unselfish, co-operative and self-reliant adults, who react instinctively according to the code without any apparent effort at self-discipline or self-control. Pat found no man or woman with an automatic impulse to rebel. Occasionally people disagreed with group actions and would go their own way, but in this they were not following any individual preference but the dictates of their dreams.

Extensive research had confirmed Pat's early observations concerning their social behaviour, which was characterised by an almost complete lack of discord. Except for the single instance already recorded, he encountered no friction between the groups. There were occasional disputes between unrelated individuals over women: these were heard by a jury and the matter settled by the payment of a fine by the offending party. But quarrels between relatives within the group were unknown. Odd individuals, who might otherwise have caused trouble by reason of their bad-tempered, selfish or anti-social actions, were invariably regarded as backward, overgrown children and treated with tolerant good humour. Pat encountered no theft, no sexual offences and no offences against children. Homosexuality was unknown, and tribal customs included no practices such as cannibalism, head-hunting, child-betrothal, immolation of widows, or ritual mutilation of the body.

Anthropologically, such a racial personality was a unique phenomenon, and Pat collected a formidable amount of psychological data to account for it. He was assisted in these researches by Dr. Kilton Stewart, today a well-known psychotherapist in New York, who is successfully applying techniques learnt from the Temiar in his treatment of neuroses and other forms of mental illness.

According to Stewart the secret of the emotional adjustment of the Temiar is a psychological technique they stumbled on probably many centuries ago. It is associated with their dreams, and was developed to provide a type of dream action to conform with their religious beliefs.

No racial group has been described in anthropological literature in which the dream and trance play so great a rôle in the daily lives of the people as they do among the Temiar. To them the dream is a mystical experience which occurs when one of a person's souls[1] leaves the body during sleep and wanders about the jungle in search of guidance. Therefore important decisions are seldom made by a group without one of its members having had a dream that prescribes a certain course of action. If a man dreams of a particular spot in the river, he will fish there. If his dreams suggest a valley or settlement in which he should seek his bride, he will certainly follow his dream directions. Most Temiar inspiration comes from their dreams. Pat met men who had dreamed mechanical inventions such as fish-traps, complicated puzzles, decorative patterns and medicinal remedies. All their epic poetry, all their dances, all their rhythms, all their songs are dream-inspired.

Because of the great social significance attached to dreams the

[1] The Temiar believe that a man possesses several souls which animate different organs or functions of the body. The principal souls are the head-soul, the eye-soul, the breath-soul, the heart-soul and the liver-soul. The last named, which is primarily concerned with learning about the future, is the peripatetic soul, although the head-soul, and therefore the thinking soul goes out on special errands and to gain experience.

children at a very early age are encouraged to talk about their dreams, and Stewart holds that it is the special advice they get from their parents regarding their dreams that has the effect of turning them into nature's true gentlemen.

The key to the system is action. The child is not just told to sleep and dream, he is taught how to dream correctly, and in particular what he should do in his dreams. To begin with he must never be afraid in his dreams. If he dreams of smoke he must not avoid it as he would smoke during his waking hours, because it stings the eyes: he must go boldly into the dream smoke, for only thus will he conquer the smoke spirit and bend it to his own will.

By the same token he must attack dream animals, dream monsters and dream ghosts that try to block his path. If he defeats them they become his slaves, but if he runs away they will persecute him until he seeks them out and fights them. This, according to Stewart, is sound psychiatry, since every image that appears to the dreamer is charged with the force of the dreamer's subjective emotions, and the image must be destroyed in order to release his objective emotions which are associated with it.

For example, when a person does something, even if it is a good act, an image is left in your mind that is filled up with your subjective reactions, possibly anxiety, guilt, fear, envy. In your dream the person's image will possess these subjective attributes, but if you destroy the dream image you have paid him off subconsciously and thereafter you will be able to regard him and his act with complete objectivity.

The dream is an emotional safety-valve to clear the mind and heart of prejudice, intolerance, and feelings of inferiority. However, if the dream is not correctly used it can react against

43

the dreamer. If his subjective emotions are not released, they can build up to react against him and his associates.

If the Temiar child dreams of soaring or falling he is told to relax, as these sensations represent the efforts of his head-soul or other souls to get free of his body. If, however, he has a fear of hitting the bottom or of reaching too high, then his souls will be impeded in their need to arrive somewhere—and it is necessary for him to arrive somewhere in his dreams if he aspires to being a *halak* or shaman. Behind this precept is the belief that a man can only gain ultimate power over the forces of evil if he has courage to reach out boldly, while on the other hand fear makes his souls withdraw deeper into the body, becoming repressed and paralysed.

That is Temiar theology, but the psychologist's interpretation of such dreams is that they represent an impulse on the part of the dreamer to break away from his relatives and express himself as an individual. The bold seeking of dream adventure and the fulfilment of arriving somewhere satisfy the impulse, so that the effect on the dreamer is towards greater identification with the group, a greater desire to co-operate and better team spirit.

Implicit in all dream instructions is the idea that a man, with the co-operation of his fellows and the assistance of friendly spirits, can dominate the forces of evil, provided he has spiritual courage to assert himself. The important thing is that he cannot do it alone. He is as dependent on his relatives and friends as they are on him, and if he helps other people while he is awake he can call on their souls to assist him in his dream exploits.

The same laws of sharing and co-operation are applicable in the dream as during waking hours. The child is told that if he finds food or treasure he must share it with the group. If he does not he allies his head-soul to the earth demon, and is therefore in danger of losing control over it and so being drawn down into the material slough of selfishness and stupidity. Yet with truly extraordinary psychological insight, the Temiar do not forbid violently anti-social actions in a dream if the dreamer has no alternative.

For example a boy may find himself in conflict with a dream image of his father or brother. If the image opposes him he must fight it to the death, as it is probably an evil spirit masquerading in the guise of his relative. Similarly if a dream image of his mother or sister tempts him into a taboo love relationship he is justified in completing the act. The emotional safety-valve is permitted to function. However, the child is held responsible for all his actions in a dream, and since violence is not socially admissible he is bound in conscience to reveal the dream to the person whose image was involved, and to apologise just in case the image was a legitimate soul whose intentions were mistaken by the dreamer. As dream antagonism is also regarded as a possible omen of some future trouble, the two concerned must try to avoid it.

As Stewart maintains: "The Temiar Senoi doctrine is like the Biblical statement that 'offence needs must come, but woe to him by whom it does come'. The offence charges the image of the offender with a force antagonistic to the offended. You offend a child if you cause him pain as you pull a sliver from his foot. But the pain is only a fragment of the total situation. The fear occasioned by the pain often disguises itself in the image of a friend. The Temiar Senoi dream-education proves that this fear, which makes the dream character antagonistic, is released and dispersed as the dreamer outfaces and kills or conquers the antagonistic dream character. It is also released if the dream character stabs, or kills, or strikes the dreamer. It is as if the dream character gives up its individual existence whenever the dreamer, who created it in past time, is willing to re-experience the shock

45

or pain that turned the image against the individual, in the original painful experience."[1]

Dream interpretation and manipulation are not of course the whole picture. There are other important factors in the emotional development of a Temiar child in the deep jungle. To start with he receives no punishment, nor is he reprimanded for something he has done wrong: instead the act itself is discussed and condemned if it is anti-social, or has anti-social overtones. The only sins the Temiar recognise are those against one's fellows.

From its earliest days the child is aware not so much of his own identity as that of his group. Within a huge extended-family longhouse he is secure with his relatives from the terrors of the surrounding jungle, and protected by the *ruwai* or group-soul from evil spirits seeking his destruction. Moreover there is never any instability in group life: definitely no financial instability, since a *parang* is all that a man really needs to be rich in the jungle. If the child's parents separate or die he is cared for by the group. There is no concept of illegitimacy, there are no distinctions, and as a dreamer he rates as a full member of the group almost from the time he can talk. In the morning councils the elders will cite not only their own dreams but those of the children when projects are under discussion. This inculcates a sense of responsibility.

Stewart believes that the Temiar child, emerging from such a background, is not only receptive to direction into the right social attitudes, but gets the best possible start from the psychological point of view. Group comment on his actions weans him off nursery behaviour, while the correct use of the dream process provides a salutary means of satisfying impulses which otherwise would accumulate in the unconscious mind.

From the dream collections Pat and Stewart made in various

[1] *Mental Hygiene*, Vol. XXXVIII, No. 3, July 1954, p. 400.

Reinvigorating the group-soul. Field staff at the Research Station dancing the Jinjang. Alcohol is unknown to the Temiar

Famous shaman Angah Sideh leading a dance. Shortly after this photograph was taken he achieved the catatonic trance state

Senoi nose-flutes, the origin of which is lost in aboriginal history

Richard with Pangoi (right), a 'tough nut', and his son Alok, who earned $13,700 in rewards. They are examining a poisonous ipoh tree

age-groups, it was apparent that an individual's dreams consistently evolve from childhood to adolescence. Gradually the child learns to carry out the dream directions it receives from the adults. Towards adolescence it begins to get somewhere in dreams, to bring back things for the group, to fight and destroy enemies. Then by adolescence a boy usually begins having a type of recurring dream, and from its pattern the elders can generally tell if he has in him the makings of a shaman. The shaman is a vital element in group life, and the man who will eventually take over the function has to be trained very young.

The Temiar are animists. They believe that the whole of nature is impregnated with spirits, some of which are associated with particular places, while others are unattached to any material thing and free to wander about at will. Some of these spirits are good, but many are evil and at variance with living humanity, causing crop failures, floods and other calamities, and even death by stealing away a soul which had temporarily left the body during sleep or sickness.

The group has a special place in cosmic creation, as a link between the world of spirits and material nature. The group must maintain the balance between the two, making use of nature without offending her susceptibilities. The intermediary between the group and the spirits is the shaman. He can invoke their benign, protective power, and he does this with the assistance of his *gunigs* or spirit guides.

Here the dream is used as a ritualistic mechanism, for it is the only means by which the shaman can contact his *gunigs*. When the shaman sleeps his head-soul leaves his body (as it always does during sleep and sickness) and goes wandering in the jungle. Also wandering in the jungle is a *gunig* who has previously selected the shaman as a medium, and when they meet the spirit persuades

47   c

:cept it as a protective or guardian spirit. Once the
s got over his initial fright, for the *gunig* may be a bad
spirit in disguise, he is only too willing to accept the *gunig*, and
learns from it how to make contact if its help is needed. This is
usually done through its personal dance, with accompanying
words, steps, rhythm and tune, and decorations (fragrant leaves
and certain flowers which vary according to the dance).

The young Temiar who aspires to be a shaman will try to
persuade others to follow the dance taught him by a *gunig*
encountered in a dream. The group will always be prepared to
give him a chance, though if the conditions he imposes are too
difficult he may be told to get himself a less exacting *gunig*! A man
has to prove the originality and efficacy of his dances before he is
accepted as a shaman, but the great shaman can demand food
taboos, fasts, even continence, and the group will accept them.

The *halak*-dance[1] is the principal religious and social function
during which the shaman invokes the spirit and leads or directs
the dance it has shown him. The climax is the trance state which
they believe occurs when the spirit suddenly enters the shaman
and through him the other dancers. The trance usually begins as a
catatonic condition in which the subject collapses and lies rigid or
writhing. His voice drops an octave lower than normal during
this phase, and he may snarl like a tiger: the Temiar say that the
forces of good and evil within him are struggling for possession,
and among the spiritually immature the torment may sometimes
result in violence. But within a few minutes the catatonia
subsides, and the subject gets up and wanders about in a state of
dissociation, now speaking in a voice an octave higher than normal.
He may blow on people or make sucking noises through his
clenched fist, recite mystical spells of unintelligible spirit talk or

[1] There are other less formal dances for amusement and entertainment.

48

converse with spirits inside or outside other people's bodies. He is no respecter of persons, and is likely to tell individuals in the audience a lot of home truths, but he is amiable about it and motivated by a desire to impart the tonic effect of the spirit essence.

During the trance the shaman may be prompted to ascertain the state of the group's luck by grabbing a handful of tapioca cut into small pieces, then assuming a posture of great tension, and throwing with his hand half-open. Their luck will be good if an even number of pieces remain in his hand, bad if an odd number. Experienced shamans can diagnose illness, prescribe treatment, even prophesy during a trance. But these are side-effects compared with the essential purpose of the ceremonial dance, which is to preserve and reinforce the *ruwai* or group soul of the community, to ward off evil and to strengthen the protective spirit itself. Just as man needs the spirit, so the spirit needs man. The spirit is better for hearing its song sung and seeing its dance performed, because its power and prestige in the spirit world depends on the extent of its recognition by humans. Therefore the group must honour its spirit guide in order to obtain the full benefit of its protective influence.

The character and behaviour of the members of the group are also believed to reflect on the spirit guide. Reprehensible actions may cause it to lose power, while a crime committed by the shaman himself may result in the total loss of its efficacy. Conversely good conduct has the opposite effect, and in order to please and honour their *gunigs* many shamans lead austere lives. Their influence is greatly for the good and it undoubtedly accounts for the high social morality of the Temiar.

There are no absolutes in Temiar society, no rigid laws to make the system run smoothly. There are taboos of course—food taboos and sexual taboos—but individuals may break any of them in response to dream directions. Provided a man does not harm or endanger others by his actions he may do as he pleases. He is not even entirely responsible for his misdemeanours: if he commits a crime or offence against an individual of another group, all his relatives in his extended family are collectively accountable and liable to be fined by a jury of headmen who gather from far and wide to hear the case.

As the individual has the choice of complete freedom of action in matters affecting nobody but himself, so the group has the sovereign right to live within its limits and seek out its own salvation. Authority within the group is the voice of the majority. The office of headman[1] is alien to Temiar culture and resulted from appointments made originally by the mikongs, who used to function as the liaison between the aborigines of the *ulu* and the *kampong* Malays of the lower reaches, although they no longer have any influence.

The two mikongs, one at Temengor and the other at Gua Musang, are relics of the Siamese domination of the Peninsula: their ancestors married aborigine women and, according to the Malays, got to know the magic of the hill people. There is a third hereditary chief, the To' Pangku of Lasah, appointed by the Sultan of Perak, who performs the same function with the aborigines of the Plus valley. The ancestors of these chiefs not only appointed group headmen, but senior headmen who became the overall chiefs of the *sakas*.

The headmen are hereditary. Usually the eldest son succeeds to the title, though if this is not possible it is by no means rare for an able-bodied son-in-law to take over when his wife's father dies or

[1] The usual title for a headman is 'Penghulu' or more rarely 'Menteri', both Malay words. The title 'Batin' is applicable only to senior headmen of the Aboriginal Malays, although a few Temiar headmen have adopted it for themselves.

becomes too old. When in the course of time a group becomes too large and splits into two or more separate households, the eldest son of the middle generation generally becomes headman of the splinter group.

The headman has the place of honour in the long-house: his family usually occupies the dais at one end. He is treated with respect. But at the morning councils, when group matters and projects are discussed, he has like the other male adults only one vote.

To Pat's way of thinking these happy, carefree, peace-loving people had created for themselves a truly Utopian democracy. Pat was an idealist. No wonder he was enamoured of the Temiar.

It was during the summer of 1933, according to Puteh, that Pat fell in love with Anjang. He had discovered a prehistoric site near Jalong, and was visiting it from time to time to make sketches and take photographs. On these occasions he would call at Dato Bintang's long-house where he would see her.

That October he went to Celebes. Dr. Callenfels had invited him to come and visit a proto-neolithic site he was excavating on the Karama river in central Celebes, and the Malayan Government, having nearly axed Pat earlier that year because of the slump, now sanctioned an eight-week tour of the Netherlands East Indies for purposes of comparative study.

He returned to Taiping in December. He was due six months' home leave in the spring of 1934, but before he left Malaya he went to see Dato Bintang, and after the customary exchange of civilities asked for his ward in marriage.

"Dato Bintang, I wish to give my work for your people," Pat told him. "I wish to live with Temiar, to be like the Temiar."

"*Tuan*, what will you give for a bride-price?"

"I have brought it with me," Pat assured him. "There are

beads, cloth for sarongs, *parangs*, salt, brass wire for spiral bangles, and fish-hooks."

"It is a fair price," the headman said gravely. "Take my niece if she desires you." He called to Anjang, who came and stood before him, her arms down by her sides. "Do you desire this man?" he asked her.

Anjang turned and looked at Pat. She nodded her assent.

"*Tuan*, take the girl," Dato Bintang said.

"I will marry her when I come back from my country," Pat told him.

---

5 . The Prophecy

For Richard, in the fifth form at Aldenham, a red-letter day was 25th May 1934. It was the day his brother was invited to lecture at the school and show a film of his work in the deep jungle.

The film was marred somewhat because the headmaster insisted on the removal of all scenes which included bare-bosomed aborigine belles. However, in deference to Richard's avowed interest in anthropology, he was allowed to assist Pat in the editing, and that night Aldenham was edified by an entirely masculine version of Temiar life. Cleverly cut in were shots of the expedition on the march, of Pat interrogating aborigines about their customs, and being exorcised by a medicine man as he lay sick with malaria in Kelantan.

It was a thrilling account and Pat left with three rousing cheers from the entire school. He had caught the boys' imagination, being both athletic and brainy, with a ready wit, a sporting sense, a young heart and a youthful appearance.

This last was an embarrassment to him. He was twenty-six, though he looked four years younger, and as he once told Richard: "The trouble is I can never get anybody in the scientific world to take me seriously."

Nevertheless the Oxford and Cambridge Joint Faculty of Anthropology met for a second time that year, an unprecedented thing, to hear his lecture on "The Dream Psychology of the Senoi Shaman", and later when he gave the same lecture at the Musée de l'Homme in Paris, the entire audience of several hundred people rose to applaud him.

In October, Pat returned to Malaya, having turned down an offer of the Chair of Anthroplogy at Cambridge. But his first letter home caused something of a stir. He announced that he had become engaged to a girl he had met on the voyage. The family did not know her, but from all accounts she seemed suitable.

That winter H.V. took Sheelah out to Malaya. He had recently published a monograph on the stone implements of Bandarawela in Ceylon, and particularly wanted to inspect some undisturbed neolithic slab graves which Pat had discovered near Slim in Perak. They returned to Europe in March 1935; then in July, when Richard left school, he and his mother went out to Malaya for six months.

Pat was then excavating Gua Baik, his prehistoric site near Jalong, and he took Richard up to see the work. A trial trench had been put down in a cave shelter under a limestone cliff at the side of the Korbu river, and Pat had already discovered two skeletons, as well as pottery, stone implements, bones and skulls.

They spent the afternoon at the site, and that evening after dinner Pat picked up a bottle of whisky in one hand and a cushion in the other. "Come on, Dick," he said. "We're going to watch the dancing in Dato Bintang's long-house. The party may go on all night. You can sleep if you like during a dance, but it's bad form to leave the long-house, unless for a very good reason."

To a stranger a Temiar long-house is a mysterious and not particularly inviting structure, raised on stilts, with matting walls, leaf thatch and the airy impermanence of a house built of cards. It may attain to two hundred feet in length, as Dato Bintang's did, his group being one of the largest in the area, that year totalling nearly a hundred individuals. As they had settled down permanently, in the centre of five large *ladangs*, which they worked in rotation, the house was older and rather more dilapidated than most in the Temiar country. Anyway darkness had repaired it temporarily.

The interior was decorated with jungle flowers, fibres, and palm leaves cut and plaited into a variety of ingenious patterns. The only light came from blazing wood fires in earthen hearths around the large central floor, and these illuminated the convulsive movement of glistening bodies circling to a slow dynamic rhythm which kept the springy floor in a state of constant undulation. The entire structure shook to the rhythm, and all the dancers and many of the onlookers were singing. The men on the floor were garlanded with leaves, swaying and waving whisks of foliage held in either hand in an elaborate scythe-like motion, while the women in contrast moved almost mechanically, upright and restrained, hands limp by their sides. Several women were weeping as they danced, their limbs heavy, it seemed, with an ineffable sadness.

In compartments round the floor were the uncertain silhouettes of children and old people, many smoking their hill tobacco rolled in dried *nipah* leaves. As Richard followed Pat to a dais at one end of the floor, he saw a child of two at its mother's breast let go of the pap and reach out for her cigarette. The mother put it in the mouth of the child, who puffed at it contentedly.

A few yards from the dais sat the orchestra—a line of girls beating a log of wood with short sections of bamboo. The sections varied in length and thickness to produce sounds of differing tone and volume, the combined effect of which was weirdly attractive. The orchestra sang as they pounded the log, echoing phrase by phrase the words of a gaunt, wild-eyed old man outside the circle of dancers, singing or rather groaning out his song in low-pitched agony. At moments he would become convulsed with a shuddering that was transmitted to his fluttering leaf-whisks.

"That's Dato Bintang," Pat told his brother. "He's the greatest shaman of the Temiar."

As they sat on the dais Richard noticed that the girl in the orchestra nearest to them was smiling at Pat as she sang.

"A friend of yours?" Richard asked.

Pat studied his brother. Then he said quietly: "That, dear boy, is my wife."

The impact left Richard speechless. He looked at her, trying to adjust himself to the idea of having an aborigine, a jungle girl, for a sister-in-law. She was beautiful enough, with a round, serene face, and thick hair that hung down to her shoulders in waves. Her skin, of a honey colour, was flawless in texture, and her arms and breasts were exquisitely shaped. She sensed the brothers were talking about her, because she looked away in embarrassment, pounding vigorously with her bamboos.

"I thought you were engaged to somebody you met on the boat coming out," Richard said after a while.

"A very nice girl, but we both realised it wouldn't have worked," Pat said. "She later became engaged to a fellow named

Goode, and some wag in the New Club said it was a case of 'Goode after Noone'."

"This girl's not just your mistress?" Richard asked. "Most of the bachelors I've met out here seem to have a Chinese floozie somewhere in the compound. There's no reason I suppose why you shouldn't have an aborigine."

"No, Dick, she's my wife," Pat told him. "I'm married to Anjang in the sight of God and the Temiar." He signalled to her. "Dato Bintang sent word round to the *ladangs*, and headmen came down from the Plus, the Yum, the Mu, the Legap, and the upper Korbu. There were about two hundred people. We killed a buffalo and several dozen chickens. The party went on for three days and three nights."

"Have you told anybody else in the family?" Richard asked.

"No, it's going to be damned difficult."

Anjang had come up to the dais and was standing before Pat, her hands by her sides. Strands of beads were draped crosswise from her shoulders and under her arms, and white, waxy, frangipani were blooming in her hair. Pat spoke to her in Temiar, and she fetched two bamboo drinking-cups and a length of bamboo containing water. She placed the cups and water near Richard, then returned to her place in the orchestra.

"Open that bottle, Dick, and let's have a drink," Pat said.

Dato Bintang now joined the circle of dancers, and Pat said: "The basic pattern of this circular type of dance is always the same. It begins with a slow, rhythmic movement, which relaxes the bodies of the dancers and gives them the heightened co-ordination and elation the Temiar call the *hab* of the dance."

He listened for a while. "He's singing about us. He's glad we are here. His spirit guide, who incidentally is his wife, is glad we are here. We have come from a far-away *saka*, but we do not

56

come to steal their *saka*. We do not poison their fish. We do not tap jelutong, nor do we live in a *kongsi*, nor do we rape their young girls, nor do we explode gunpowder in their rivers. We come as brothers. We bring good things. We bring good luck. We have many dollars. (Heavens, how that man is mistaken!) Our medicine is good——"

"I'm glad we're acceptable."

"These people are going through a profound social crisis, and for them this dance is a spiritual lifeline," Pat said. "It's what they call a Chinchem, and its origin suggests there are far stranger things in the jungle, Dick, than are dreamed of in our philosophy."

Pat went on to tell his brother how when he returned to Jalong after his leave in England he found the group in a bad way. They had had an influenza epidemic which had caused several deaths. Their crops had failed. There were cases of their girls being seduced by the Chinese. To add to their troubles it seemed that Dato Bintang, their great shaman, was losing contact with his spirit guide. Instead of warding off their persistent bad luck, he was expending all his spiritual energies fighting for the life of his wife, Siti Minang. She was dying of T.B. but he should have known the case was hopeless and left off his ministrations.

Pat explained that psychologically it was very dangerous for a shaman to get himself too deeply involved in an attempt to cure somebody who is incurably ill. The belief is that sickness is caused by Sankal, the spirit of a great female giant, who has waylaid one of the sick person's souls and imprisoned it in her armpit. To recover the soul, and thus effect a cure, the shaman has to go into a trance and send his liver-soul to the island in the lake where Sankal lives. He has to come upon her stealthily and tickle her in the ribs until she throws up her arms laughing and so allows the captive soul to escape. The shaman has of course to make sure not to get caught himself, and the Temiar consider that it requires great courage to approach Sankal's lake, let alone take on Sankal herself. Courage is not enough. The shaman must also be able to tell when a patient's life is coming to its natural end, and give up the struggle, or else he may find himself contending against the irresistible forces of nature. If rashly he should persist his own life may be forfeit.

Unfortunately for Dato Bintang he had allowed his shamanistic judgment to be overruled by his love for Siti Minang. She died while he was in a trance, trying to tickle Sankal, and when he came round in his triangular temple hut in the centre of the long-house floor and heard she was dead, the shock nearly drove him out of his mind. He developed a high fever, but insisted on attending his wife's funeral.

Her body was rolled in the mat on which she lay and bound with three lashings of *rotan*. A long pole was inserted through the roll to enable it to be carried, and it was borne to a place on the other side of a stream, where a grave was dug, a slit-bamboo sleeping platform inserted in it, and the corpse laid on the platform with all her intimate possessions. These are always buried to make sure the ghost will not return to the long-house to claim what it owns. A covering of poles, slit bamboo and banana leaves was put over the body, and the grave was then filled with earth, till a simple mound was heaped over it. On the grave the woman's family placed little offerings of food and tobacco, and a low leaf-shelter was erected over it. The area was fenced round with bamboo, and fires were lit at the corners to help the spirit on its way. Then the mourners returned to the long-house.

By this time Dato Bintang was really ill. That night he became delirious, and all the next day he raved. He slept fitfully during the night. But the following morning when he awoke his fever had gone, and he announced to the group that his wife's spirit had appeared to him in a dream, and that she had spoken to him.

"Bintang," she had said, "I have left you behind in the *saka*, and I now dwell in the place of spirits. I am very lonely, for there are no birds, and I yearn for the smell of burning incense."

"Why have you come back to me now, Siti Minang?" he asked.

She said: "There is a reason why I have come to you, and that is to teach you about food. You eat rodents, which are unclean, and pigs which grow fat with gross feeding on filth. If you stop eating this unclean food the Malays will not despise you."

She then told her husband to perform her Chinchem dance. "My Chinchem," she promised, "will drive the black spirits of disease and calamity back into Sankal's navel."

"How do you wish me to dance your Chinchem?" he asked, and she taught him the step, the tune, and the sad theme of the song, full of regret for lost happiness, and compassion for the dead.

Dato Bintang had asked for a sign to prove she was not an evil spirit in disguise, and Siti Minang said that if the group danced her Chinchem the following night her betel box which had been buried with her would be returned during the dance.

"And was it?" Richard enquired.

"Dato Bintang swears it was," Pat said. "There was a woven grass mat on his sleeping platform, and during the dance the betel box is supposed to have suddenly fallen on it. Kilton Stewart and I questioned him under hypnosis, to see if we could find out how he managed to bring off the betel box trick. But his account under hypnosis agreed entirely with his original story, and with the evidence of others in the long-house who saw the box fall."

"Surely there must be an explanation?" Richard said.

"I could find no evidence of deception," Pat said. "Dato Bintang showed me the box, which they were all certain had been buried. Everybody had been told about the promised sign before the dance started, so you can imagine the effect on them when it did appear. The shaman let out a shout, and about half the group had seizures. When they came round a cold wind was felt blowing through the long-house, and all those who were sick were cured that night."

The rhythm of the Chinchem had become faster, and the dancers, nearing the point of exhaustion, were becoming more abandoned. Suddenly with a piercing cry Dato Bintang leapt up into the air and collapsed on the dance floor. The orchestra broke off abruptly, and almost in the same instant some of the men and all the women dancers staggered and dropped to the floor, where they lay in a sweating, writhing heap.

Their frenzy lasted possibly five minutes, during which time the other dancers struck them with whisks, and relatives pulled them away from the heap and laid them out on their backs.

The old shaman was the first to get up. He walked round the long-house, making impulsive flourishes and rattling his leaf-whisk. Presently he approached the dais, and Pat went down and brought him over to where Richard was sitting.

"Feel his sweat—it's ice-cold," Pat said. He spoke to the shaman in Temiar, then he told Richard: "I've asked him to prophesy through the spirit of Siti Minang."

Dato Bintang flourished his whisks. He threw one of them down, and blew on the brothers in turn through the fingers of his fist. His breath came out cold and icy like his sweat. He began speaking and Pat interpreted.

"He has a vision of Siti Minang's Chinchem sweeping across the country of the Temiar. He sees many dark spirits, and black trees, and red suns. He sees the navel of Sankal like a black pit from which the spirits come up bubbling. He sees evil men

invading the *sakas* from the distant *kualas* where the jungle
ends."

The shaman made several passes with his whisks. Then he went
on speaking.

"He sees in us the future hope of the Temiar—this Chinchem as
the spiritual agency to fight these perverted evil forces, and our-
selves to lead the Temiar against them. You're definitely in it,
Dick. He says that after me you will become their Tata."

Thinking back through the years on that night of flickering
firelight and glistening bodies stamping strange rhythmic
patterns, of hollow bamboo music, of too much whisky and the
smell of wood smoke, hill *tembakau* and drying foliage, Richard's
most vivid memory is of the old shaman during those tense
minutes of prophecy, and Pat's interpretation that charged the
jabbering with tremendous significance. Richard was eighteen.
Though he would not have admitted it then, his resolution to
become an anthropologist was strengthened by a sense of having
already been ordained for a high purpose by the spirit guide of the
most powerful shaman of the Temiar.

A few days later a party of nine Temiar braves arrived from the
Rening river with an invitation from Pat's great friend Along,
Chief of the Pahang Temiar Reserve, to visit his long-house.

"I can't leave the excavation just at the moment," Pat told
Richard. "But why don't you go? The men say that if their Tata
cannot come, then their Little Tata must. They won't take no for
an answer."

"Little Tata?"

"That's what they called you."

"Well I think Big Tata might be more fitting, since I stand six
feet two in my socks, fully six inches taller than Tata!"

So Richard went to the Cameron Highlands, from where he

was taken down the Telom river to the Rening. Here he met Along and all the other headmen of the area.

In February 1936, Richard travelled back to Europe with his mother. Sheelah was married in Paris to Dennis Trumble, an officer in the Malayan Customs, and after the wedding Richard went on up to Cambridge, where he entered Pat's old college, Corpus Christi.

Meanwhile the family heard very little from Pat in Malaya: later when Richard inherited H.V.'s file of his brother's letters, he found only four written between October 1936 and October 1938, when Pat returned to England on his next leave.

All four letters are mainly concerned with the causes leading to his financial difficulties. There was, for instance, the Coronation Carnival in Taiping in 1937. As he explained: "I was asked to put on a Sakai raft on the lakes for the Carnival, not officially, but in a friendly sort of way, by one or two of the Committee. All the other rafts and barges were run by clubs or *kongsis*, like Planters or Miners, etc. I ran mine out of my own pocket, and did not realise until the show started that people were going to move from craft to craft and refreshments had to be offered. I was given a prize of $30 but spent in all $600! I thought of putting in a claim afterwards, but I am no good at that sort of thing."

The following year he had again got into debt with tradesmen, and when H.V. asked an old family friend to inquire tactfully into his son's affairs, it was found that possibly three-quarters of his salary was being spent on aborigines. The friend wrote to say there were rarely less than twenty or thirty staying at his house in Taiping at any time. They would come out of the jungle with some petition or complaint, and Pat would not only be expected to feed them but pay for their transport back to the point at which they entered the jungle.

At the same time he was running several schemes which he considered a practical means of solving problems arising out of the culture contact, and it meant his having to pay men he had trained to supervise the work.

The schemes included model settlements to show certain groups how to adapt their traditional pattern of life to conform with encroaching rubber, mining and lumbering interests. In Sungei Siput he had employed at his own expense a Malay irrigation expert to whom he sent lowland Temiar to learn about wet cultivation, to save their having to go on felling valuable timber to clear fresh *ladangs* for dry cultivation.

At the Cameron Highlands he maintained one of his personal jungle guides to act as a gillie for trout fishermen who came up from the plains: the idea being to encourage other local aborigines to take up this sort of work. He had also engaged additional field staff for his ethnographic research, as well as a stenographer whom he paid out of his own pocket, since he had to travel about the districts, advising the District Officers on aborigine problems, and his secretary in Taiping was also the Museum caretaker.

In April 1938, in a rafting accident, Pat lost a lot of his field notes on the Temiar, together with his Temiar-English dictionary, and his cine-camera.

"It was a terrible blow," he wrote. "Months of intensive work were lost in those rapids. But I look back on it now as both a test and a purging. In my blank despair the realisation came to me that the great deal I had to do could never be achieved if I did not pull myself together and become a reservoir of basic wealth, which would be behind me in all I did. I felt my word was not carrying enough weight in some quarters, because I was becoming known as an eccentric scientist who was quite unreliable over money. This thought was suddenly quite intolerable to me, and I determined that those who may hope to discredit my efforts in the humanitarian field because of these previous failings of mine would from now on be grievously disappointed. I gained an altogether objective view of myself as I sat on the bank below the rapids, my clothes wet, staring at my bearers trying to recover what was left of the raft.

"I saw in those moments of insight that I have had, on the one side, too much flattery, and then on the other side, too much jealousy. Flattery did not spoil me, but it did make me drive my convictions forward without the roundabout nonsense and timidity which characterises minute-paper government. This I know has aroused resentment in certain quarters. I could see the reaction in my own department to my misfortune, for the Director of Museums wants me to be a museum curator first and a field ethnographer afterwards. So I decided not to report the full extent of the loss, and the next day I began to re-record all over again."

In another letter he told his parents: "The record is now creeping back and accumulating fast. It has been hard work, and still will be, but in the end I can see my way to a beautiful plan for a thesis, whereas before I could not see the wood for the trees."

There was other important news. It concerned his famous aboriginal enactment. For years he had been urging the Government to adopt a coherent policy towards aborigines. He had warned administrative heads of the dangers of the culture contact, and of trouble breeding where Chinese jelutong-tappers and tin-miners had come up and settled in Temiar territory. He had pointed out the hereditary right of the aborigines to jungles they had occupied for centuries; long before British enterprise opened up the interior.

In an "Examination of the Present Circumstances Affecting the

Status of the Ple-Temiar Senoi"[1] he had elaborated: "Previous to the intervention of British rule, the Ple-Temiar pursued the independent existence of a hill people on the mountains of the Main Range. Only the decision of the British Government that the boundaries of the states of Perak and Kelantan should be defined by the watershed has made the Ple-Temiar the subjects of anybody. It is maintained here that full recognition of this fact should influence our dealings with the Ple-Temiar. From the point of view of the British Government, however, the Ple-Temiar have been assumed to have been the subjects of the Sultans of Perak and Kelantan. At the present time the whole question is very open. The Ple-Temiar are not Mohammedans, and there is no reason to suppose that they show any tendency to become such in bulk. If it is maintained that the Senoi are the subjects of the Sultans a definite policy which recognises their rights must be instituted. The present situation is full of anomalies. For example, up to now, no facts about land tenure of the Senoi were available. A simple device was to assume that they had no ownership of land. In some cases their land was given to Chinese squatters and they were ejected. In one district compensation was given to Senoi groups whose land was alienated to European estates. But no compensation was given for the land alienated in the Cameron Highlands (Semai Senoi). On the present State map of Perak large areas of exclusive Ple-Temiar land are designated 'Malay Reservation'; most of it is unsurveyed. If we are to have a reservation, let us at least reserve the land for the people who occupy it."

He had justified the right of the Ple-Temiar to pursue their own way of life, and suggested that recognition be given to tribal laws and customs. He had argued that Ple-Temiar culture was in

[1] *Report on the Settlements and Welfare of the Ple-Temiar Senoi of the Perak-Kelantan Watershed.*

harmony with their environment, since they lived in an ecological balance with wild life, and their system of cultivating *ladangs* did not lead to deforestation. He had indicated the strategic importance of the jungle routes the aborigines kept open, and their value as guides, porters, and trackers. (The Police often made use of them for apprehending tin-stealers and runaway criminals.) He had shown that there was not even an economic argument in favour of allowing Chinese tappers to exploit jelutong, as their methods were found to destroy the trees, whereas the Temiar method did not have this result. "Relatively vast areas of the Peninsula are still undeveloped jungle," he wrote, "so that today timber, wild life and primitive people coincide in a single area. It seems not unreasonable that the interests of the inhabitants should have their protectors as well as the timber and big game." In fact he had put forward so many recommendations that a number of senior M.C.S. officials had taken exception to a "mere scientist sticking his nose in matters of high Government policy".

Fortunately Pat had supporters as well as detractors in upper Government circles, and many of his ideas and suggestions found their mark. The outcome was the Aboriginal Tribes Enactment—Perak: No. 3 of 1939, establishing reservations for the jungle folk, which Pat drafted himself. As he informed his parents: "It was quite without precedent. Every step had to be thought out and principles laid down out of my own head." Under section 5 of the enactment, provision was made for the appointment of a Protector of Aborigines by the Sultan in State Council, and Pat was appointed the first Protector of Aborigines on 21st December 1939.

The current Aboriginal Peoples Ordinance—No. 3 of 1954—which is a Federal ordinance, was drafted almost entirely on Pat's enactment, which it repeals.

During Richard's last year at Cambridge, Pat returned to the university on study leave, to work on a thesis for his Ph.D. He rented a small flat in a lane off the market square, where Puteh, who had accompanied him, acted as his cook, valet and house-keeper. One of Pat's close friends at the time was Noël Ross, an M.C.S. officer, who was also at Cambridge on study leave and was taking a 'ghost' course in anthropology. Ross had a bigger flat, overlooking King's Parade, and here quite frequently they got together for an evening of aboriginal music and dancing and Scotch whisky. Puteh would beat out the rhythm on a python-skin drum against recordings of dance music Pat had made, and Ross and the Noone brothers would dance in loin-cloths.

During one of these sessions there was a knock on the door, and Pat opened it to find a policeman standing outside. He had come to investigate what appeared to the people in the house opposite to be a nude orgy: they had only been able to see the dancers' bare upper bodies. However the constable was reassured by the loin-cloths, and after accepting a drink continued on his beat.

Kilton Stewart was also in England at the time, engaged in writing his own thesis for a Doctorate of Philosophy of London University, and he spent most of his week-ends at Cambridge with Pat. Having worked together in the jungle on the dream psychology of the Temiar Senoi, their thesis subjects were similar, although of course they each treated different aspects. Stewart dealt more with the application of the dream as an instrument of socialisation; while Pat showed how the dream had been used to shape the whole pattern of the lives and culture of the people.

Every year a thesis is selected to be read in outline during the Cambridge May Week festivities. In 1939 it was Pat's, and Stewart recalls how he read it before a distinguished assembly in his fine, resonant speaking voice that filled the hall.

After the outline had been read, the subject was thrown open for discussion, and one of the professors raised what Pat had anticipated would be the only serious objection he would have to contend with. This was that since every premise had been based on dream experience, how was he to prove that the various dreamers were in fact telling him the truth.

Pat had an answer ready. He described how on journeys through the jungle he would get up during the night and sit listening to his aborigine porters talking in their sleep. In this way he frequently heard a dream unconsciously being described as it was happening. He heard songs and poetry composed with lines being improved and better words and meanings tried out. He heard discussions with dream characters. So when the same dream was recounted to him in the morning he was able to check the dreamer's accuracy. He found no case of a narrative of a dream experience being substantially falsified.

One night he and Stewart had heard a shaman porter receive a dance instruction from his spirit guide. It had rained a lot during the journey, the path was very slippery, and the men were not keen to take them over a difficult pass the next day. But the shaman announced in the morning that if they performed the dance he had received in his dream, then his *gunig* would enter the tin boxes they carried and make them empty. The dance was performed that night, and the following day they continued the journey. No longer did the men complain about their loads, which they said now felt as light as if the boxes were empty. The extraordinary part of it was that they were able to pick them up as though they were in fact empty boxes. And as they walked they seemed to be expending far less effort than that which should have been required for the job.

Pat stayed at Cambridge for three terms, then he went to stay with his parents in the South of France, where he began writing up his thesis. After a few weeks he went on to Malaya. Meanwhile Richard had got his degree in anthropology, and H.V. decided to send him out to join Pat to get field experience working under him. Richard sailed from London on 24th August 1939. He was at sea when the war started—a war that was to sweep away the old Malaya.

PART TWO . DÉBÂCLE

★

6 . Little Tata

Pat was living with Anjang in Museum House when Richard arrived in Taiping. But as she was one of about thirty other aborigines who occupied the house and the servants quarters in the compound at the back, her presence aroused no comment in European social circles.

Richard thought she had grown a little taller when he was introduced to her in the front porch of the house. She greeted him in Malay as they shook hands, then she turned and spoke to Pat in Temiar.

"She says," Pat interpreted, "that I must tell you the correct relationship-term for you to use when addressing her. It is '*teneh*' and it means elder sister. She will call you '*pe*'—younger brother."

"*Selamat teneh*," Richard said to her, and she and a crowd of her relatives who had gathered on the front steps to welcome him laughed happily.

Pat took a parcel out of his car—he had met Richard in Penang, and they had motored up to Taiping together. He handed the parcel to Richard and told him to present it to Anjang. She accepted it decorously, but a moment later she was tearing off the wrapper to release a pile of vividly-coloured sarongs. Pat mentioned that there was one for each of the women in the house, and eight of them surrounded Anjang in a laughing, tugging,

70

female scrum. Soon they vanished into the house, scurrying up the stairs to the bedrooms where their screams and giggling could be heard. They emerged later wearing the new sarongs, most of them with their foreheads and cheeks freshly decorated with red and white dots. Anjang had not painted her face, but she had put some frangipani blooms in her hair. Richard noticed the reddish tints in the thick dark-brown waves, which he had already heard described as one of the elements in the Temiar racial livery.

Meanwhile, however, he had been swept bewildered into the ménage. Aborigines appeared everywhere, and the house reeked of their hill tobacco. He was shown to a bedroom. It was already being used by two other couples who had rigged up split-bamboo sleeping platforms.

"Sorry about the crush," Pat said. "But all the bedrooms are crowded. Anyway you'll soon get used to communal life."

Richard did, and in the succeeding weeks he discovered an entirely new side to Pat—that of the gentle, imperturbable Tata. He did not seem to mind what his crowd of guests did in his house. They played his gramophone, sometimes all day. Taps were left running. Lights burned all night in the house, as there were always some of the crowd awake, talking and smoking and moving about. At meals the brothers sat alone at the dining-table, served by Puteh, but there was always an audience of aborigines in the dining-room, watching them eat and discussing the *tuan's cuisine française* which Puteh had learnt while he and Pat were in France. At times an aborigine might come up to the table and examine a plate at close quarters, then return to his place on the floor and describe it to the others.

Richard had started learning Malay, and in the afternoons he would go round to the museum, where Pat had planned for him a course of anthropological literature on Malaya. A lot had to be crammed into a short time as Pat was due to leave on his next expedition on 24th October and he wanted Richard to accompany him.

The purpose of the expedition was to study some of the Negrito groups near the Siamese frontier, since Pat was now responsible for the welfare of the entire aborigine population of Perak.

They went first to Grik, the administrative capital of the District of Upper Perak, although the telephone line from the south stopped fifty miles short of the town. Grik was a natural outlet for Negritos who brought down jungle produce, such as *rotan, atap* thatch and bamboo, which they traded for *parangs* and salt. The District Officer, a Malay, had offered to call in some of them from the neighbouring jungle, so Pat and Richard waited at the rest-house.

The following day three appeared on the rest-house veranda. They were not particularly healthy specimens, as two had skin disease, and the third, the headman of the group, had a couple of angry-looking sores on one leg, but they were true Negritos— negroid pygmies, with glossy black skin, woolly hair, flat noses, thick lips and large, shining eyes.

After much palaver the headman promised to return the next day and lead the *tuans* to their encampment. Yet as Pat half expected none of them turned up.

"They've heard there's a war on," he explained. "They're probably scared we might try to conscript them to fight."

The expedition continued up to Kroh, in two Austin Seven cars, which were then the only vehicles capable of negotiating the thirty-mile mountain road connecting the two towns: the baggage went by elephant along a path through the jungle. The motor road, where it dipped down into valleys, had been banked up with the red earth of that part of the country, there being no bridges or culverts, but as it was the rainy season many of the low-lying stretches had dissolved into soft clay. The drivers' method of tackling these morasses was to rush them in bottom gear, revving hard and hoping for the best. Somehow they invariably made the other side, although on occasions they came very near to going over the side of the embankment. The country was a pattern of intense green, jungle-clad hills and shimmering valleys cleared for *padi*, with flimsy Malay villages along the way, leaving an impression of tall, slender, areca-nut palms, languid Malays and suicidal chickens crossing the road.

For the earlier part of the journey they could see the twin limestone peaks of Kendrong and Krunei rising almost perpendicularly from the surrounding jungle. From Klian Intan, where the Rahman Hydraulic Tin Mine had cut away half a hillside just above the village, there was a good road all the way to Kroh.

From the rest-house, where they stayed, stretches a vista of gardens with tropical flowering shrubs, playing fields, a lake, an avenue of scarlet flame-of-the-forest trees leading away to the Chinese shopping centre, and beyond that the surrounding intensely green hills. Every evening a number of Europeans, mainly tin miners and planters and their wives, would arrive at the rest-house for a round of golf on the nine-hole course, spend a couple of hours drinking and gossiping on the rest-house veranda, then return to their homes.

A few of the local officials might stay on for dinner at the rest-house, then the talk would usually come round to one subject in particular—Captain Hubert Berkeley.

Berkeley was a thin, sour-looking man, who had been District Officer of Upper Perak from 1906 to 1928, a power and a personality known to every Malay in the district. Richard heard him accused of keeping it backward because he didn't believe in progress: Berkeley resented interference, and there was the famous story of how he once put the British Resident off a proposed tour of inspection. There had been floods that year, and Berkeley sent a message down to Taiping to the effect that there was no bridge at the fifteenth mile. Thinking that he would not be able to cross the river the Resident decided against the journey. The message was true. There wasn't a bridge at the fifteenth mile —there never had been.

But Berkeley had loved the people he administered, and he had had the political foresight to negotiate the absorption of the independent state of Rahman into his district, so that Perak would thereby gain control of the headwaters of the Perak river.

Kroh was redolent of Berkeley. At the side of the lake below the rest-house was the little wooden house he had built for himself. In the garden (for he was a keen gardener) was a wide variety of beautiful tropical shrubs and creepers, and on the road to Betong in Siam was the hot spring where Berkeley would go in the cool of the morning with his lovely Malay adopted daughter. They would change into bathing sarongs and stand for half an hour in the large concrete bath through which the steaming sulphurous water flowed.

It was one of Berkeley's halting bungalows on a jungle path eight miles from Kroh that Pat used as a base for the expedition. There were two plank huts on stilts connected by a wooden platform in a wide clearing by the side of a small tributary of the Rui river. One of the huts leaned over drunkenly with its roof collapsed, and elephant tracks in muddy patches in the lawn of short, tough grass surrounding the bungalow suggested who had been the culprits.

The other hut was dank and dirty, but it was soon cleaned up, and with their camp equipment laid out it was made quite comfortable. The Malays—and there were seven to start with—were accommodated in tents round the halting bungalow. It was the Moslem fasting month of Ramadan, which meant that they could not eat, drink or smoke anything from four a.m. until after the sun had set, so none of them felt inclined for work in the afternoons. But the villagers in the nearby Siamese village of Belukar Semang were Buddhists, and they made up for the Malays' lack of enthusiasm by bringing gifts of fruit and vegetables and offering help in any way they could.

The village headman knew a Negrito group that was encamped in the neighbourhood, and he promised to get a few of them to come to the halting bungalow and meet the *tuans*.

A few days later three shiny black little figures with blowpipes and quivers and *parangs* stuck through their loin-cloths emerged from the gloom of the surrounding jungle and cautiously approached the camp.

Pat saw them and immediately went out. He greeted them in Malay and offered cigarettes, adding that he was the *tuan* whom the Government had entrusted with the care of the jungle folk. They stayed a while, and before they left he gave them a bag of rice and told them to come again if they wanted anything, particularly medicines, which he and his brother would give.

It was the start of a long and patient wooing which was interrupted after a week by the arrival of H.V. at Kroh. Pat went off to meet him, leaving Richard to cope with what had developed into a daily sick parade of Negritos with sores, cuts and skin diseases, and a variety of undefined pains and aches. While examining his patients Richard would take the opportunity of obtaining their anthropometric measurements.

Two weeks went by, then one morning two of the Negritos came to say their chief had hurt his leg.

"Give us medicine for him," one of them said.

"Let him come here and I will heal him," Richard replied.

The men went off, and Richard decided he would have to inform Pat immediately of what had happened, as this was the sort of opportunity they had been waiting for. If the chief was badly hurt and could not be moved, the chances were he would invite them to the group encampment to attend him. Richard returned to Kroh, where he found Pat and H.V. at the rest-house.

Early next morning, when the two brothers returned to the halting bungalow, they met a visiting party of Negritos, who came to say their headman's leg was getting very painful. They asked if the *tuans* would bring medicine to him.

They started out, escorted by the Negritos, along a narrow jungle track, crossed a stream and struggled up a steep hill, eventually arriving at a small flattish area higher up a stream. A small natural clearing appeared in the jungle, and here they suddenly saw the encampment.

The track led through an opening in a circle of simple lean-to shelters, so arranged that their outer leaf-walls also acted as camouflage and a flimsy stockade. There were eleven shelters furnished with sleeping platforms consisting of no more than a few lengths of slit bamboo resting on logs laid on the ground. In front of each shelter was the family cooking fire. In the centre of the circle, perched on the stump of what had been a fairly large sapling, was a small *pano* or medicine hut, pyramidal in shape and measuring about three feet at the base. Except for the headman, who lay on a sleeping platform, the encampment was deserted.

"We'll stay just as long as it takes to see to the old man," Pat said. "We mustn't show we're interested. And for heaven's sake don't go near that *pano* hut."

The chief had sprained his ankle and lacerated his foot. Richard cleaned and dressed the wound, bandaged the sprain, and gave the man three aspirin tablets with a drink of coloured water. Then they walked straight out of the encampment, and the escort took them back to the halting bungalow.

That was the first of several visits to the encampment. The brothers were regularly taken to attend to the chief, and when his leg got better they went at his invitation. By this time the women, wearing short fungus skirts that hung like hanks of thick black string around their waists, and naked children were to be found in the shelters when they arrived. Later, when these got used to the *tuans'* visits they would go about their daily household duties instead of just sitting and staring.

Unfortunately the Noones learned nothing from the group beyond what they had observed, because one morning their escort did not turn up for them at the halting bungalow. Pat thought that they might have gone out hunting. But when after four days they still had not appeared, he and Richard went up to the encampment to investigate. They found the place deserted. The shelters had been left, but the *pano* hut had been taken away.

They never discovered why the group had suddenly decided to leave or where they had gone. But as Pat explained, that was more or less how Negritos had behaved towards every anthropologist who had ever tried to study them. It may have been that the group had eaten all the edible roots and tubers in the surrounding area of jungle and had just moved on to another place without bothering to say good-bye, or that, being nomads, they had suddenly felt restless and decided to go, or perhaps that something had been done or said to upset them. Pat and Richard would never know.

Pat had to return to Taiping, but Richard stayed on at the halting bungalow with two Malays, in the hope of being able to contact another Negrito group that was thought to be in the area.

t to Pong, a journey of nine leech-infested miles, in
ird group. There he heard that Ering, the Negrito
met at Grik, was in the lock-up at Kroh. He had
rying to sell a baby tapir, a protected animal, and
Richard hurried back to see if he could help him and thereby win
his confidence.

Richard paid the man's fine of twenty dollars, which seriously
taxed his finances, but the following day Ering vanished again.
Richard then heard of yet another Negrito group near Klian
Intan, and cycled there with Yaacob, one of his Malays, but again
he was disappointed. The Negritos had moved off with all they
possessed, leaving their pathetic circle of leaf-shelters and a
number of deep holes here and there in the jungle, where they had
burrowed in search of tubers.

Richard found a message from Pat when he returned to the
halting bungalow, with instructions to go down to Grik to refit
for a solo expedition to Ayer Chepam on the Perak river to make
an intensive study of a group of Lanoh Negritos, who had inter-
married with Lower Strata Temiar and were now living a settled
life in the Temiar style. The headman, Goh, was a friend of Pat's,
and sent a party of his braves to Grik to meet Richard and take
him down river by raft to their settlement.

There was no question of Richard's having to woo this group.
They were waiting to welcome him. He was taken to the long-
house on a bluff overlooking the river and ceremoniously
received by Penghulu Goh, who invited him to stay as long as he
liked.

Richard stayed three months, until Pat (now Acting Director
of Museums) wrote asking him to return to Taiping. He added
that he had received a letter from H.V. in Colombo suggesting
an interesting plan for Richard's future.

The female orchestra at an informal dance when Richard and the author visited a Temiar settlement in the Fort Kemar area. The music is weirdly attractive

Kabun, the orphan aborigine boy, who has led a Communist armourer out of the jungle to surrender with a quantity of arms and ammunition

Anthropological research. Richard photographing two Temiar girls in the Ulu Jemheng

Richard returned to Taiping, but he was not enthusiastic about the plan, which was that he should join his father in Colombo and study under an archæologist at the university there.

Instead Richard got a temporary job with the Public Health Department of Perak. His assignment was to carry out a field investigation into the economy and nutrition of a rural Malay *kampong*. There was only a small government grant of thirty dollars a month for the investigation, but Richard looked on it as an excellent opportunity to improve his Malay and to get to know the people. The place selected for him was Kampong Perak, not far from Taiping.

However, H.V. was not satisfied. He wrote to say that if Richard wanted to study nutrition, one of the world's greatest experts on the subject was in Colombo, and had already indicated his willingness to accept him as a pupil. A cheque for a passage to Ceylon and travelling expenses was enclosed in the letter, which ended with positive instructions for Richard to take the next boat to Colombo.

"I really don't want to go," Richard told Pat. "Now that I have learnt Malay I can be useful here. But in Ceylon I would have to start again from scratch."

"H.V.'s going to be very angry if you oppose him," Pat said. "He'll probably cut off your allowance."

"I'll have to risk that."

As Pat predicted, H.V. cut off his younger son's allowance. Richard had counted on the passage money to keep him going for a while, but Pat borrowed most of that to pay his grocer's bill. Eventually H.V. relented and started sending the allowance again eight months later: but in the meantime Richard had had to manage on his thirty dollars' grant from the Public Health Department. He had bought a ramshackle Malay house for fifty dollars, and had lived as a Malay, eating Malay food and working

D

with the villagers in their *padi* fields and the *ladangs* which they cleared on the outskirts of the jungle.

The experience he gained at Kampong Perak, and the friends he made there were to prove an immense value to him later.

7 . *The Frontier Patrol*

It was January 1941. The Japanese had occupied Indo-China, and to the military chiefs planning the defence of Malaya this constituted a threat to the whole Peninsula.

At the time very little was known of the northern boundary along the Siamese Frontier. The boundary was barely mapped, indeed parts of the District of Upper Perak depended on a survey that was over thirty years old; in his search for Negritos Richard had found some rivers flowing in the opposite direction from that indicated on the existing map.

It was therefore decided to have it thoroughly reconnoitred and for this purpose a secret organisation known as the Frontier Patrol was set up. It consisted of five Europeans with jungle experience, who were each given a sector of the frontier for which they were responsible, under the overall control of E. O. Shebbeare, the Chief Game Warden of Malaya. The Noone brothers were among the five. They had adjacent sectors, Pat based at Grik, and Richard at Kroh.

Each patrol officer was left to recruit his own men and organise his patrol as best he could, so Richard went to Kampong Perak where he engaged eleven of the best men he knew and transported them and their families, lock, stock and barrel, to Kroh. Here they built their own houses by the side of a stream just outside the town, with a house for Richard to stay in when he tired of the rest-house. Later they were joined by another two Malays from Sik, and one from Negri Sembilan and two from Taiping. These, with Richard's boy Yaacob, completed his permanent establishment.

Richard first had them trained. He fetched three of Penghulu Goh's braves up from Ayer Chepam as instructors in jungle craft and raft construction and navigation. Then he took them all out together with porters and baggage elephants and showed them how he wanted the job done. Finally they were split into five sections and left to operate independently from advanced posts along the frontier. He visited each frontier post in turn collecting their reports on tracks they had reconnoitred and any other information they had picked up.

Richard's second in command was Osman, who later ran the entire patrol on his own when Richard was sent out on a special assignment. He was paid thirty dollars a month. The quartermaster, who was also responsible for porters and elephants, was a Sik Malay from the Ulu Muda, an honest-to-goodness personality named Palang Gadok. He earned twenty-five dollars a month. The rest of the permanent staff were paid between fifteen dollars and twenty dollars.

In addition Richard had eight secret agents whom he sent over the border to get what information they could of Japanese activities in Siam. It was known that the Siamese were secretly collaborating with the Japs, and it seemed possible that preparations were being made for an attack. Early in December the Far Eastern Fleet, with the *Prince of Wales* and *Repulse*, two of the most powerful ships afloat, seemed a sufficiently formidable deterrent.

The best of Richard's secret agents was an old Patani Malay, the Haji Awang Halir, who lived at Simpang Perak, a small village of not more than four houses at a point where two tracks coming down over the mountains from Siam converge to lead off again in three directions southwards. It was through this village that the rubber smugglers from Malaya, and the buffalo smugglers from Siam, and any others wishing to avoid the main route, had to pass. It was an ideal place to pick up interesting gossip.

The Haji was a relative of the deposed Raja of Yala in Siam, and had formerly lived there. Somehow he possessed a Siamese passport, and this enabled him to make frequent trips over the border to collect information from some of his relations who were also in Richard's pay. Being Patani Malays they were violently anti-Siamese. This was a traditional bitterness that dated back a hundred years to two terrible battles in which the Siamese had badly beaten the Malays. Moreover within the last few months laws had been passed forbidding the drumming to call the Moslem faithful to mosque, and the wearing of the sarong, the Malays' national dress, and these and other petty restrictions had stirred up the old hatreds. There had been no difficulty in recruiting the Haji's relatives as British agents.

Every few weeks Richard would go up to Simpang Perak. He loved the spot with its overgrown ditches and ramparts where the Patani Malays had made a last stand. It was full of memories and ghosts. He built a little bamboo house near the Haji's, and here they would sit talking by the light of a kerosene lamp late into the night.

"Well, Haji," Richard would say, "I trust you found your relatives well in Thailand."

"I found them well, *Tuan*, but not happy," the Haji would reply, bursting to impart the information he had brought back.

For instance, on one trip he informed Richard that the aerodrome at Patani was being enlarged, that the Japs had established a headquarters at the Zoo Hotel in Haad Yai, an establishment owned by a German, that Japanese officers had come down to Betong to make a reconnaissance of the frontier area, that two Japanese agents were on a Siamese rubber estate not four miles from the border, that large units of the Thai Army had been moved down from the north, and that a concrete road block was being built just outside Betong under the guise of a ceremonial arch for the approaching Thai national celebrations.

The Haji had a natural flair for his new rôle. Indeed in one affair of counter-espionage he completely outwitted a senior officer of the Thai Military Intelligence who had been sent into Malaya to find out all he could about the Frontier Patrol. The officer had the misfortune to come through Simpang Perak.

"*Tuan*," the Haji told Richard on his next visit, "the hated enemy have sent over a spy."

"How do you know this, Haji?" Richard asked.

"Because, *Tuan*, this man who says he is a Malay is not circumcised. I saw him bathing."

"So he is a Thai."

"Yes, *Tuan*."

"But why should he be a spy?"

"Because he asked many questions. I too am a spy, and I know that such meaningful questions do not come from mere idle curiosity. *Tuan*, his interest is in the Frontier Patrol. He wanted to know about you, and I told him many things. I told him how you followed the jungle tracks and wrote reports in your house here."

"But, Haji, why did you tell all this to the man, knowing him to be a spy?" Richard asked.

"I told him no more than he already suspects, and now he is certain to come to you. Then you can kill him."

Richard laughed. "Why should he come to me?"

"I told him you are always ready to employ a good man and you paid well," the Haji said.

A week later Richard was sitting in Kampong Lallang, sipping jet-black coffee with the rest of his men, when a man walked into the *atap* shelter of the coffee-shop. Richard did not pay much attention to him, as a crowd always collects when there is anything interesting happening. Presently the stranger began talking to some of the men, and after a while Osman came up and said that the newcomer wanted to be taken on as a porter.

Richard called him over and asked who he was. He replied that he was a Kedah Malay, and had once been in partnership with his father in Penang as a procurer of women, but that business had fallen off, and he had come over to the mainland to look for coolie work. He spoke perfect Malay but looked more like a Siamese, being unusually tall, with a long, thin nose, jet-black, gently wavy hair and striking, beady eyes. In view of what the Haji had said Richard was immediately suspicious.

"All right," Richard said, "I will take you on as a porter. What I am looking for is a man who can write English. I would pay him twenty-five dollars a month and enlist him in the patrol."

"I can write English," the man said.

"Then you are the one for me. Even Osman here cannot write English," Richard said.

Yap, which was what the ex-procurer of women called himself, was engaged forthwith, but when they got to Kroh Richard telephoned the Officer Commanding Police District.

Yap was arrested and found with an automatic pistol and a large sum of money in his possession. He was in fact the Siamese spy whom the Haji had first spotted, and spoke not only Malay and English, but Chinese, German and Dutch as well.

. . . . .

One evening in October 1941 Richard was at the rest-house at Kroh, when a short, stocky man with a grey moustache arrived. He registered under the name of Johnson, and from what Richard overheard of his conversation with the Chinese boy, Johnson intended to stay a few days. Presently he joined Richard on the veranda and they got talking. "What are you doing up here?" he asked Richard.

"I am in the Game Department. I've just got back from a trip to Sik. I have been trying to investigate the movements of a herd of elephants." It was Richard's usual cover story in reply to embarrassing questions.

The telephone rang, and the Chinese boy answered it. He kept saying there was no *Tuan* Nixon staying at the rest-house, whereupon the stocky man darted inside, grabbed the telephone from the boy and took the call.

When he came out he said: "Your name's Noone, isn't it?"

"Yes," Richard said, "but who are you, Johnson or Nixon?"

The stocky man laughed. He produced his identity card, which proved he was Nixon, a major attached to General Headquarters, Singapore. "I am from the Special Operations Organisation," he said. "I have come up here to see you about a special job."

"I am under the G2 (I), 3rd Indian Corps, sir," Richard said. "He's said nothing to me about this."

"I'll get 3rd Corps to signal you to work directly under me in this affair," Major Nixon told him. "Meanwhile let's go to my room. What I have told you is to be treated with the utmost secrecy."

In his room Nixon explained that he was responsible for establishing a secret route through the jungle to link Kroh with the British-run Pinyok Tin Mine in South Siam. In the event of the Japanese attempting an invasion of Malaya through Siam, the route was to be used for infiltrating infantry to Pinyok, from where it would be possible to cut the strategic Betong-Yala road at a point some fifty miles north of Betong.

The Major said: "I shall want the route completed and a series of huts built at intervals of a day's march. The huts will have to be stocked with food in case the route has to be used by British families being evacuated from the mine. But that can be done on a second trip. The important thing now is the route. That's urgent. Can you leave tomorrow?"

"I think so, sir."

"How old are you, Noone?"

"Twenty-two, sir."

"A bit young for a job like this—but you'll do."

Richard spent the next ten days on an expedition with a party of porters and baggage elephants. They cut a route to an agreed rendezvous, a mountain called Bukit Bubus, on the frontier, and established three huts at intervals of a day's march. On his return Richard reported to Major Nixon and heard that the people at Pinyok had failed to locate Bukit Bubus after two attempts, but did not want to try again for fear of arousing suspicion. They had, however, reached a pass farther north, so when Richard returned to stock the huts with food in special sealed containers, he linked his route with the pass.

Then it was decided that he would have to return again along the route, this time with a wireless set and a supply of arms and ammunition to be dumped at the pass for the British personnel at the mine, who were now required to defend the road until the infantry arrived. But since the arms and wireless set were not immediately available, Richard went with Pat to spend the week-end in Penang where Sheelah and her husband were stationed.

In Penang the prospect of war still seemed very far away. They looked in at the Eastern and Oriental Hotel before lunch on the

Sunday. The bar was crowded with Europeans and so was the lounge. It was a typical, pleasant Sunday morning's drinking session. Eleven days later Japanese bombers attacked Penang and for three days the island was subjected to a series of terror raids. Casualties were terrible, both from the bombing and machine-gunning in the crowded streets. The town went up in flames, but nobody bothered to try to put out the fires or to check the looters, as most of the Asians had fled to the hills and all but four Europeans had fled to the mainland. The four who remained were a doctor, a Church of England minister, a Catholic priest, and an adjutant of the Salvation Army.

Meanwhile, however, Pat and Richard had motored back together from Penang. At Kroh rest-house they had had a final drink, touching glasses to Pat's toast of *Nong pai* (Temiar for 'new path'), his slogan for his welfare campaign for the aborigines. They had said good-bye at Kroh and Pat had carried on to Grik.

Then next day Major Nixon signalled cancelling Richard's gun-running expedition, and a little later orders came through from 3rd Indian Corps for Richard to disband his Frontier Patrol sections and to report to the 3/16th Punjab Regiment stationed at Kroh: he was commissioned a second-lieutenant with immediate effect.

Richard knew the unit well, having carried out a number of track reconnaissances for them and having helped to train them in jungle craft. He at once cycled round to their camp camouflaged under rubber trees on a large estate, and found Colonel Moorhead in the headquarters tent. Moorhead said: "Sit down, Richard. The situation is grave. We have just had orders to advance into Siam. It's a big operation called Matador, in which we form part of a column of infantry and some sappers known as Krocol. Our objective is to deny the port of Patani to the Japs in the event of an attempted landing. I am in command of Krocol and have been appointed Military Governor of all the Siamese territory Krocol occupies. You will be my political officer."

On the night of 6th December word came through that a Japanese convoy had been sighted in the China Sea steaming south, and Krocol received orders to prepare to advance.

The following evening Richard went up to the rest-house where he was expecting to meet the Haji. A tin miner from Klian Intan was sitting on the rest-house veranda drinking a whisky. Richard ordered one himself and sat down. Nothing seemed to have changed.

"I'm up here on a few days' leave," the miner said. "I hear there are some cute little Siamese dancing-girls in Betong. How would you like to drive out there tonight?"

"No, thanks," Richard said. "I have been called up. We're standing by."

"Bloody inconvenient."

"We're about to be invaded."

"Oh, the Japs won't get very far. Malaya's the easiest place in the world to defend with four-fifths of the country impenetrable jungle. They'd have to use the roads and there are only three from north to south. We've enough troops to stop them anywhere."

British propaganda, primarily intended to bluff the Japanese into thinking that Malaya was impregnable, had succeeded only in misleading most Europeans into a false sense of security.

Later the Haji came up to the veranda, and Richard took him into his old room.

"Old friend, what news have you brought?" Richard asked.

"*Tuan*," Haji replied, "the Thai Police have been given rifles and machine-guns by the Japanese. They have been told to shoot any British soldiers who cross the frontier."

At four a.m. on Monday 8th December, word came through that the Japs had landed at Singora in Siam and at Kota Bharu in Kelantan, but the sun rose and Krocol still waited.

Later that morning Richard, who had returned to the rest-house to pay off the last of his Frontier Patrol men, heard what sounded like distant thunder.

"The Navy must be doing a bit of target practice off Penang," said the tin miner on leave. He looked bleary-eyed after a late night at Betong. Actually the thunder came from Sungei Patani where the Japanese were bombing the aerodrome, destroying on the ground most of the front-line aircraft based there.

When eventually the order to advance came through, at one-twenty p.m., Patani in Siam was already in the hands of the Japanese, and Moorhead's objective had been limited to securing the Pinyok Tin Mine. The route that Richard had prepared with so much effort was never used. Krocol's advance began at two p.m. It was the first move of the fiasco.

8 . *The Fiasco*

As the Haji had predicted, the first shots at Krocol were fired by the Thai Police. As the leading scouts crossed the frontier and took over the customs post, two gendarmes happened to be strolling up the road to relieve the frontier guards. They dropped their shoes, which they were carrying in their hands, and dashed into the jungle after firing a few shots. But a few miles farther on Krocol was stopped by about fifty police, who were behind rocks, up in trees and covering several road blocks made by felled trees, It took some time to clear them out.

The Punjabis drove on to Betong where the Chinese population turned out with white flags, fruit and cigarettes to welcome them. Nailed to the concrete triumphal arch which the Haji had reported was an enormous white flag signifying the town's surrender. The Thai District Officer was there, bowing to the advancing Indians. He told the leading company commander that he had received orders from Bangkok not to oppose British troops, but when Richard arrived to question him he was nowhere to be found: he was in fact on his way to Yala by car.

Meanwhile the gendarmes had taken up positions twenty miles north of Betong, where the road snakes through a gorge and the Patani river rushes along below the road. With some sixty convicts, whom they had released from a penal settlement nearby and armed with Jap rifles, they succeeded in stopping Krocol until on 10th December the first Japanese tanks and mountain artillery arrived with three battalions of infantry in close support. In their first encounter with the little yellow tanks the 3/16th Punjabis lost nearly a whole company.

They fell back to a bend in the road, where they dug-in, covering a road-block. Sections were spread out down to the river on their right, and up over the ridge on their left, with two companies in reserve. Next day the Japs succeeded in infiltrating past their right flank, but were successfully driven back. Then they attacked the opposite flank and were again repulsed with heavy casualties. But their mountain guns were now in position and the Punjabis were subjected to a ceaseless bombardment.

By dawn the following morning, 12th December, the Japs had their heavy machine-guns on the eastern slope of the ravine overlooking the slit trenches of the defenders, who were presently subjected to intense fire. The ridge was attacked again, and overrun, while B Company astride the road was pounded hard with shells and mortar bombs.

D Company, led by an Indian officer, Second-Lieutenant Zarif, attacked the machine-gun positions, and lost half its men in the first wave. Gathering the rest together, Zarif led the final assault with a magnificent display of verve and gallantry, and captured the machine-guns. But the Japanese were also in strength higher up the ravine and farther down river. From here they could not be dislodged.

As Krocol was now in danger of being encircled, Moorhead obtained permission to withdraw. Richard was in a slit trench with B Company when the withdrawal started. They had to run back along the road, a gauntlet of about five hundred yards, with the Jap machine-guns sweeping it with tracer ammunition and their artillery firing over open sights. When B Company re-assembled behind cover of a bend in the road, only sixteen men remained out of the company's original hundred.

They marched back two miles to where the unit transport was parked along the side of the road facing Malaya, ready for the withdrawal. They had taken up defensive positions in the ditch, north of the line of transport, and were waiting for the order to embus, when a light truck suddenly appeared round a bend, moving very fast. It slowed down as an officer of the 5/14th Punjabis leaned out and shouted that the enemy tanks were just behind. Then the truck drove off leaving panic among the men waiting to continue the withdrawal.

Trucks were suddenly moving off while men were still clamber-ing aboard, and Richard, who wasn't quick enough, got left behind. However, the C.O. of the 5/14th Punjabis came up in his truck and gave Richard a lift. They drove back another five miles to where a concrete bridge was being prepared for demolition, and got out. But Richard did not see the others getting back into the truck and he was left behind again.

He was joined after a while by three officers of his own unit, who had also been left behind. They started walking back towards Betong. As they passed trucks ditched in the quagmire on either side of the road, they put some of them out of action by dropping a grenade under the bonnet. Then they found a deserted Bren-gun carrier and managed to get it working. Finally they heard the bridge go up, and a few minutes later the sappers' truck went hurtling past, followed by Colonel Moorhead in a second carrier, sitting at the guns. There was nobody alive between him and the Japanese.

Back over the border in Malaya the Punjabis took up prepared defensive positions on the road from Kroh to Baling. This left the Grik road undefended, and at dawn on 14th December Richard was sent out with a reconnaissance patrol to see if it was being used by the Japs in a thrust towards Grik. He took the patrol along jungle paths he knew well from the expedition to study the Negritos, and reached the road at a point above Klian Intan. The Japs were streaming southwards in the cars and trucks they had captured, with nobody to stop them except the Argyll and Sutherland Highlanders at Grik. Pat was with the Argylls.

When Richard got back to the Kedah Positions as they were called, he found only dead Punjabis, blasted pill-boxes and the two Bren-gun carriers knocked out. So he took his patrol back into the jungle and led them over the Kedah Divide to Baling by a route he had used two years before. There the remnants of the 3/16th Punjabis were gathered. They were executing their first fifth columnist, a Formosan, who had sniped a dispatch rider. The Formosan was struggling and screaming as he was tied with a length of webbing to a rubber tree. Then a shot rang out and the screaming stopped.

Soon the Argylls, less Pat's Company, arrived to relieve them, and the 3/16th Punjabis were brought down to Selama, where a stand was to be made all along the Krian river.

There followed the débâcle of the Jitra Positions, a solid line of trenches and concrete pill-boxes in North Kedah which had taken months to prepare, but were now waterlogged for the most part. Anyway the Japs infiltrated past them through the jungle, and attacked from the rear. The 11th Indian Division defending the positions was badly mauled and fell back.

The Krian river was successfully held for a time, until the Japanese column which was thrusting down from Grik threatened to cut off the 11th Indian Division at Kuala Kangsar.

The east bank of the Perak river was to be the next major line of defence, but there were neither sufficient troops to hold an extended front, nor reserves or air support to counter-attack at any break-through. Step by step the division was forced back, with remnants of the units combining to form single units.

Richard was attached to his battalion headquarters, which Colonel Moorhead generally established in some Chinese *kongsi* or Malay house: he never picked a comfortable European house and consequently they escaped a lot of the bombing attacks which knocked out several other battalion headquarters.

Most of Richard's time was spent interpreting. Men were brought in every day for interrogation, some suspected fifth columnists. At Siputeh a Chinese dressed in white was seen standing in the middle of the road waving a white topee during a dive-bombing attack. He was arrested and brought to Richard. When the man was searched yards of thin strips of white cloth were taken from his pockets. They were of the kind used as ground markings to direct Jap pilots at special targets. Colonel Moorhead ordered him to be shot.

Although there were a number of Chinese fifth columnists, the majority were Malays and Tamils, who were paid colossal sums to go forward and obtain information about the defensive positions, and also to guide the infiltrating Japanese infantry along jungle paths in their terrifying encircling movements.

These guides were given orange arm-bands, but the usual uniform of a collaborator was all white with a red head-dress. Collaborators' houses were marked with paper rising-sun emblems. These kept the inmates free from molestation by the Japanese.

The terror of the civil population was the curfew. When the 3/16th Punjabis were still in Kedah the Government issued an order that any civilians found outside their houses between dusk and dawn would be shot. But there was nobody to let the people know of the order, for the usual means of disseminating information to the *kampongs* had broken down.

Richard got permission to take four men and tour the neighbourhood, explaining why the order had been issued and what would happen if anyone did not comply. But in other areas where this was not done many innocent people were shot.

All the way down the Peninsula the Government departments had packed up and fled long before the Japanese were anywhere near, thus leaving a deep zone of chaos through which the defenders had to retreat.

In places Sikh police constables banded together into looting parties, broke into wine shops and roamed about drunk, terrorising the townsfolk. Bands of raiding Chinese also visited the *kampongs* and broke into rice stores. Most of the European estate houses were looted. The least fortunate were the sick. At Kampar an Army ambulance unit arrived to find the hospital full of civilian patients. The hospital had a fairly large European staff, but not one doctor or nurse had remained in the building. They had loaded their luggage into hospital transport and left without even telling the patients. Richard helped to evacuate some of them in requisitioned buses.

At Kampar the 11th Indian Division changed its tactics. Instead of defending a line, some battalions were left to defend fortified localities while the remainder were held in reserve for counter-attack. It was Moorhead's idea: he was now a brigadier in command of the 15th Indian Infantry Brigade. But the Japanese outflanked them by coming in from the sea and landing at Telok Anson, near the mouth of the Perak river. The Argylls were rushed to hold them there and the rest of the division had to fall back again to positions on the Slim river. Then the Japs made further landings in quick succession down the west coast of the Peninsula, and the retreat continued, hastened by the break-through of the Japanese tanks at Slim river, and the loss in some places of whole battalions.

What was left of the 3rd Indian Corps withdrew by a long and unnecessary march through the positions of the fresh Australian troops of half of the 8th Australian Division.[1]

But after four days the British and Indian troops comprising the 3rd Indian Corps were back in the front line again, side by side with the Australians.

During the reorganisation, Moorhead was a colonel again, in command of the combined 3/16th and 2/16th Punjabis: he was to take over the next brigade to be formed as soon as reinforcements arrived. But he never got his brigade. At Parit Sulong the Japanese had taken a hill which jeopardised the Punjabis' flank. Colonel Moorhead personally led a counter-attack with two

[1] The other half was in the Middle East.

companies, and took the hill. They were consolidating the ground when a chance grenade landed right at the Colonel's feet. He was killed outright.

Richard was not with the unit at the time. He had been summoned to Singapore on 12th January and arrived in the city just before nine o'clock that night. He went to Raffles Hotel to get himself a room and was astonished to find a dance in full swing. Most of the Europeans were in evening dress. There was no accommodation available, so Richard went on to Malaya Command Headquarters. He had been told to report to Lieutenant-Colonel Dalley, and found him in the Command Officers' Mess. Dalley had been Director of the Criminal Intelligence Branch at Kuala Lumpur before the invasion. He knew the Noone brothers, and had been one of the recipients of the Frontier Patrol's intelligence reports.

"Have you had any news of your brother?" he asked.

"No, sir, not very much. I met up with some Argylls who were with him in C Company at Grik. They told me he was sent up with a platoon to hold the Japs on the road down from Kroh. Then the Company got orders to withdraw and Pat's platoon was left behind. If he's alive he probably took to the jungle."

"Well, it's the best place for him as far as I am concerned," Colonel Dalley said.

He went on to explain that he was raising a unit called Dalco, made up of men with a knowledge of the country and the language. The object was to provide special reconnaissance patrols and guerrilla parties to be left behind the enemy lines.

"I particularly asked for you, in view of the excellent track recces you carried out on the Siamese frontier," Dalley said. "I want you to do the same thing in Johore."

It was by using side-roads and tracks that the Japanese were able to infiltrate their infantry, and even their tanks in some places, past the defenders' positions. Very little was known by the British commanders of these side-tracks, as few were shown on the operational maps.

Richard now had to help remedy this situation and spent most of his time driving round Johore in a small Vauxhall with a planter named Donald Farquharson. They collected all the estate maps they could lay hands on, piled these into the back of the car and reconnoitred the roads shown on them. They worked in close touch with unit commanders, who wanted to know exactly where the gaps lay in their defences. Richard and Farquharson had to look for and report the gaps.

After their setback near Segamat, several Australian battalions found themselves cut off with the Japanese already astride the main road south of their positions. They would have had to abandon their transport if Richard and Farquharson had not provided them with an alternative route through a network of cart-tracks and estate roads. At one place where there was no road, Richard and Farquharson had organised Tamil coolies to build an embankment up to a section of railway line, and planks were laid across this to take motor traffic. Although very rough and ready it enabled the Australians to by-pass the Japanese trap.

Unfortunately the detailed reconnaissance of the country had been left till too late, and after two and a half hectic weeks Richard and Farquharson completed their last drive from Kota Tinggi to Johore Bharu. Six bridges had been blown up, but by detouring through estate roads they were able to get round the obstacles. This was reported to the Royal Engineers, who then mined the remaining free roads before the Japanese came down.

At Johore Bharu the decimated battalions of the defenders were retreating over the causeway to Singapore Island. Dalco's job was done, and Richard and Farquharson received orders to report again to Colonel Dalley, who was forming another special unit in Singapore City.

9 . *The Black Pall*

Colonel Dalley's special unit was an act of desperate military and political expediency. It was called Dalforce and consisted of an infantry battalion manned by the very Chinese Communists that he and his Special Branch officers had previously spent most of their time trailing.

When the idea was explained to the Communists they flocked to join Dalforce, eager to fight the Japanese. But there was no transport or equipment for them, and their weapons consisted of an assortment of sporting rifles, some new, some practically museum pieces.

Most of the recruits were completely untrained. They were given two days' training, then sent into the front line along the perimeter defences.

Unfortunately some of the units were not informed that they were to be reinforced by Chinese, and the inevitable happened. They were mistaken for Japanese and shot up before they could even take up their positions. At one place a party of British soldiers, also thinking they were Japanese, surrendered to them and threw down their arms.

Actually Richard never served with the Chinese. He and Farquharson were again detailed to go collecting all the detailed maps available in Singapore of the estates, mines, towns, ports, harbours, estuaries and railway installations in Malaya. They were told that these maps would be vital for planning the re-invasion.

They lived first at the Belgian Consul's house near Tanglin, but later they moved to the Dalforce rear headquarters in a Methodist church at Fort Canning. Here they stayed to the end. During the last few days their final map-collecting efforts were slowed up when their car was smashed by a party of Australians who used it to break in the doors of a wine-shop.

One night Richard and two other officers set out to locate a light flashing from an upper storey of the Cathay Building. They could not find the man who was obviously signalling to the Japanese from the huge skyscraper, and after an hour or so gave up the search and headed for the Raffles Hotel for a drink. As they entered the gate they heard a shot as a bullet glanced off the roof of their car, followed by three other shots in quick succession from behind a hedge. They ducked and rushed round to find an Australian lying on his back on the ground, with his rifle on his knee, firing up into the air. In the hotel, the lounge was a scene of massed Australians caked with mangrove mud, sprawled about on chairs and on the floor.

On Thursday 12th February, a rumour spread that a message had been sent from General Wavell in Java to the effect that as the troops in Singapore had put up such a bad show no further reinforcements would be sent, and that if any man left the island without a written order he would be shot.

The message was a fact, but it merely hastened the complete breakdown of discipline and morale during the last three days before the surrender. Men swarmed on the docks trying to get away, and machine-guns badly needed at the front were brought down to the docks to prevent unauthorised persons attempting to leave.

On 13th February, the order came through for the Dalforce Communists to be disbanded. They had fought gamely, but unfortunately had proved almost as great a danger to themselves as to the enemy. Also it was thought unfair to leave them to be captured by the Japanese while bearing arms against them.

Somehow the Communists got to hear about the order and disappeared with all their weapons and ammunition, leaving only their dirty blue uniforms in tidy little heaps on the floor.

Next day the officers were given written permission to leave the island, but as the last ship had already gone only six of the twenty-five were prepared to attempt an escape. Richard was among the six.

It was almost eleven a.m. when the written order came through, and they set out for the docks to see if they could find some sort of craft. The place was deserted save for a few Tommies looking very desolate after discovering that the old training hulk, H.M.S. *Laburnum*, had no engines. The *Laburnum* rode majestically against the wharf, her rigging draped with an assortment of clothes, bits of wood and parts of go-downs. The docks were strewn with wreckage. Trunks and suitcases were spilled open, their intimate contents soaked with rain and mud. Golf-bags were littered about. Flashy cars of the élite of Singapore, gashed and peppered, lay in every conceivable position.

On a grassy stretch of ground behind the go-downs were two anti-aircraft guns with piles of shells inside their tidy, sand-bagged emplacements. They too had been deserted, so that their long gleaming barrels pointed silently upwards at the dense black pall of smoke rising from the holocaust of the city.

Most of the buildings seemed to be on fire, feeding the pall, which was supported by thick black mushrooms rising from the burning rubber dumps and oil installations. Aircraft were circling under the pall among little white puffs of bursting anti-aircraft shells. From the other side of the city the noise of the battle would flare up to die down again. To the east, and much nearer, could be heard the unmistakable stutter of Japanese medium machine-guns, and the poop of mortar bombs going up.

Major Colin Marshall, the senior officer, told Richard and a young officer named Kitchener, who had been in the Game Department, to wait on the waterfront while they went off in search of a Chinese junk at the other end of the harbour. Richard and Kitchener waited half an hour, then a motor launch appeared coming in from the end of the mole. There was only one man, a European, on board, and he was heading for where they were standing on the wharf. A few artillery shells whistled overhead, landing first in the placid waters of the harbour, then in the middle of the dock area. The two who were waiting bolted behind the go-downs, and flattened themselves to the ground. After a while the shelling stopped, and they came out again.

The man in the launch was a civilian. He had hidden the boat under the mole the night before, and had now come to collect some other Europeans of his firm, who presently came out from behind the go-downs and got into the launch. There were altogether ten of them, and the man at the wheel said they could take a few more. Richard mentioned the Dalforce party, and they waited for them to return, but when they did not he and Kitchener got on board, and they set out towards the distant islands at full speed.

They passed a yacht in which the occupants were trying desperately to get the engines to start, and threaded in and out between the masts of junks and other shipping sunk in the harbour. From the mole Richard looked back at the dying city.

Orange flames from a number of fires were licking the black pall. From a flagstaff over Fort Canning a Union Jack was fluttering gaily.

At two o'clock that afternoon they were about seven miles out when Richard, who was standing on the gunwale, saw what he took to be a reef in the water. He reported this, but was told he was merely looking at a reflection in the water of the smoke rising from the blazing oil tanks on the island to the east. They went on. The shadow in the water under them became darker.

Richard called out again to the helmsman that they were over a reef.

"Don't worry, old boy," he replied. "I know these waters. I've sailed them for twenty years."

A moment later there was a grinding shriek and a jolt that threw them all in a heap to the bottom of the cockpit. The launch was firmly stuck, though fortunately there did not appear to be any damage.

For half an hour they tried every conceivable means of freeing her, but all to no avail. She was firmly embedded in living coral, and to make matters worse the tide was going out. They could do nothing but wait until it rose again and the boat could be floated off, but in the meantime it had to be propped up with bits of timber from inside.

Luckily the smoke from the burning oil installations thickened, screening them from the planes which circled overhead all afternoon. They spent most of the time hiding under the lee of the launch, in the nude as they did not want to wet the only clothes they possessed. Then as evening came they had a meal—corned beef, biscuits and two bottles of whisky.

The tide was inordinately slow. They watched its progress up the taller spikes of coral. Then just before nightfall, they were at last able to push the boat backwards off the reef and all clambered aboard once more.

It was useless trying to press on in the darkness without chart or compass, so they made for the lee of an island and put in as it was getting dark. They pushed the anchor overboard, but it would not hold as the tide was pulling them on to the reefs that fringed the island, so they had to keep watch all through the night, easing the launch off every time she drifted in too close. They could hear the crump of Jap shells finishing off their work on Singapore, and the rumble of the defenders' own heavy artillery in the background. Dawn came: it was Sunday, 15th February 1942. They set out, steering south in the direction of Sumatra.

On 6th March Richard disembarked at Fremantle, in Western Australia, nearly three weeks after leaving Singapore. He and Kitchener had parted company with the other Europeans at a little island in the Riouw Archipelago, preferring to continue the voyage by Malay sampan, while the others had gone on in the launch. Eventually the two had got to Sumatra. They had travelled across it to a port on the south-east coast, and on to Java, from where they had been evacuated in the Dutch liner *Zaandam* to Fremantle. They were then taken with the rest of the Army personnel to Perth, which is a few miles inland, and issued with new uniforms and quartered in a school building.

Next day Richard was walking along one of the main streets in Perth when he bumped into one of his fellow passengers on the *Zaandam*.

"I saw a notice asking for information about you in the Malayan Agent's office," the man said. "It was signed H. Something Noone."

"H.D.—could that have been it?" Richard asked. "H.D. is my brother."

"I can't be sure," the other said. "But why don't you go and see for yourself? It's just round the corner."

Richard dashed to the office and went to the notice board. The message was from H.V. whom Richard had thought to be in Ceylon. He went round immediately to the address given in the message, and was astonished to find not only his parents, but Sheelah and her small son who, strangely enough, had also appeared in Perth a few days before and traced H.V. and Mrs. Noone through the Malayan Agency. Then a few days later Sheelah's husband knocked on the door. He had gone into the Navy, when the Malayan war started, and now his ship had put in at Fremantle.

The whole Noone family could now be accounted for, with the exception of Pat. Of him, unfortunately, there was no news at all.

10 . *"Have Contacted Noone"*

Richard was posted to S.O.E., the Special Operations Executive (Far East), the headquarters of which was in Melbourne.

In July 1942 Force 136 was formed in Colombo. This was a unit of special agents who were to be sent into Japanese-occupied territory to organise its underground resistance. Richard volunteered for Malaya but was turned down. He was told that the Army was not prepared to risk his falling into enemy hands as he knew too much about special operations. However, as he was in the Intelligence Section of S.O.E. he was able to keep in touch with Force 136 activities.

In May 1943 Richard heard that the first party of Force 136 agents under John Davis had been put ashore on the west coast of Malaya from a Dutch submarine. One of their main objects was to contact Pat, who they believed was possibly the only European still alive in the jungle. Later Davis reported that although he had heard that Pat was alive, he had not actually contacted him.

A second party went in. Then a message was received in Colombo which read: "HAVE CONTACTED NOONE". Later it turned out that it had been wrongly deciphered. 'NOONE' should have read 'NO ONE'.

The war continued. Richard was married in Melbourne, and became the father of a daughter. The tide turned in the Pacific, and as the Americans pushed the Japs back through the islands, S.O.E. headquarters moved up to Hollandia, in Dutch New Guinea, then to Morotai in the Moluccas. The war ended while Richard was on leave in Melbourne. He heard from H.V., who cabled that he had instructed his bankers to put a sum of money to Pat's credit in Singapore.

Heartening news came of Pat—a cable from Aunt Daisy, Mrs. F. H. Layard, in Ceylon: "HEARD UNOFFICIALLY PAT WELL".

It was followed by a report in a Melbourne newspaper that Pat was known to be living with Sakai in the deep jungle as their 'king'. "It is expected that Noone will return to civilisation when information comes to him through the native grapevine that the British have reoccupied Malaya," the Singapore correspondent of the paper concluded. That Pat had not heard the war was over was a reasonable assumption, particularly in view of the administrative chaos immediately following the Japanese defeat.

Next came two cables from Force 136 officers. The first stated that Pat had been seen a year before in the Ulu Kelantan, the other that he had last been reported to be with aborigines six months before.

H.V. wrote to John Davis who had led Gustavus I, the first Force 136 operation. Davis replied: "Unfortunately I did not get to the Main Range (near Bidor) until October 1942 and I heard that Pat had passed through there two or three months before. He then crossed the Cameron Highlands into Kelantan where he met and stayed with Creer. Throughout 1944 we made constant inquiries for him without success. There were a number of rumours that he had gone north to the Temengor area, and in June 1944 we heard a rumour that he was dead. None of them could be substantiated. Later, and particularly since the Jap surrender, stories have been rife about his appearing in a number of places. Unfortunately all have proved untrue."

A party of British guerrillas had been left behind in Malaya when the Japanese thrust down to complete their conquest of the country. The guerrilla leader was Major F. Spencer Chapman, who later joined the Chinese Communists and lived with them in the jungle. In April 1944 he undertook a journey in search of Pat, and reached Jalong, where Dato Bintang told him that nobody in the group had heard of Pat since the war started.[1] In the light of what was later established, Dato Bintang was not telling the truth.

It was known that Pat too had been with Chinese Communists, and Spencer Chapman's strangest story concerning this was of a chance discovery he made while on a march with a party of them in June 1944. He noticed that they were rolling their cigarettes with paper that had something written in English on it. He took the paper from them and, piecing the strips together, found that

[1] *The Jungle is Neutral* by F. Spencer Chapman, D.S.O. (Chatto & Windus).

it was a fragment of a memorandum written by Pat, giving the reasons why he parted company with the guerrillas.

All who were involved in the search for Pat were baffled, not only by Pat's disappearance but by the fact that they could get very little help from the aborigines. In some groups the very mention of their beloved Tata's name was taboo.

Davis gave an explanation for this in a second letter to H.V.: "It's possible Pat died while in the care of Sakai, and they became so frightened of possible reprisal by us that they made a taboo of the matter. This, however, is only a guess. The Sakai must know what happened, and I am sure we shall find out the truth from them as soon as things have settled down and someone can go in to make a thorough investigation. Rest assured this will be done."

But this was not done, and the Noones could only write to everybody they knew in Malaya, asking that any information received about Pat should be passed on.

Pat's friend Noël Ross had been District Officer at Grik at the time of the invasion. He was caught by the Japanese and spent the rest of the war in a prison camp in Siam. He wrote to Mrs. Noone that he had last seen Pat at Grik, just before he left with his platoon to hold up the enemy advance down from Kroh:

"He was cut off, and I heard no more till 1943, when I met an Argyll sergeant in a camp in Siam. He told me he had been with Pat, who had looked after them magnificently, taking the party through the jungle to near Jalong. There Pat decided to stay with two sick Argylls, while the sergeant went on with some Dyaks. Later he had a note from Pat saying both men had died and he intended staying with his folk, the Temiar."

A Game Department officer named Dolman, who had been in the Frontier Patrol, had seen Pat in the jungle during the first few weeks of the occupation. He wrote: "I met Pat first (and for the only time) in the Sungei Siput area, in January 1942. He had some Argyll other ranks with him, and as he was down with a light attack of malaria I preceded him, on his advice and with his help, towards the Cameron Highlands. He later crossed in that neighbourhood and I had a note from him (some time in March 1942) saying that he had been able to get plenty of food, but as he could not get quinine the Argylls with him had succumbed. He seemed quite cheerful and said he was coming to see me shortly. But circumstances forced me and my party to capitulate before we met again, and I am afraid I have so far been unable to get any reliable information as to what happened later."

Another friend of Pat's, a Danish planter named Anker Rentse, had been searching for him since June 1944. Rentse was with Force 136, and had dropped a section of his men by parachute at Pulai, a Chinese settlement in the jungle south of Gua Musang, in Kelantan. Later Rentse went into Pulai himself and heard from two Chinese Communists that Pat had been there less than a year before. He had stayed a while, then left with a party of aborigines, promising to return. He did not return, but was said to have been seen later on the Telom river. Rentse went up the Nenggiri river looking for Pat, as far as Kuala Betis. But all he was able to establish was that Pat had never been anywhere in that area during the occupation.

Meanwhile, however, H.V. had been in touch with the Colonial Office in London. The next information he received was that two Europeans had been traced who could give particularly valuable information about Pat. They had actually lived with him in the jungle during the occupation.

11 . The Terrible March

The two Europeans were John Creer and Robert Chrystal, but Pat's cook-boy Puteh had also been with him in the jungle. Puteh, when he was traced at his *kampong*, was able to provide the first part of Pat's war-time adventure.

Puteh was at Tapong, their advanced Frontier Patrol base on the Upper Perak river, when a wireless message was received instructing Pat to report to the Argyll and Sutherland Highlanders at Grik. Pat was then on his way up the river in their motor-boat, returning from his week-end with Richard in Penang.

When Pat arrived at Tapong and saw the message, he told Puteh that he would start for Grik at first light next day with the families of the aborigines who had been working for him in the Frontier Patrol. Puteh was then to recall the sections still out on reconnaissance, and they were to bury the wireless and other equipment, and come down to Grik by raft, bringing all his books and field notes, and as much tinned food as they could manage.

This was done, but it took time, so that when Puteh and the rest of Pat's men arrived twelve days later at Kendrong, the river village which serves as the port for Grik, they heard with dismay that the town was deserted.

Their informant was Mat Piah, the little Malay who had a small store on the river bank. "Nobody is in Grik. Even the dogs have gone," Mat Piah announced.

"And *Tuan* Noone?" Puteh asked. "Has he gone too?"

No, *Tuan* Noone had arrived there a few hours before with twenty-four British soldiers and two Dyak trackers. Two of the soldiers were wounded. Twenty of the party, including the wounded men, had boarded the ferry and pushed off down the river, using it as a raft. (Later Puteh heard that the ferry had cap-sized in the fearsome rapids farther downstream and all aboard had been drowned.) However, Pat with the remaining four soldiers and the Dyaks had gone to Kampong Bersia, a few miles up-river.

So Puteh and the others with him humped all the boxes of food and notes which they had brought down from Tapong, and set off to find Pat and the remainder of his party. They were at Bersia with Anjang and the other aborigine women and children.

Pat told Puteh of their battle with the Japs the night before. The platoon had occupied Kampong Lallang on the Kroh road. At ten o'clock two Chinese came in with a dozen bottles of beer which they offered for sale: they were very likely spies sent ahead to ascertain their strength and dispositions, because at midnight the Japanese attacked. They were beaten back, but at four in the morning they attacked again in greater numbers, and the platoon was forced to withdraw. When they got back to Grik they found their company had gone, taking all their transport.

Early next morning they all set out on a march through the jungle in an attempt to come out somewhere below the British line of defence, avoiding the direct route south, as Pat thought they might be overtaken by infiltrating Japanese. Instead he took them north up the Perak river in a detour which Puteh remembers as the greatest ordeal of his life. In normal circumstances such a journey would have taken them ten days. They did it in four.

Pat and Anjang led the way, with Puteh at his usual place behind them, followed by the Argylls, Sergeant Connolly and Privates Westhead, Richardson and Boult. Then came the Dyaks, and lastly the aborigines, of whom there were twenty-eight adults and two children, a boy and a girl of about ten.

At Kuala Temengor they cached the tin boxes containing, among other things, a large quantity of Pat's research notes: they

Police Aboriginal Guard (P.A.G.) and his wife at a jungle fort. A few months previously this man was a member of the Communist Asal Protection Corps

A northern Temiar settlement. Communist terrorists helped to clear the *ladang*

were buried behind one of Berkeley's halting bungalows at the village, and the headman was told to keep the spot a secret which he must not reveal until the war was over. This he promised faithfully he would do, and they turned up the Temengor river, reaching Kampong Temengor where they spent the night in a Chinese house near the village.

Next day they reached Kuala Jemheng and slept that night in an aborigine settlement, continuing at dawn the following morning with a guide named Asoh. He took them right up the Jemheng river, over a high shoulder of Gunong Besar, and down a very steep track the other side. It rained heavily most of the afternoon, and the leeches were particularly bad. They massed in bunches round previous bites, attracted by the smell of blood, but there were few opportunities to stop and get them off, as Pat would allow nobody to halt. They marched until past ten that night, then camped at a spot by the side of the river, too tired even to erect shelters or cook a meal.

But before dawn the party was on the march again, following the track by torchlight. While they were crossing the Piah river, one of the Argylls dropped his rifle in midstream, and two hours were lost before it could be recovered. They pressed on, climbing a steep path up a small tributary of the Piah to a ridge which they followed westwards along a game trail until it led them down to the Gambir river. The Gambir was their goal, for it brought them down at last to a settlement just above Kampong Lasah. Here they literally dropped on to the long-house floor, where their hosts gave them a little food before they fell asleep.

They were exhausted and bruised, and their feet were blistered and swollen with leech bites. The soles of some of their boots had worn through, and Pat's boots had split. But they had reached Lasah, from where he hoped it would be a simple matter to contact his unit.

He sent Puteh to the village in the morning to telephone Sungei Siput for a car or truck. To their horror Puteh came back with the news that the Japs were already in Sungei Siput. There was no time to lose. They pulled on their boots again and set out right away, continuing the journey south, and reached Dato Bintang's long-house at Jalong at ten that night. They hoped to come out of the jungle next day at Tanjong Rambutan.

In the morning before they left Jalong, Puteh heard Pat speaking to Anjang.

"Things are bad for my people," he was saying. "The Japs have come down from the north killing and causing explosions. I must go with the soldiers to fight them." He held both her hands and looked into her soft, shining eyes. "Teh," he used her pet name, "it is better that you should stay here with your own people."

Her eyes brimmed. She shook her head.

"Teh, some time may pass before I can come back to you again. It is not right that you should be left alone when I go." He turned and put his hand on the shoulder of a young brave who was standing by. "Uda is as my younger brother. He will marry you and look after you until I return."

She burst into tears. She would have none of it, and Pat finally compromised by letting her accompany him as far as Tanjong Rambutan.

That evening they were in the hills above Tanjong Rambutan, when they heard that Ipoh had fallen. Their next hope was the Cameron Highlands, from where they could get down to Tapah, but as they were all too worn out to attempt the journey, they decided to seek shelter in the long-house of a man called Along Lindong.

There they spent Christmas.

They moved back to the Jalong area, to a settlement where Lung, one of Anjang's five elder sisters, was married to the headman. But that night a young brave arrived from Jalong with the story of a strange little man with glasses, who had come up from Sungei Siput in a car, saying he was the son of the Sultan of Selangor and wanted porters and guides to take him through the jungle to the Cameron Highlands. He had a pistol, several hand-grenades at his belt, a wireless, and apparently a large sum of money. Four aborigines had agreed to accompany him, and they had set off in great haste.

As he was obviously an enemy agent, their wisest course would have been to continue their journey. But Westhead and Richardson had fallen ill with malaria and could not attempt it. So Pat decided they should move to a concealed position up a small tributary of the Korbu river. Here they built a house. Sergeant Connolly, however, wanted to press on, so Pat arranged for guides to take him and the Dyaks through to the Cameron Highlands.

It was Puteh's job to buy food for the party: they had started with about $200 between them, as well as a quantity of opium which Pat had taken out of the Government shop in Grik and which they used as currency, particularly with the Chinese. Puteh shopped in Lasah, and it was on one of his visits there that he encountered Dolman, with two British soldiers, Sergeant-Major Foley and Private Driscoll. They were the sole survivors of a platoon of the East Surrey Regiment, which Dolman had brought down from Baling.

Puteh led them straight to Pat who by this time was also down with malaria. They stayed the night and went on the next day.

Westhead and Richardson died towards the end of January, within three days of each other. Then Boult also got malaria, and without quinine his condition became steadily worse. Quinine was the only hope of saving him, so Pat decided he would have to go up to the Cameron Highlands where he was sure he would be able to get some.

Before leaving he sent Puteh back to his *kampong*, as he did not think it fair to his family to keep him in the jungle any longer. At first Puteh had refused to leave, saying: "*Tuan*, you have treated me like a son. It is my duty to stay and serve you."

But Pat had replied: "My Senoi friends will do that. You can serve me better as my agent outside the jungle. When I need anything I will write to you, signing myself 'Mat Yaacob'."

So Puteh returned to his home near Parit Buntar on the west coast, and Pat set out for the Cameron Highlands with Anjang, Uda and Boult, who had refused to be left behind with the aborigines at the nearby settlement. The night before he had amused them with his rendering of 'Tiger Rag', but he was too sick to have attempted the journey. The route lay over Gunong Chingkai, which aborigines believe to be haunted, and the guides were anxious to get to the other side before nightfall. Boult slowed them up, so Pat told Uda to stay with him, while he and the others went on ahead to prepare a camp. A couple of hours later Uda caught them up. He said Boult had collapsed and died as they toiled up the slope. The date was 3rd March.

Six days later the rest of the party arrived at Penghulu Angah's long-house on the Rening river, where Pat heard that Dolman, Connolly and Driscoll were living in the house of a Christian missionary named Siantoeri, only a few miles away. Foley had died, and the Dyaks had gone off on their own.

After a few days rest Pat went on to see Siantoeri, and arrived to find that the three Europeans had just left to give themselves up.

"*Tuan*, they were desperate," Siantoeri explained. "They had no quinine, and no money to buy any, and then we heard that the Japs were coming to round up all Europeans in the jungle."

Siantoeri was a Batak and an upstanding, well-intentioned young man. He urged Pat to follow their example. "*Tuan*, Singapore has fallen and all hope has gone. If you do not give yourself up, you must either continue your miserable existence in the jungle, or commit suicide." And he added: "But suicide is forbidden by the good Lord."

"No, I won't surrender to the Japs."

"Thus said *Tuan* Creer."

"*Tuan* Creer?"

"The District Officer of Kuala Lipis," Siantoeri said. "He is now staying at Jelai Kechil, with another *tuan* named Hubback."

Pat intended visiting them, but Creer forestalled him by arriving unexpectedly one morning at Angah's long-house with the news that he and Hubback had been attacked by Chinese at Jelai Kechil, and had got separated in their flight into the jungle.

Creer went on: "I was at Siantoeri's place last night when a couple of Sakai came in to say two hundred Japs were on their way down the Telom looking for you. Frankly I don't think we've got much time to lose."

They set out immediately with Anjang and Uda, heading up the Rening river for Kelantan. But that night, just before their meal, a runner came up from Angah to say that the men seen coming down the Telom were Chinese, not Japanese. So the party returned next day to Angah's long-house.

On 3rd April, Pat, Anjang and Creer moved into a little hut the group built for them nearby. They lived there for five weeks, Uda remaining in the long-house and working in the *ladang*. Creer was sick with malaria most of the time, and would have died but for the quinine bought by Siantoeri, who also provided books, a blanket, shoes and clothing from the Methodist mission bungalow in the Cameron Highlands.

About the end of April, Angah's group moved down to Krani Hondai's long-house near Kuala Rening to help him open a new *ladang*, and early in May Pat suggested they should follow Angah's group as it was quite two hours' walk up the river bank for anybody bringing them food; one day nobody had come and all they had had to eat was the pith of a *bayas* palm.

They moved down to Krani Hondai's settlement and stayed in his huge long-house. Hondai was one of Pat's oldest aborigine friends and sponsors. He had a little *pano* hut in the centre of the long-house floor, which he would enter and sit in for hours calling to his spirit guide, while everybody had to stay quiet and smoking was forbidden. Again Creer would have died of malaria but for Siantoeri's quinine.

Another hut was built for Pat, Anjang and Creer, and they were joined there by Anjang's stepbrother who had come over from Jalong to work for Pat since Uda, it seemed, had gone his own way. The next couple of months passed uneventfully, except for another scare when Japanese were reported within an hour of the hut, and for a second time they took to the hills.

During July a message came from some Chinese guerrillas in Pulai, inviting them to join the band, and Creer left with two Chinese on 5th August. Pat followed him a month later, after persuading Anjang to stay behind with Krani Hondai's people.

Pulai is a strange and oddly attractive anachronism—a long, secluded valley of craggy limestone outcrops and flat *padi* fields on the high upper reaches of the Galas river, inhabited by the descendants of a wandering Chinese tribe who fled their country and settled here over two hundred years ago. Little has changed in that time, for the people still speak an archaic Hakka dialect and worship gods long since forgotten.

In 1942 it had recently become the centre of the Kuomintang guerrillas, a loose association of jelutong-tappers and timber-fellers who carried out sporadic attacks against the Japanese. It was the sort of set-up they had been hoping for—a base where there was enough food and security to make life tolerable, and keen fighting men whom they could organise into a local resistance movement against the enemy.

They were made welcome, and the guerrillas seemed particularly pleased with the revolver and four rifles they had brought. But Pulai proved a disappointment. There was a lot more talk of ambushing Jap trains and convoys than action, and most of the time Pat and Creer were kept concealed, as the headman was afraid of their being seen by spies.

After a month of this Pat got bored and decided to return to the Rening. But before he left he and Creer had the greatest difficulty in persuading the guerrillas to return one of Pat's four rifles in exchange for his revolver. In the altercation that ensued Pat was hit across the shins with the butt of the rifle he was demanding. He got it back in the end and set out with his guide for Pahang. Creer stayed on.

When Pat returned to Krani Hondai's long-house, he heard that two Europeans were living near Jalong in a Chinese Communist camp. So after staying a couple of weeks on the Rening river, he and Anjang set out for Perak.

---

12 . Pat's Propaganda Tour

Chrystal, who had managed a rubber estate near Sungei Siput before the war, had joined one of Spencer Chapman's left-behind parties, and with another planter named Robinson had arrived in late November 1942 at the headquarters of the Perak Communist guerrillas, who were part of the M.P.A.J.A. (Malayan People's Anti-Japanese Army).

The Perak guerrillas were termed the 5th Corps, in the typical grandiloquent fashion of the Chinese, although the total forces controlled by them could not have exceeded a hundred, in small sections of ten or twenty men and women. Corps headquarters comprised the five leaders and the headquarters company of about thirty guerrillas. The commander was Lai Foo, a well-educated Chinese from the Sitiawan district, with two political officers and a senior and junior captain in charge of operations. Lai Foo's wife also assisted in political matters. She was a charming and accomplished beauty.

At the end of November their camp was high up in the hills four miles east of Kampong Chemor in Central Perak. It was well-concealed behind a limestone ridge called Bukit Rimau. A mile or two down the track was a small aborigine settlement.

One morning Lai Foo handed Chrystal a note which had been brought in by one of their collaborators via the aborigine settlement. The note was from Pat, who mentioned that he had come over from Kelantan and that he heard there were British officers staying in the Communist camp. He asked if he could come up to meet the Europeans.

Lai Foo questioned Chrystal and Robinson for some time about Pat. The matter was then discussed among the political leaders, and finally it was announced that Pat would be admitted.

Before he came, however, Chrystal wrote advising him to think twice about it. Chrystal explained that he might find it difficult, if not impossible, to leave the guerrillas once he joined them, since they were loath to let either Robinson or himself out of their sight. Still, as Chrystal also pointed out, Pat would possibly be given far more freedom in view of his valuable aborigine contacts.

On 1st December there was a ceremony in the camp to inaugurate the opening of two large huts for the men. Several outside agents and all the leaders were present. There was the usual concert, community singing, sketches showing the prowess of the brave Chinese ensnaring Japanese agents, and long speeches extolling the glories of Communism. In the middle of all this Pat made a sudden and dramatic entrance with his bodyguard of aborigine braves, and got a great welcome from the two Europeans and all the Chinese leaders.

Chrystal and Robinson, with an English-speaking Chinese boy, had arranged to do a sketch in which Chrystal was a planter, Robinson a Bengali watchman and the Chinese a Tamil coolie.

They put it across with great gusto, as they thought, but the only applause they got was from Pat: apparently, according to Low Mah, the interpreter, they had been expected to provide some propaganda deriding the British imperialist, not the farce they had devised for everybody's amusement.

When the show ended, and they had all drunk numerous mugs of hot potato-water sweetened with sugar as a special treat, Chrystal and Robinson took Pat to their hut, where he told them the story of his adventures. Pat added that before leaving Pulai he had arranged with a Chinese medical dresser, who had friends in Kota Bharu, to procure a wireless set and bring it back to Pulai. Pat's idea was that if a messenger could be sent through Siam to Chungking, which was practicable for a Chinese in civilian clothes, an air drop might be arranged with equipment and operators in Pulai settlement.

The plan gave some hope of success, and was later put up to the Communist leaders. They promised to pass it on to their

No. 1 in Johore, the famous Lai Tee, who was deposed when the war ended. Pat made repeated efforts to have some action taken to put his plan into action, but eventually he was told that the Malayan Communists were already in touch with Chungking and they would act in their own time.

By then Chrystal and Robinson had completed the training of the guerrillas which they had begun with Spencer Chapman in a camp on the Slim river. They were now asked if they would share sentry duties with the other guerrillas. Robinson agreed, but Chrystal, who refused, was assigned to writing and illustrating a musketry manual which was being translated into Chinese. Chrystal was also writing anti-Japanese propaganda for the Tamil clerks and others on the estates, though most of his efforts were rejected because they did not stress the need for a new outlook in Malaya with Communists in control.

Pat was soon tackled by Lai Foo and the other leaders about his views on Communism. They held long discussions, and at first it appeared to Chrystal and Robinson that he had become converted. The leaders were greatly impressed by his knowledge of the Malayan races, and they actually invited him to join the Malayan Communist Party, an honour in their view, and one that had never been offered before to any European.

He had been particularly questioned as to the best method of converting the Malays from devout Moslems to fanatical Communists, and was asked to write a treatise on the subject He discussed this with Chrystal and Robinson, and was inclined at first to do something about it. Later he changed his mind when he witnessed something of the Communist justice meted out to several unfortunate Chinese who were only suspected of having passed information on to the Japanese.

The procedure was to report the case—often it was no more

than trespassing—to the Politburo in Johore. Their decision was made and passed back to the jungle camp, where everybody then assembled in one of the big huts and the 'trial' began. A number of speakers would condemn the accused and his anti-Communist activities. Perhaps one or two would rise to plead for leniency. Then the court comprising Lai Foo and two of the political leaders would give their verdict. It was always the same verdict—death.

Only once was this carried out by shooting. That they said was a waste of one round of ammunition better reserved for the Japs. The usual method of execution was by beating with *changkols* (large heavy hoes) or bayoneting.

So Pat was lost to Communism, and though he had promised the treatise he never got beyond a few scrawled pages. He put off inquiries on the matter by saying he was giving it much thought.

For some months before Pat joined the 5th Corps the rule had been no smoking. This was as an exercise in self-control. Even the commander, a chain-smoker of cigarettes, had to fall into line. Chrystal was a non-smoker at the time, but Robinson had to take his pipe outside the camp whenever he wanted a smoke. Pat, an inveterate pipe-smoker, refused to conform, and soon the other smokers in the camp were also breaking the rule. Eventually it was abolished.

Chrystal remembers Pat as a good-natured individualist who was incapable of toeing any line. He was the revered Tata of the aborigines and he dressed the part, wearing nothing but a pair of brief shorts, with a sort of black cummerbund tied to leave the front hanging below his knees like a Temiar loin-cloth. He would use this periodically to wipe the straws with which he cleaned out his pipe. He rarely had any shoes, and wore a pointed beard and his hair cropped very short.

He took liberties with the Communists which might have resulted in severe penalties for anybody else. Once when they were at a lower camp in the jungle, near Dovenby Estate, Chemor, news came through that a large Jap force was coming up the track from the foothills. All the guerrillas fell in on the parade ground, and had to stand for a considerable time listening to Lai Foo giving a pep talk on Communism and the need to be brave if caught by the Japs. Pat laughed out loudly as he commented on the commander's performance, and when asked what he thought was so funny, retorted that it was such an inopportune moment for talk, with the Japanese imminent, that he couldn't help being amused.

Lai Foo was rather put out, and demanded to be treated with more respect. But Pat had made his point, and the order was made to withdraw. They were able to get away without any casualties, as the Japs could not come up except by a narrow path.

Pat was extremely useful to the Communists and they knew it. His main job was to establish and maintain a system of aborigine agents in each settlement, who would pass on messages to the Chinese and give warnings of Jap movements. He also acted as a liaison between the guerrillas and the aborigines, and but for him there might have been serious trouble between the two.

On one of his trips he arrived at a group long-house in the Kinta area, east of Ipoh, to find a state of war existing between them and the local Communists. Apparently two aborigines of the group had told the Japs, under pressure, of two Chinese who lived near the settlement. The Chinese were caught and executed, and as a reprisal both aborigines were killed by the Communists. Unfortunately for them they went too far: they killed a third aborigine for good measure.

The group were prepared to admit the fault of the first two, but they were very bitter about the third killing, so to even matters they ambushed a party of Communists returning to their camp. One Chinese was blow-piped with a dart tipped with lethal anti-personnel poison. He fell dead, while the others were liberally peppered in the buttocks with unpoisoned darts.

The headman considered the matter was now squared, and asked Pat to persuade the Communists not to kill any more members of his group or they would have to continue the blood feud. Pat was able to make the Chinese see the aborigine point of view, and there was peace in the jungle once again.

Pat's trips to the settlements were made with the interpreter Low Mah, whom he got to dislike intensely. Pat had on one occasion to report him to the commander for his overbearing attitude and for interfering with the work. Low Mah was officially reprimanded.

Between Pat's trips, the three Europeans would discuss their future. What particularly worried them was the restriction on their movements, and the continual anti-British propaganda they were forced to listen to. Also, as time went on, they were treated not as advisers who had helped to train their peasant army, but as refugees of a race now openly despised. Their great hope was Pat's plan for starting a wireless station at Pulai and sending a messenger with a code signal to Chungking, and they eventually decided that they would try to persuade the Perak leaders to let them go to Pulai. If that failed they would get out of the camp on their own, and take a chance on being caught either by the Japs or their hosts.

On New Year's Eve Pat arranged for Lai Foo and his wife, with two of the political leaders and the Europeans, to be invited to an aborigine feast of rice and wild pig. After the feast there was dancing. The guerrilla leaders were pleased and impressed, and

Pat suggested to Chrystal and Robinson next day that it might be an opportune moment to broach the subject of the proposed trip to Pulai.

Lai Foo was definitely not pleased, nor were the others, and while not actually refusing permission they made it clear that the Europeans would not leave the camp with their goodwill. Later Chrystal, Pat and Robinson were tackled individually in an attempt to dissuade them from their purpose. Nothing definite was settled, though for the next few days the three secretly reconnoitred the hills above the camp, and found a path which would take them east without risk of running into Japs.

A few days after their first mooting the Pulai trip, Pat was asked to go out with a select party to Lasah to kill a Malay who had given away some British troops in late 1941 and had recently also caused the capture of some aborigines from Jalong. The aborigines were accused of helping Pat, and carted away by Chinese detectives working for the Japs. The Malay was none other than Yeop Ahmat, Pat's museum collector.

Pat borrowed Chrystal's revolver for the assignment. Three nights later he returned very exhausted and a little under the weather from drinking *samsu* the previous night with a Chinese squatter. He told Chrystal how he and the guerrillas hid in the jungle outside Lasah, until it was fairly late and they were sure the *kampong* was asleep. They then went to Yeop Ahmat's house and hid in the dark shadows under it. There was no sound from within, and Pat called out: "Yeop—Yeop Ahmat! It is old friend, *Tuan* Noone."

No answer.

Pat called out again, saying that it was his old friend, who was very much in need of his help.

They heard a movement on the wooden floor. There was some

urgent whispering, and presently the boards creaked as bare feet walked over them.

Pat came out from under the house and stood in the open. The window slats were pushed open and Yeop Ahmat leaned out. Then, as Pat told Chrystal, he shot the traitor and saw the blood on his chest as he fell back with a groan into the house.

A few days later Pat heard to his disgust that Yeop Ahmat was seen in Taiping, apparently unscathed.

Soon after this incident the matter of the Pulai trip was settled. Chrystal was called to the leaders' quarters, and harangued for about two hours on the advisability of staying with the 5th Corps. However, when he firmly insisted on going, even without their goodwill, they gave their consent, but added that he would never be able to return or get any further help from them.

Next Robinson was interviewed: he soon came back to say he had agreed to stay. Then it was Pat's turn, and he too returned to say that the Communists had persuaded him not to leave. They had convinced him that he could best aid the anti-Japanese cause by continuing his liaison work with the aborigines.

Chrystal was taken aback by this, as the original suggestion that the three should go over to Kelantan had been Pat's. Anyway it was agreed that Chrystal would go and join up with Creer, then, if the radio set materialised and contact could be established with China, Pat and Robinson would come over to them later.

Early next morning, 12th March 1943, Chrystal left camp with Pat, Low Mah, and one of the guerrillas for Jalong. There was a feast in the long-house that night and there Chrystal met Anjang for the first time. Then the following morning Pat arranged for guides to take Chrystal across the Main Range to Pulai, which he reached eleven days later.

There Creer told Chrystal of the Kuomintang guerrillas' attack on Gua Musang some weeks before and the reprisal on Pulai by the Japs, who had burned down many of the quaint Hakka houses. Unfortunately for their plans the dresser who was to obtain the radio had fled. Also, Creer added, a Communist gang had taken charge of Pulai, having driven out the Kuomintang guerrillas to a camp some nine miles east of Gua Musang.

On 10th July of that year Chrystal and Creer left Pulai during a Japanese attack on the settlement. They returned to the Telom river area and were surprised to find Pat living at the settlement of a headman named Achok, near Kuala Bertam.

Pat reported that he had set out from 5th Corps headquarters in June on a propaganda tour of Perak and Pahang, the purpose of which was to give the aborigines anti-Japanese pep talks, and to extend the network of agents in the various settlements. While he was on this trip, he said, the Japs had raided most of the Perak Communist camps on information given them by a captured Communist leader, and Robinson with the headquarters company was on the run somewhere in the hills west of the Cameron Highlands. Pat added that he had finally broken with the Communists, and he told Chrystal and Creer how it had come about.

Pat had been suffering from repeated attacks of malaria on the tour, and one night in a long-house, when he was presumed asleep or semi-delirious from fever, he had overheard Low Mah haranguing the aborigines in his best Malay. The gist of his speech was that the British were finished in Malaya, and that the best policy for aborigines would be to throw in their lot with the Chinese Communists who were going to rule the country when the war was over.

It had struck Pat as he listened that he was being used as a tool by the Communists for the spread of propaganda which might react dangerously after the war. He knew too this was not the first opportunity Low Mah had taken to exceed his instructions. Then at last he had been convinced that Low Mah's particular brand of anti-British propaganda was uncompromisingly the Communist one. So in the morning when he wanted to move on, Pat had told him outright that he intended to stay at the settlement, and that when he was better he was going on to Pulai.

Pat was a stark figure when Chrystal and Creer joined him on 23rd July 1943. He was very thin, with a spleen enlarged from malaria that gave him a pot belly. In a holster at his hip he wore a revolver belonging to the Communists, which they were demanding back. Anjang and Uda were staying with him, and aborigines from the surrounding settlements brought him tapioca, rice, chickens, cuts of deer and wild pig and jungle fruit. They were anxious to fatten up their Tata.

He was wanting to go back to Pulai, but hesitated on hearing Creer's account of what the Communists were doing there. Then Creer mentioned that he had sent a supply of quinine to Jalong intended for him, so he decided to go there for it. He set out with Anjang and Uda, but turned back on hearing that Japs were at the settlement of a pro-Jap Temiar headman in Kelantan named Menteri Awol. Then towards the end of August a letter arrived from the Chinese in Pulai, complaining about Creer and inviting Pat to join them. Against Creer's advice, Pat set out for Pulai with Anjang, Uda, Achok and a few other aborigines.

Details of Pat's visit to Pulai were given by an English-speaking Chinese named Lawrence Keong, who had worked for the Asiatic Petroleum Company before the war and was then living in Pulai with his wife. Pat and his party stayed with the Keongs, and it was with them that he first got his idea of founding a jungle settlement of his own. It was to be in a beautiful valley of the Upper Korbu river, difficult of access, with an escape route into the hills. He was to be headman, and he was to be joined by the Keongs, with some Chinese friends of theirs, and some of his own special friends among the aborigines. It was to be truly international and democratic, and would incorporate all that was best in all their cultures.

So on 12th October he set out to return to Jalong, from where he intended to recruit most of the aborigine members of his group and also procure salt and quinine. On 15th October the Keongs received a note by hand of one of the guides who had led the party out of Pulai up to the Pahang Divide. It read:

"Dear Mr. & Mrs. Lawrence, Just a line to thank you both again for the warm hospitality I enjoyed whilst at your house. Meeting people like you makes the Japanese occupation of Malaya easier to endure. We are staying one more night here with Wong Shing Lee (two nights in all) and leave early tomorrow morning. I look forward eagerly to our next meeting, and my only object now is to get the essentials for our new settlement and be back again with you both.

"I hope to appear again between Nov. 15-20, but do not worry even if you have to wait until the end of November. Unless I die I will be back in any case, and I have a feeling in my bones that my journey will be successful. But we will choose a happy place anyhow. Look after yourselves. Yours ever, Pat Noone."

Pat appeared at Kuala Bertam at the end of October. He stayed only a few days with Chrystal and Creer in their little hut, then left to continue his journey to Sungei Siput on about 7th November. He was accompanied by Anjang, Uda and another young aborigine brave named Busu, who had been following him around for some time.

Pat had an attack of malaria coming on, and said he intended stopping a couple of days with Krani Hondai. He said good-bye and promised to be back within a month. Then he stepped on to the path and headed northwards up the Telom river with the aborigines following close behind. It was the last Chrystal and Creer ever saw of him.

---

13 . The Telom River

Chrystal had a duodenal ulcer. He had given Pat a letter to an Indian medical dresser named Rozario in Sungei Siput, asking for stomach medicine, and was anxiously awaiting Pat's return as the ulcer had flared up. So when news came ten days after Pat had left that he was still at Krani Hondai's place, Chrystal went up to investigate.

He was told by Krani Hondai that Pat had already continued his journey, avoiding the usual route up the Rening river so as to by-pass the group of the pro-Jap headman Menteri Awol. Instead he had taken an alternative route up the Telom river, via Penghŭlu Ngah's group. These were the people of Pat's old friend Dato Along, who had since died.

Chrystal went on to Ngah's long-house and was surprised to find Anjang, Uda and Busu there without Pat. Apparently he had changed his mind about taking Anjang, since in view of the delays he now intended returning almost immediately. He had told her to wait for him with Ngah's people, and had carried on up the Telom with Uda and Busu, who accompanied him as far as a settlement near the Blue Valley Tea Estate. At this point, Uda said, Pat had decided to go on with fresh guides, and instructed Busu and himself to return and look after Anjang.

"I will return within ten days because *Tuan* Chrystal is badly in need of medicine," he was reported as saying.

Chrystal returned to the little hut he shared with Creer at Kuala Bertam. They waited for Pat, but when after another two weeks he still had not turned up, they went back to Ngah's settlement to see if there was any news.

Anjang and Uda were still there, though Busu, it seemed, had left two days before to rejoin Pat, who had sent a message to say he had not been able to get a guide to take him on into Perak. Chrystal and Creer carried on up the Telom river for another two days, but were not able to find anybody who had seen either Pat or Busu. Baffled, they returned to their hut.

On 28th December, Creer left for Kelantan, to join the Kuomintang guerrillas west of Pulai. A fortnight later Chrystal went to see Uda again, and was told that nothing further had been heard of Pat. Anjang seemed particularly worried in case he should have fallen into the hands of the Japs.

On Chrystal's suggestion it was agreed that he, Uda and Anjang should go over into Perak by the route Pat had taken and make inquiries, but Uda thought they should give him another two weeks to show up.

Chrystal went back to Kuala Bertam, yet when he returned to Ngah's settlement after the two weeks he found that Uda and Anjang had left for Jalong without him. He could not get a guide then or later, and so was not able to make the journey into Perak to investigate.

After the Jap surrender Chrystal went to Sungei Siput to try to find out if Pat had ever got there. Chrystal met the medical dresser Rozario, who assured him that he had neither seen Pat nor received the letter Chrystal had written asking for medicines. Rozario was also able to say that as far as he knew Pat had not appeared in the district in 1943 or 1944. In view of this both

Chrystal and Creer shared Davis's belief that Pat had succumbed
to malaria, but that the aborigines were too afraid to admit it.

At the same time the possibility of Pat's having been killed by
either Japs or Chinese was not to be ruled out. Of the two the
Japs were less suspect. Had they captured him dead or alive they
would certainly have made a great show of the achievement to the
Malayan people, as Pat had symbolised the deep jungle resistance
which they were never really able to overcome. They were
convinced he was the master mind directing the activities of all the
guerrilla forces.

Throughout the occupation senior Japanese officers had called
at the Perak Museum inquiring of Pat's whereabouts from the
staff. They thought he might still be in touch, as indeed he was.
An Indian named Kuppusamy, who took over as curator, received
a secret visit in January 1943 from the Batak missionary, Siantoeri:
Kuppusamy had been past president of the Home Missionary
Society. Siantoeri brought a message from Pat begging Kuppusamy in the name of anthropology to locate and preserve his
research material. Then in February 1943, the Ipoh branch of the
Kempeitai, the Japanese secret police, got hold of Yeop Ahmat,
who was still on the museum staff, and an attempt to capture
Anjang was planned in the hope that this would finally lead to
Pat's being taken. Next Yeop Ahmat betrayed two of Pat's
aborigine agents at Jalong, and Pat's unsuccessful attempt to kill
the traitor followed. As a result of that, Puteh was arrested a
week or so later.

Puteh had already had two visits from Kempeitai agents since
leaving Pat in the jungle twelve months before. He had been
cross-questioned but said that Pat had come out of the jungle at
Tanjong Rambutan, from where he had been evacuated south in a
Punjabi truck as he was ill.

Now Puteh was asked about a letter he had received that very morning, and when he replied that it was from a friend asking him to go fishing he received a blow on the head.

The Japanese and Chinese detectives who had come to see him next produced a copy of the letter, which was a request for a supply of blank exercise books and was signed "Mat Yaacob". This was indeed incriminating evidence and Puteh was accused of being Pat's agent, taken to Taiping and interrogated all that night. He learned during the interrogation that he had been under surveillance for several months, and the detectives produced two other letters from "Mat Yaacob" which they had previously intercepted. These were requests for money and quinine to be sent to Jalong.

Puteh was encouraged to answer their questions by a thick stick applied always to the same spot on his head. But, as he recalls, he was genuinely unable to reveal any more information about Pat than the letters already did. Then in the morning Yeop Ahmat was brought into the room, and Puteh now heard of the scheme to kidnap Anjang, who had been reported living at Jalong.

They went to Lasah, where after a long wait Yeop Ahmat contacted his alleged aborigine spy, a youth named Hitam. They returned to Ipoh with Hitam and all spent the night together in the Kempeitai headquarters. Then very early next morning they set out for Jalong in two cars.

Nobody, Puteh says, knew exactly what they were going to do when they got there. Pat had a formidable reputation. Highly-coloured reports of his activities had reached the Kempeitai, and they genuinely believed that he lived in feudal grandeur in a bamboo fastness up in the hills, the accepted chief of all the aborigines, with a bodyguard of braves armed with blow-pipes and darts tipped with deadly poison. So there was an air of nervousness and uncertainty about the expedition.

The road winding up from Sungei Siput came to an abrupt stop at the swiftly-flowing River Korbu, and still the party had not made up their minds as to how they should set about capturing Anjang. The Kempeitai agents were not jungle men, and did not appear to relish the thought of venturing along the narrow path to Dato Bintang's settlement some distance away.

At last after lengthy discussion Hitam was sent to see how the land lay, being carefully instructed at the same time that he was to come back to the road and report on how many men were in the long-house and how many were working in the *ladang*. He went off promising to return within the hour, while the others lit up cigarettes and tried to agree on some plan of action. The hour passed, then another and another, but still Hitam had not appeared. Yeop Ahmat pointed out that aborigines had no idea of time, but that was little consolation for the impatient Japanese. Then another hour went by, and another, and still there was no sign of Hitam. It was now one p.m. and the Kempeitai were getting bad-tempered. At four p.m. they were worried and nervous; at six they were really scared.

The sun had dropped below the great trees, intensifying the gloom of the jungle, and the insects were making such a racket they could hardly hear themselves speak. The situation had also become ridiculous, because somebody should have gone in hours before to see what was keeping Hitam, and now they couldn't very well return to Ipoh without something to show for the expedition. However, their faces were saved when Hitam showed up a little after six.

The reason he gave for the delay was that his father had sent him to work in the *ladang*, and he could not refuse without arousing suspicion. Anjang was not there, and if they wanted proof he would take Yeop Ahmat in to see for himself. Yeop Ahmat declined the invitation.

The senior Jap then decided they would all return to Ipoh, and with great courage Hitam agreed to accompany them: he knew that while the party had been kept waiting an urgent message was being rushed to the Chinese guerrillas, who by now would be in position on the road ready to ambush the cars. Fortunately for Puteh the guerrillas had not had sufficient time to make a road block. He was in the leading car which dashed through the hail of bullets without any of its occupants being hit. All except Hitam in the second car were killed. Yeop Ahmat was in the second car.

The Japanese made no further attempts to get hold of either Anjang or Pat, and from all accounts appeared to have thought right up to the time of the surrender that he was with the Communist guerrillas.

Far more suspicion rested on the Communists as far as those investigating Pat's disappearance were concerned.

One Force 136 officer, Frank Quayle, strongly held the view that they knew far more than they cared to admit. He had joined the 5th Corps headquarters about the end of August 1943, when their camp was on the Jor river to the west of the Cameron Highlands. Here he met Robinson, who at the time was expecting Pat to return shortly from his propaganda tour of the aborigine settlements.

Robinson said that Pat had had some quite strong arguments with the leaders about the nature of the propaganda, and it was finally agreed that the sole object would be to boost the guerrilla movement and to counter the Jap efforts to win over the aborigines with gifts of sugar, tobacco and cloth.

Then three weeks later Robinson died of malaria and was buried near the camp, and about a month after that Low Mah returned to say Pat had quarrelled with him and had decided to sever his connection with the Communists.

Before this it seemed that Pat had been quite popular with Lai Foo and the other Chinese leaders, but now nothing good could be said of him. They called him a deserter, adding that he had been given a revolver before going out on the trip, and since he had kept it the obvious deduction was that he meant to steal it.

Quayle had stayed with the 5th Corps for the next six months, during which time he repeatedly asked Lai Foo if he had received any news of Pat. The reply was always the same—that nothing was known of his whereabouts. Although they had both the men and the opportunity they apparently made no attempt to organise a thorough search, which to Quayle had sinister significance. He pointed out that several hundred people had already been butchered for lesser crimes against the Communists than desertion and attempting to frustrate their activities. Pat had done them great service, but he was no longer indispensable to them, since, from what they now made out, Low Mah had not let the grass grow under his feet. He had been building up his own aborigine contacts in the settlements on his trips with Pat, and could now carry on independently. Because of this, from the Communists' point of view, Pat was a definite obstacle to their plan for subverting the aborigines since he had too great a hold over them for anti-British propaganda to make any impression while he was alive, and the Communists had already made it clear that the anti-British slant was an essential part of their propaganda campaign.

A number of stories were in circulation as to how Pat met his end with the Communists. One newspaper, quoting an unnamed Malay, suggested that he was tried and shot at one of their traitor-killing camps. Another paper reported that he had been shot in the back while resting on a march. A third that he had been stabbed.

Yet, from Creer's account, letters from 5th Corps addressed to Pat continued to arrive at Kuala Bertam for some time after he had left them on 7th November 1943. They were all peremptory summons for him to return to duty, and one delivered in December read: "Come back at once. Major Chapman is here. If you are sick you may take enclosed quinine." A few tablets came with the letter.

Several months later Low Mah himself came to Kuala Bertam, looking for Pat. The Communists wanted to bury the hatchet, he said.

After the war, when several Communist leaders came to London for the Victory Parade, H.V. managed to contact Low Mah and invite him to tea. He accepted, and told H.V. that from inquiries he had made it seemed that Pat had disappeared somewhere in the vicinity of the end of the Cameron Highlands road. This, Low Mah said, was not far from one of the groups which had been accepting gifts from the Japs.

14 . *Anjang's Secret*

In the summer of 1946 a special meeting was held at the Royal Anthropological Institute in London to discuss what action should be taken towards organising a search for Pat's missing research material.

As a result of the meeting, a letter was sent to the Colonial Secretary asking for his assistance. He was informed that the general body of British anthropologists regarded Pat's work as of the first importance. It was explained that he had been "developing an entirely new line of research of brilliant originality and very great promise for the understanding of the highly complex cultures of such primitive tribes as the Temiar Senoi. His method, which involved a combination of the techniques of social anthropology and social psychology in a manner never previously attempted, excited profound interest among anthropologists experienced in the application of anthropology to the problems of colonial administration, when he read his notable paper[1] on the dream experience of the Temiar Senoi to a full meeting of this Institute in 1939. Films which he showed at this and other meetings were of a quality quite outstanding from the scientific point of view. At the same time it must be emphasised that he was able in 1939 to give only some slight indication of the extent and nature of his field research and it is known that he had collected by 1941 a very great mass of material of vital importance to both anthropological science and for administration, the working up and publication of which was eagerly awaited.

"His presumed death is regarded as one of the most serious losses suffered by anthropology during the war, and it would be doubly regrettable if the material which he had already collected could not be found and made available for study . . ."

On receipt of the letter the Colonial Secretary ordered an official search for the material.

This naturally began at the Perak Museum, where Pat was known to have left a lot of his notes, ciné-films, photographs and recordings. But when Kuppusamy was questioned he said that the filing cabinet containing all the material had been looted by Malays and Chinese before the Japs occupied the town in December 1941. It seemed odd that the only other things looted in the museum had been the collections of Malayan *kris* and embroidered sarongs from the upper floor of the building.

[1] *A Study of the Role of Dream Experience in Culture-Contact Among the Temiar Senoi of Malaya.*

Nothing had been touched on the ground floor, where most of the exhibits remain exactly as they were in Pat's time, and the office and library, which were also on the ground floor, seemed otherwise intact. But Pat's notes were gone without hope of recovery.

Puteh was then contacted, and he reported the thirteen boxes of notes and books buried at Kuala Temengor. These, as far as Richard knew, constituted most of Pat's field notes for his psychological study of the Temiar, and the District Officer at Grik arranged for a party to go up to fetch them from the *kampong*. But when they got there the headman said that one of his neighbours had informed the Japs of the cache. As a result a section of Jap soldiers under a ferocious commander named Aromoto had arrived, and, as the headman admitted, he had been forced to reveal where the boxes were. The Japanese had then dug them up, expecting to find arms, but when only papers and books were discovered, the commander ordered them to be burnt. The headman added that he had been forced to assist in the burning.

During the occupation Pat had continued his research, but left most of the exercise books he used at 5th Corps headquarters. Quayle had seen them with some of Pat's belongings in their hut. But these too were lost: Quayle explained that they were left behind when the camp was raided by the Japs and everybody had to get out in a hurry.

The Royal Anthropological Institute and, more particularly, the Noone family were bitterly disappointed by the loss of Pat's monumental work.

In 1948 London courts ruled that Pat's death might be presumed to have occurred in about November 1943, and his estate was wound up. Yet in Malaya there were people who were not prepared to accept the ruling. One was H. T. Pagden, then

Director of Museums, who planned an expedition, intending to follow Pat's proposed route over the Terla pass into Perak, and down the Kinta river. Puteh was to accompany him. They were to scour the settlements, looking for clues, and try to find out what happened to Uda and Anjang, who they believed could lead them to Pat if he was still alive. But Pagden fell ill at the last moment, and the expedition was off.

Then in June 1948 the Emergency began and within a few months there were several rumours in circulation of a bearded white man having been seen in the jungle by Security Force patrols. In 1948 and 1949 a white man was reported as having appeared in Kedah. In 1950 a white man answering to the same description was reported in Perak. A patrol of the Suffolks were convinced they had seen him in a terrorist ambush party in Selangor, and in 1952 a patrol of Malayan Police claimed having seen a white man with some terrorists near Tapah. In 1953 some aborigines from Pahang reported the presence of a terrorist camp on the Jelai Kechil river. They also told Barbara Penington, a member of the Department of Aborigines who was interrogating them, that there was a wireless set in the camp. They added that the operator was a white man, who had striking blue eyes and a beard. The mysterious white man was thought to be Pat, who it was suggested had become involved with the Communists against his will and was helping them only to safeguard the interests of the aborigines.

Meanwhile Puteh had joined the newly-formed Department of Aborigines. He too had never given up hope of Pat's being alive, and believed that the reason why Uda and Anjang had never been traced was that they were with him somewhere in the jungle.

From the day he joined the department Puteh had made inquiries about them among the aborigines he met in the course of his job. He was encouraged in this by Peter Williams Hunt, then Adviser on Aborigines, who had promised Pagden that he would do his best to get to the bottom of the mystery.

In August 1950 Williams Hunt and Puteh went to Ipoh, where Williams Hunt had to call on the Assistant State Secretary, an Australian by the name of Wood. Puteh was waiting outside the office in the departmental jeep, when his boss suddenly came out of the office to say he had just heard from Wood that Anjang had been located. She was with a group that had been brought down from Kuala Legap, where they had been helping the terrorists, but now had a settlement on the north bank of the Plus river, two miles upstream from Lasah.

At last it seemed that the truth would be discovered about Pat, but when Williams Hunt and Puteh visited the group next day they found that Anjang was dying. She lay on a pandanus-leaf mat with a piece of flowered cloth lightly over her body, which was so thin and wasted that the ribs stuck out. She recognised Puteh and her eyes filled with tears. She made an effort to speak but could not, and the headman explained that she was suffering from advanced ulceration of the throat. The condition had lasted nine months, getting steadily worse.

As she was too weak to be moved, Williams Hunt gave some tins of milk to the headman for her, and he and Puteh left promising to return with a doctor as soon as possible. But as it happened the doctor in Sungei Siput could not leave for several days, and when they got back to the settlement they were told that Anjang had died. In the doctor's opinion the cause of death was bronchial septicæmia.

Puteh was desolate. Anjang was a link with the past, with the twelve happy years he had spent in the service of his beloved *Tuan* Noone. But they had found her too late.

"She knew the secret, and she has taken it with her," he said.

PART THREE . THE CAMPAIGN

*

15 . A Pattern of Terror

After the war Richard had got a job in the Australian Intelligence Department and settled down in Melbourne, but unhappily his marriage went on the rocks, and in November 1952 he had returned to Malaya, where he joined General Templer's staff as Secretary of the Federal Intelligence Committee. In the autumn of 1953 the interview with General Templer took place which has already been described, and as a result Richard was made head of the Department of Aborigines. He was ordered to reorganise it on an Emergency footing.

The struggle with the Communists had then reached a dangerous stalemate. They were back practically to where they had been in 1942 as guerrillas of the M.P.A.J.A. hiding in secret mountain camps. The only difference was that there were many more of them, they were far better trained and armed, and they had completed the total domination of the aborigines in the deep jungle. These factors made their military position far more dangerous than it had been during the occupation, when their guerrilla activities against the Japanese had been on a very small scale, and from all accounts they had killed many more alleged traitors than they did Japs.

During the war the policy of South-East Asia Command had been to build up the M.P.A.J.A. as a resistance movement to fight behind the Jap lines once the Allied landings began according to the grand strategic plan for the re-conquest of Malaya. Liaison teams were dropped by parachute or landed by submarine, and when satisfactory contact had been established with the M.P.A.J.A. large quantities of automatic arms and ammunition and other equipment were dropped to them. It was to have been their task to disrupt the Japanese lines of communication, but in August 1945, a few days before the invasion fleet was due to leave ports in India and Ceylon, Japan surrendered.

During the interval between the surrender and the arrival of the Allied troops, the M.P.A.J.A. came out into the open in many parts of Malaya, claiming that the victory was their doing and that they would now take charge. It was a brief but unforgettable reign of terror in some places, the Communists purging all those who had opposed them politically or merely refused them help. Meanwhile their organisers were busy creating Communist cells under the name of 'trade unions' among workers engaged in every form of employment, from gardeners to cabaret girls.

It was not until the beginning of December 1945 that arrangements had finally been made by the British Military Administration for the M.P.A.J.A. to be demobilised. The guerrillas were paid off and told to hand in their arms. But most of those which had been dropped to them and a large quantity of Japanese war material found its way to secret dumps in the jungle. These were kept for the day when the Malayan Communist "People's Republic" would be created by force out of the political and economic chaos of South-East Asia, as captured M.C.P. literature clearly indicates.

The M.C.P. wasted no time in implementing their policy. They followed the usual Communist tactics, infiltrating into key positions in the newly-formed trade unions which the post-war Government was trying to foster, so that by early 1948 control of

The author with Aweh, his bodyguard (right), at a rock pool in the jungle

Richard and the author (right), interrogating Akob

Negotiating a rapid with a load of *rotan* and leaf thatch

The author rafting down a placid stretch of the upper Temengor river

these unions had passed to the Communist-dominated Pan-Malayan Federation of Trade Unions, which had steadily begun to frustrate the genuine efforts of labour leaders to develop responsible trade unionism. Unions were being forced to call strikes on trivial pretexts and the attempts of leaders at negotiation were sabotaged at every turn. The Communist weapons were intimidation and blackmail. In May 1948 the Commissioner of Police in Singapore informed the Federal Legislative Council that orders had already been given to Communist Party members in trade unions to resort to violence to secure their ends. He quoted six political shootings which had taken place the month before.

Efforts were made to meet labour discontent and to improve working conditions all round. But the employers too were being threatened if they came to terms. In April 1948, a new scale of wages for most classes of workers had been recommended by the Council of the Employers' Association in Penang. The recommendation was carried unanimously, but when the Council met to confirm the scales not one Indian or Chinese employer attended. They were far too scared. Not long before an employer had been shot dead in a street in Penang for giving evidence in court against a Communist trade union leader who had intimidated him.

Numbers of Chinese had already been deported for subversive activities, and there had been several prosecutions for intimidation. But the powers of the Civil Police were still heavily curtailed and there were hardly enough men to cope with the sudden increase in lawlessness.

The labour struggle reached a climax in Singapore when the Pan-Malayan Federation of Trade Unions announced its plan to hold a mammoth public meeting followed by a procession of 100,000 people on May Day 1948. The Police Commissioner agreed to the meeting but banned the procession, which would have been beyond the capacity of the Police to control. In reply the Communists threatened to hold the procession in defiance of the ban, and the Government reacted by banning the meeting as well. As a reprisal the Communists burned down one of the largest factories in Singapore.

By the middle of May there was gun law on virtually every labour front. For instance, in Johore Communist agitators seized a Chinese rubber estate and held it for a month. In Singapore a rubber factory was surrounded by men with rifles and knives and its workers were ordered to strike. At another factory armed men called a strike, one of the grounds for which was a demand for a particular type of machine which had in fact been used in the factory for the past twenty years. There were a number of strikes in support of demands for wages that were actually lower than those already being paid. Wholesale armed robbery of vast quantities of rubber from the estates and warehouses took place, estate offices and factories were burnt down, managers were attacked, and a number of loyal Asian employees were murdered.

Then on 16th June the manager of the Elphil Rubber Estate outside Sungei Siput was shot through the window of his office. He had just written in his log book: "I have to point the company's attention to . . ." when he died. Two other European planters on the estate were then taken outside the office by a gang of armed Chinese, who tied them up and shot them.

A state of Emergency was immediately proclaimed in the Sungei Siput district, and in parts of Johore, and on 18th June, after a police station had been attacked, the Emergency was extended to the whole of the Federation. Special powers were adopted to deal with terrorists, and the Communists, to avoid wholesale arrest, took to the jungle, those in the trade unions decamping with the union funds. Overnight they had mobilised as units of the M.P.A.B.A. (Malayan People's Anti-British Army), though they later called themselves the M.R.L.A. (Malayan Races Liberation Army).

Their initial aim was to disrupt the two basic industries of tin and rubber on which Malaya's economy largely depends, to kill as many Europeans as possible, and to create terror among the Asian population. During the ensuing chaos, they hoped for the support of a mass uprising which would enable them to neutralise the Police and the Army and thus overthrow the Government. They counted on being in a position to declare Malaya a Communist People's Republic by August 1948.

In the first wild phase they murdered not only Europeans but Asians of all ages, sexes and races without particular discrimination.[1] Some of these atrocities were characterised by insensate brutality. For example in Kampar, Perak, a grenade was thrown into a roadside circus, killing five people including a pregnant woman and her two-year-old child. At Kepong, Selangor, a gang fired into a crowded cinema, and five people were killed including women and children. In the Plentong district of Johore a man and his wife were killed, their hut set on fire and their eight-year-old daughter thrown on the flames.

Membership of the M.C.P. at the time of the declaration of the Emergency was about 14,000, of whom more than ninety per cent were Chinese. Men under arms numbered over 5,000, and there was a large, well organised auxiliary force known as Min Yuen (literally 'the helpers'), whose function was to collect food for the fighting men and extort money for party funds. Some of the richer Chinese had to pay up to $50,000 to ensure their safety.

The C.T.s (Communist terrorists) were competently led by

[1] Of 4,651 civilians killed, wounded and missing up to 31st August 1957, 3,063 were Chinese, 721 Malays, 450 Indians, 184 Europeans, 137 Aborigines and 96 of other races.

experienced commanders. They had weapons of all kinds and they struck unexpectedly, ambushing military convoys, attacking police outposts, estate offices and mines, derailing and shooting up trains, setting fire to buildings, and slashing thousands of rubber trees. They always had the advantage of surprise, and for the first few weeks it was touch and go.

However they failed to cause anything like the disruption they intended, as most European miners and planters and a high proportion of the men and women working for them stood firm. The Communists made a desperate propaganda appeal to the nationalism of all Malayans to support them in their struggle for independence, but they had alienated the very people on whom they depended for their mass uprising. The Malays in particular were determined to oppose them and flocked to take up arms in defence of their villages.

The M.C.P. had made the mistake of committing its forces prematurely, without sufficient men or supplies. The Army and Police fought back, and gradually, with the build-up of the Security Forces and an Emergency organisation, the Government gained control of the situation.

It was a desperate task at first, with jungles and swamps on the side of the C.T.s, and a large section of the Chinese public behind them either by force or inclination.

The C.T.s' main support had come from the Chinese squatters. These were mostly immigrants who had entered Malaya as labourers between the wars, or displaced persons, the jetsam of the Japanese occupation. Under threat or persuasion they had supplied the C.T.s, sheltered them, and furnished the recruits necessary to keep the M.R.L.A. up to strength. There were over half a million of these Chinese squatters settled in primitive encampments in jungle clearings on the fringes of civilisation, on open ground near towns and tin mines, on the edges of rubber estates. It was not possible to station troops and police in every squatter settlement, some of which were accessible only by jungle paths, and many even nearer roads and towns had hardly been brought under normal Government administration. The terrorists' guerrilla strategy had been based on the fact that the Government could do nothing about blocking their access to all the squatters all the time. This was another miscalculation, for the Government, after deporting some to China, resettled the bulk of the half million in some 550 'new villages' behind barbed wire, with Police and Home Guards to prevent terrorists from getting in and squatter sympathisers from taking food out.

So effective was the Government food denial campaign that Communist despatches captured in 1952 indicated that it was only their shortage of food supplies which prevented them from concentrating men in numbers large enough for a reasonably effective attack. They were being forced to limit their effort to small-scale ambushes, while on the other hand the Security Forces were steadily being expanded, with already some 350,000 Malayan volunteers to assist them, including 170,000 Home Guards.

The terrorists were soon being hunted relentlessly, their camps bombed, their cultivation areas in the jungle poisoned from the air, their morale weakened by an intensive psychological campaign in which millions of leaflets were dropped to them, and voice aircraft flew low over the jungle, telling them that they were being duped by the Communist masters, that they were suffering unnecessarily, that if they surrendered they would be treated well. They surrendered in large numbers.

The M.P.L.A. had suffered nearly 8,000 casualties when Chin Peng, their leader, ordered the withdrawal of most of the fighting men into the remote *ulu* of the Main Range. Here, at the time of

Richard's assignment, they were living on the aborigines, who had opened up numerous *ladangs* for them and surrounded their hide-outs with a protective screen of listening posts to provide timely warning of the approach of deep-probing Security Force patrols. As a result it had become increasingly difficult to eliminate C.T.s in the jungle. Again and again patrols reported following C.T. tracks to a camp, only to find it recently deserted. The M.C.P. policy was now to hang on indefinitely. The Government, they felt, must eventually come to terms, rather than continue waging what had become one of the most costly and complex small wars in history.

As General Templer had summed it up, the day he gave Richard his assignment: "The aborigines hold the key to the deep jungle situation. Without their food the C.T.s couldn't subsist, and without their tactical intelligence the C.T.s couldn't stay a move ahead of our patrols most of the time. The answer, Noone, is to deny the aborigines to the C.T.s in the deep jungle. It will require a major propaganda and welfare campaign to bring them under our influence, but it will have the highest priority, and all your reasonable needs will be met."

16 . Senoi "People's Republic"

In October 1953, the headquarters staff of the Department of Aborigines was accommodated in the Museums Department office in Kuala Lumpur: in actual fact all Richard inherited were three tables, a typewriter, a filing cabinet, a map of Malaya, and a telephone which he shared with the Curator of the Museum, who sat opposite.

Richard's Assistant Adviser was Barbara Penington, a tall, bustling South African, who had been virtually running the department since the death of Peter Williams Hunt the previous June. The year before, Barbara had done some good work with aborigines in Tapah, when her husband was in command of the Police circle there. She had set up a medical clinic where aborigines who had been resettled in the area began coming to her for treatment. She had gained their confidence and obtained a lot of valuable information about local C.T. activity, which she passed on to her husband, with the result that the Tapah Police brought off some deadly ambushes in the area. Now that he was Superintendent of the Field Force, the para-military arm of the Police, the link with the Department of Aborigines was particularly useful.

Puteh acted as a general field assistant, interpreter and contact man, with nine aborigine field staff who were accommodated at a site just outside the town. All the clerical work at headquarters was done by one typist, who was often the only member of the department in Kuala Lumpur when Richard and Barbara went into the jungle.

The states were even worse off. Pahang had a protector and three aborigine field staff, Perak had a protector, an assistant protector and two field staff, and Kelantan had two Moslemised Temiar contact men. There was no provision at all in any of the other states.

The morning Richard took over as Adviser on Aborigines he began by asking for all the available information on aborigines relative to the Emergency. He had first to know exactly what his new job entailed. Though his immediate problem only concerned those aborigines who had been dominated by the C.T.s, his actual responsibility covered the entire aborigine population which was then thought to be somewhere between fifty and sixty thousand. Of these some 30,000 lived in the main jungle, as distinct from the fringes, but this figure could be further reduced, as about 22,000 had been brought under Government control and influence through an elaborate resettlement policy and the recent establishment of deep jungle forts. That left approximately 8,000 in the deep jungles of Perak, Kelantan and Pahang. They were Senoi, of whom the greater proportion by far were Hill Stock Temiar—Pat's Happy People. Intelligence reports indicated that they were all under some form of Communist domination.

Richard classified them according to the extent of their domination. As follows:

Category A—those co-operating with the C.T.s to the fullest extent, generally armed by the C.T.s with rifles, shot-guns and automatic weapons and living near or in C.T. camps. Their main function was the subversion and domination of the surrounding aborigine groups. They were also responsible for the protective screen, and for acting as guides and porters. They were later classified 'hostile'.

Category B—those living in proximity to the main C.T. camps in the deep jungle, whose function was solely the production of food for the camps and the provision of information regarding Security Force movements.

Category C—those living at some distance from the C.T. camps but nevertheless responsible for making food contributions.

Of the 8,000 roughly 5,300 belonged to categories A and B. But all three categories were firmly in the grip of the terrorists through an efficient and ruthless system known as the Asal[1] organisations.

[1] The Malay word for 'original': the C.T.s were thus recognising the aborigines as the first inhabitants of Malaya.

The Asal organisations were a direct link with the past: in fact they were developed from the liaison work Pat had done between the aborigines of the *ulu* and the M.P.A.J.A. during the Japanese occupation.

After the surrender the M.C.P. had maintained a tenuous contact with the headmen, and there is evidence that Chinese who were experienced in dealing with aborigines were sent on occasional goodwill tours of the deep jungle groups. To some extent they took over Pat's welfare rôle, as they helped the groups by providing them with simple medicines, new seeds and a few *parangs* and axe-heads. But along with these gifts the groups had also received a special jungle version of Communist propaganda. They were told, for instance, that when the Communists ruled Malaya an aborigine would be able to walk into a shop and take anything he wanted without having to pay for it.

Aborigines are receptive to new ideas, particularly if these appear to benefit them materially, and as far as they were concerned the Communists seemed the only people who bothered about them at all: since Pat's disappearance no Government representative had been anywhere in the deep jungle.

In July 1951 the Communists had decided to consolidate their position in the deep jungle, and a Politburo directive to the state committees ordered that the aborigine groups on the Main Range were to be completely dominated. The Asal organisations were the basis of the plan.

The Asal organisations were aboriginal Communist cells which were initially responsible for ensuring that local groups substantially increased their *ladang* acreage. There was usually one to a main river valley. Each area had an Asal organiser, assisted by a nucleus of experienced C.T.s, who had to recruit a number of 'hostile' aborigine braves and train them to form a unit of the Asal

Protection Corps. Generally entire groups were enrolled, as individual aborigines seldom take an important step on their own account. These groups were told that they had been mobilised on a war-time footing, and that they were now at war with the British 'running dogs', who would suffer the same fate as the Japanese. In return for their services the 'hostile' groups were promised untold benefits when ultimately the Communists took control of Malaya: for instance one group of ninety men, women and children were guaranteed the sole jelutong-tapping rights for the whole of Pahang! At the same time the Communists stressed that treachery would be punishable only by death.

It was learned later that many of these groups seldom had much option but to accept the distinction of being picked for the Asal Protection Corps, the Communists having begun by ingratiating themselves into the area and ended by dominating it once they entered in force. The groups in categories B and C had even less option once the Asal organisations were effectively in control, and in cases where an independently-minded group insisted on staying outside the Asal there were stronger means than persuasion to make it step up food production.

There was the case of an entire group of forty people being shot by a C.T. platoon because one of the group had informed the Police that they were being forced by the platoon to give them food. Actually the platoon commander was reprimanded for the outrage, as the M.C.P. preferred to employ the gentler method of persuasion. From all accounts the most brutal Asal organisers were not Chinese but aborigines, two Semai headmen in particular, one Bah Pelankin in Perak, and the other Chawog in Pahang.

By October 1953 the Communists had completed their domination of the deep jungle area outside the protective range of

the forts, though in some places they were even able to exact
tribute of rice and tapioca from groups almost within sight of a
fort, and to Richard, who knew the Senoi as a selfless, independent,
totally democratic people, the situation was incredible. Anthropologically they were incapable of toeing any line, much less
a Communist Party line. The explanation was found in Pat's
study of the psychology of Temiar group behaviour, and it lay in
the doctrine of shared liability. As the whole group suffered for
the actions of any one of its members, individuals themselves were
not likely to act rashly. As Richard deduced—and there was a
good deal of evidence later to prove he was correct—any idea of a
group's opposing the Communists would be discussed at morning
councils. These discussions would sometimes go on for days, the
older, wiser members doubtless advising caution in view of the
Communists' threat of reprisal. This according to the jungle code
necessarily involved the whole group, and to an aborigine, group
extinction is far more terrifying to contemplate than personal
extinction.

All things considered, it must have seemed far more sensible to
take the line of least resistance. Besides, the groups in the deep
jungle had been told that if they were ever captured by the
Security Forces their heads would be cut off. Thus it appeared to
the aborigines that by helping the Communists they were helping
their protectors.

For his part, Richard realised he would not only have to
counter ten years of Communist propaganda, but convince the
dominated groups that he could provide them with adequate
protection against the Communist vengeance which would
follow their defection. In any case he first had to *reach* the groups
in order to win their confidence, so that he could put across his
message.

That day as he thought about it the task seemed nearly impossible. He had no idea at all of how or where he was going to make a start.

---

17 . "Kill Bah Pelankin"

Richard was able to postpone having to work on his plan, because the next day he was summoned urgently for an interview with General Sir Hugh Stockwell, the General Officer Commanding, Malaya, Templer's executive military commander.

Richard found General Stockwell standing beside his desk, a tall, thin, distinguished-looking English gentleman, with the huge, panting Alsatian dog that followed him everywhere sprawled at his feet.

He said: "Noone, we've just had some hot information pinpointing a very high-level Communist camp—possibly that of the Politburo. It's at a spot just east of the Cameron Highlands. We're launching a major operation—Operation Valiant—at this very moment, and I want you to go in and see what you can do about the aborigines. If you can get any of them in that area to help us, I believe we may bag the top M.C.P. leaders."

The original information had come from a small patrol of paratroopers of 22 S.A.S. (Special Air Service Regiment). Late the evening before they had been following a Dyak guide along a jungle path. Suddenly the Dyak had held up his hand and pointed. Down a side track that had been cleared through the jungle they saw a terrorist sitting on a log with a Sten-gun across his knees, contentedly puffing at his pipe.

He looked like a courier resting after the day's march, and the patrol leader shot him dead. It was too late to attempt to follow up his tracks, so they stripped the body and hid it at the edge of the track. The track was interesting. As far as they could make out it had been cleared to a width of about six feet and led up a hill.

Back at Troop headquarters the dead man's clothes aroused considerable interest. Both the shirt and trousers had been freshly laundered, and a receipt from a laundry in Singapore dated a week before was found in one of the pockets. The deduction was that he must have been a fairly high-level Party member, who had possibly just returned after a special visit to Singapore. He also had a tin of Navy Cut tobacco which suggested he might have slipped out of camp for a clandestine smoke. Did the path lead to the headquarters of the Central Committee of the Malayan Communist Party, and possibly the whereabouts of the Secretary-General, Chin Peng himself?

In case it did four infantry battalions were already converging on the area, guided in by the S.A.S. who had two squadrons in the deep jungle of north-west Pahang.

"Can you leave immediately?" the General asked. "Time is the vital factor in this operation."

"Yes, sir. I'll just call at my flat and collect my kit."

"I wouldn't bother about that. Brigadier Howard, who is commanding the operation, will be able to fix you up with anything you want."

Soon Richard and Puteh were on their way into the jungle by helicopter. They flew north-east over the tree-tops which looked like tightly-packed cauliflowers of varying shades of green with heads of red, orange and yellow occurring here and there. Ahead of them was the dim blue outline of the cloud-capped peaks of the Main Range. Soon the vast mountain system of mountains and

valleys was unfolding beneath them, with the terrifying endless-
ness of jungle stretching away in every direction as far as the eye
could see. Silver streams drained every re-entrant, feeding the
wider torrents in the valleys. At the side of the streams the palms
and bamboo clumps could be seen and occasionally the im-
maculate quilting of primeval growth was broken by an untidy
aborigine settlement with its chaotic *ladang*. The Pahang river
emerged from behind a fold of mountains like a silver snake,
twisting southwards, then round to the east.

They came down with a flight of eight helicopters like a
visitation of giant dragonflies at Bukit Betong, a railway halt on
the Jelai river. The landing zone was a scene of bustle and
ordered chaos, with infantry in battle equipment emptying out of
the helicopters and forming up at the edge of the field, unladen
helicopters taking off, and a crowd of Malays with naked pot-
bellied children encroaching dangerously near. A bicycle was
lying near the wheels of one of the helicopters, where somebody
had dropped it and fled.

Richard was taken to Brigadier Howard's tented headquarters a
quarter of a mile away.

"I want you to go on to Advance Headquarters at Kuala
Misong," Howard told him. "That's where they'll need you."

Soon Richard and Puteh were seated in another helicopter,
ascending vertically as if in an aerial lift, the people and the
dragonfly shapes of helicopters on the ground diminishing between
their feet. They now wore jungle greens still smelling of the
factory, rubber and canvas boots laced to the calf, and floppy
hats. At their belts they carried *parangs* in canvas sheaths, water-
bottles and ammunition for their carbines. In their packs were
their rations and anti-malarial tablets, poncho capes, change of
clothing, green mosquito nets, ground sheets, blankets, billy-cans,
eating irons, shaving outfits, electric torches and toilet paper.

They flew up the Jelai river valley and onwards up the Telom
river to where it was fed by a foaming tributary from the north.
This was the Misong, on the south bank of which, near the con-
fluence, a hole appeared in the jungle where the giant trees had
been felled by explosives to prepare a landing zone. It was
raining now, and the helicopter descended into the hole, down
past the swaying tree-tops, into two hundred feet of dripping
gloom.

They climbed down from the quivering thorax of the dragonfly, dragging out their carbines and packs. The landing zone was a
quagmire of red earth and blasted wood and roots, through which
they squelched, ducking under the swishing rotor blades. They
heard the swishing suddenly increase with a roar, then the steel
insect shot upwards, funnelling down a draft of atomised rain.

A poncho-caped soldier emerged from the undergrowth.

"Mr. Noone, sir?" he asked.

"Yes."

"Major Salmond is expecting you. Better get your ponchos
on, sir, or you'll be drenched to the skin."

He led them to the swollen Misong river which they crossed,
balancing along a tree-trunk that spanned its banks. On the other
side was a sandy patch—the very spot where Pat and Bellamy-
Brown had spent the night next to their moored rafts because of a
herd of elephants. Two basha huts stood on the sand, and round
them a dozen men were bivouacked in small shelters they had
improvised for themselves out of saplings and ground sheets.
This was Headquarters Troop, B. Squadron, 22 S.A.S.

Major Salmond, the squadron commander, was in one of the
bashas, reading a message as a young paratrooper at a wireless set
wrote it out on a message pad.

"It looks as though we've lost track of where the C.T. was
shot," Salmond said as Richard and Puteh came in. "The Dyak

who was with the patrol is sick, and there's nobody else who can possibly guide them back to the spot. They have been trying all day, but this damned rain has obliterated every sign of where they went."

He showed Richard on the map roughly where the wide path had been cut. "Can we hope for any help from the local aborigines in trying to locate it?"

"It's hard to tell," Richard said. "Some of the headmen round here were my brother's oldest friends. Ché Puteh knows them all, but they might be too scared to say anything."

"I think they will help us, sir," Puteh said.

"Well," said Salmond, "my patrols have reported vast *ladangs* all along the Telom. My hunch is they are all collaborating like mad."

A little later the wireless operator tore a message off the pad and handed it to Salmond, who read it and told Richard that a consignment of Javanese tobacco and other welfare goods was arriving for him at dawn next day.

"I ordered it before I left," Richard said.

That night he and Puteh shared the second basha with the sick Dyak.

Next day one of Salmond's patrols brought in a number of aborigines from near Kuala Bertam, including Penghulu Achok, near whose long-house was the hut in which Pat had stayed with Chrystal and Creer before he left on his last journey for Perak.

When eventually conversation got round to the C.T.s, Achok was non-committal. He hadn't seen any for several months, he said.

"He's lying," Richard told Puteh in English. "He has a *ladang* of about thirty acres. He shouldn't need all that for a group of no more than fifty."

"Better to hurry slowly, *Tuan*," Puteh advised. "When we win his confidence he will tell everything."

Richard hadn't mentioned Pat up to that time. So he asked casually: "Have you heard anything more of my brother?"

The Penghulu's face suddenly fell. "I know nothing about *Tuan* Tata," he replied. "I have not seen him since he and Puteh came to my father's *ladang*. Puteh was then a boy. I too was a boy at that time."

"That was more than twenty years ago," Puteh said.

"How could that be, since he lived near your *ladang* during the Jap time?" Richard asked.

"No, *Tuan*," Achok said, looking away. "He was over in the high hills in Kelantan. He never came this way."

"But *Tuan* Creer and *Tuan* Tinggi[1]—these two also stayed with you?"

"I do not know them," said Achok.

Shortly after that he suddenly decided to go, and left with his retinue.

Richard was flabbergasted at the headman's denial of Pat, but to Puteh it was a ray of hope. As he pointed out, aborigines never lie unnecessarily. "He must have very good reason. Could it not be that your brother is still alive and in this very area?"

Puteh, with the help of some aborigines from the Kuala Misong area, built a little house near Headquarters Troop site. The house became Richard's base where Temiar and Semai came from the surrounding settlements for a pow-wow and the tobacco, sarongs, *parangs* and trinkets which were doled out liberally.

He told his visitors that he had been appointed their Tata by Government, and that from now on their protection and

---

[1] The aborigines nickname for Chrystal. In Malay it means 'tall'.

welfare was his prime concern. He had begun his campaign.

After a few days Krani Hondai arrived, now a wizened gnome with a piece of cloth tied bandana-wise round his woolly head and his large, prominent teeth stained reddish black from incessant smoking and betel-chewing. His dart quiver was tied on a string at his right hip, and a naked *parang* was thrust through his loin-cloth on the other side. In his left hand he carried a seven-foot blow-pipe.

By dint of showmanship he was now the acknowledged pundit of the Telom valley, the authority on the ways of the European. He shook hands with Richard and immediately produced a grubby little notebook and a stump of pencil. With these he appeared to be taking notes of their conversation, but when Richard later examined the notebook he found that Krani Hondai had only been making squiggles.

For two days Richard worked on 'Clerk' Hondai, while the floor of the little house was spattered with the jets of red, betel-coloured saliva he squirted out from between his teeth at intervals. Then, when Richard really thought Hondai was in a relaxed and communicative mood, he quietly switched the discussion round to Pat.

"Did you know that Anjang is dead?" he asked. "Anjang who was my brother's wife?"

Krani Hondai's thick lips suddenly closed over his protruding front teeth, and his good humour seemed to shrink into the wrinkles round his face. He shifted himself on his haunches and he spat accurately through a crack in the split bamboo floor.

"She could not speak at the end," Richard added.

"I did not know *Tuan* Tata's wife."

"But I heard that he brought her to your *ladang* during the war."

"No, *Tuan*, he did not come to the Telom. He lived in

Kelantan," Krani Hondai said. He sat smoking quietly for a few minutes. Then he asked to be excused and left with his companions.

Meanwhile four battalions of infantry and two squadrons of S.A.S. had been combing the Telom valley for terrorists, and the R.A.F. had been pounding certain areas with bombs. But not one C.T. had been found dead or alive.

The only positive information Richard had been able to elicit from the aborigines he interrogated was that a big Communist camp was situated in the Semai country to the south-west, over the Perak Divide. He helicoptered back to Bukit Betong and reported this fact to Brigadier Howard. A meeting was held on the spot, and the decision made that very morning to shift the operation to the Perak jungle north-east of Bidor, the area known as the Batang Padang.

At Bidor, Richard suggested that aborigines should be used as guides instead of Dyaks. This was accepted, and he engaged three Samai from Tapah who agreed to lead columns of troops into positions in the area, provided that they themselves could also wear jungle green to avoid being identified as aborigines by any C.T.s they met. The guides got their uniforms, and the brigade, with all its units linked by wireless began a wide encirclement of the area.

Richard established an interrogation centre for himself near the main operational headquarters, but at the edge of the jungle so that aborigine visitors could feel they could come and go without being noticed. Soon he had a large number, attracted by his tobacco and gifts. He worked on them, but without apparent success, and he became despondent, wondering how he would ever succeed in putting himself and his campaign across to these people.

Then two men arrived, with shot-guns hanging from the shoulders on crude *rotan* slings. They were from the upper Sungkai river, and stayed two days in Richard's hut, smoking his cigarettes and sharing his rations.

Before they left, Richard said: "You know of course that if you shoot any C.T.s or give any information that leads to a kill, you will get a very big reward."

They thought a little, then one whose name was Abas said: "There are two C.T.s who pass through our *saka*. We have seen their tracks and they always use the same path. Every time the moon is big they go over into Pahang, and when the moon is small they come back into Perak."

"They must be couriers," Richard said. "If you shoot them you will get at least 5,000 dollars."

Abas could not understand the extent of 5,000 dollars, but when Richard explained what that amount of money could buy, he and his companion appeared very interested. They wanted to know what they should do if they shot a C.T., and Richard explained how the body had to be searched and everything in the pockets removed and brought, with the arms and ammunition, to the assistant protector at Tapah.

Soon after that the two aborigines left to return to their mountain settlement, and Richard forgot all about them in the hectic succession of events which followed during the next several months.

After nearly two weeks of fruitless search in the Batang Padang Operation Valiant was fizzling out, and Richard returned to Kuala Lumpur to find Barbara Penington in a state of excitement. In Tapah the night before she had met a headman who had told her that he knew the whereabouts of Bah Pelankin, the Asal organiser in the Batang Padang.

Bah Pelankin was a Semai headman who had turned terrorist and was already notorious for the success with which he had maintained food output among the groups in his area. He was known to have murdered and tortured several aborigines for non-co-operation, and was now touring the settlements armed to the teeth, warning aborigines of the consequences of giving any information to the 'running dogs'.

"We'll never get anything out of the Batang Padang as long as that man is at large," Barbara said.

"What's your headman friend like?" Richard asked.

"Pretty straight. I've known him for some time. He and five of his group are Home Guards."

"Do you think they have the guts to try killing Bah Pelankin themselves? It would have a tremendous psychological effect on the aborigines if they settled this score on their own."

"They're still at Tapah," Barbara said. "Let's go and ask them."

In half an hour they were on their way to Tapah in Richard's Jaguar. They found the headman (whose name cannot be disclosed) in the compound outside the assistant protector's office. He told them he knew that Bah Pelankin was in the habit of visiting a certain house at the edge of the jungle to collect rice.

"He comes every third day," the headman said.

Richard said: "He is a bad aborigine and a traitor to his *saka*. He has killed his own people."

"That is so."

"Somebody should kill him."

"Yes, such a bad man should be killed."

"There would be a very big reward for any man who killed him."

"The reward for killing him is killing him," the headman replied.

"Then you kill Bah Pelankin."

"Yes, I will kill him—then he cannot kill me for giving you this information."

"How will you do it?"

"I will take two of my brothers (relatives) and wait for him in the jungle near the house to which he comes for food every third day. There is a tree felled across the river near the house. Bah Pelankin and his bodyguard will step on to this tree-trunk. Then, as they are walking above the river, we will shoot them. They will fall into the river. That is the way we will kill Bah Pelankin and the other."

"It is a good way," Richard agreed. "But you must not lose their bodies. You must pull them out of the water and hide them so that the Police can come and identify them."

"*Tuan*, we will do as you say."

"Go then and kill Bah Pelankin."

Two days later Operation Valiant was called off, after 5,000 men had thrashed about in the jungle for nearly a month without seeing, much less shooting, a terrorist. An estimated 4,000 terrorists in Pahang and Perak had slipped away from their pursuers, a feat that could not have been managed without timely warning through the aborigine protective screen, and without aborigine guides to lead the C.T. platoons out of their camps by secret escape routes known only to the guides themselves.

As General Templer told Richard: "If nothing else, it has proved conclusively that as long as the Communists have the aborigines on their side we cannot hope to make the slightest impression on them. This deep jungle terrain is so vast and so complex we couldn't shift them with ten divisions. So it's absolutely vital to get those jungle folk on our side. We've got to deny them to the Communists."

That same evening the assistant protector in Tapah telephoned through to say that Bah Pelankin and his escort had been killed, and Barbara Penington, who took the message, let out a whoop that startled the Curator of the Kuala Lumpur Museum.

It was the first success of Richard's campaign.

18 . The Standing Committee

Richard's plan for winning over the dominated aborigines was based on the use of small welfare units he called 'field teams', each consisting of a Malay field assistant and a number of aborigine field staff. The field teams were to function at the forts and natural outlets, where they would establish intimate personal contact with visiting aborigines. At each of these centres the field assistant would run a medical clinic, a shop and a school, and by careful handling of the aborigines would attempt to win their confidence as a first step towards obtaining from them the vital tactical information without which the C.T.s could not be killed. The plan proposed an immediate expansion of the Department of Aborigines to put it on an Emergency footing and Richard asked for a total of thirty Malay field assistants and sixty-two aborigine field staff for the field teams, and, to control the teams and stimulate the flow of information, eleven assistant protectors and two protectors.

Richard submitted the plan on 21st November 1953. At six-thirty p.m. on 22nd November he received a memorandum from General Templer's office, informing him that a Standing Committee on Aborigines had been appointed, and instructing him to attend the first meeting at ten o'clock the following morning.

He arrived at King's House at nine-forty-five and was admitted to the ante-room where members of the Standing Committee were assembling: the Chief Secretary to the Federal Government, the G.O.C., the Secretary for Defence, the Secretary to the Member for Home Affairs, a representative from the Treasury Department, the Director of Intelligence, the Commissioner of Police, and various staff officers.

"I say, Noone, you haven't a hope of getting this through—it's going to cost a fortune," Richard was told by one of the members.

Another said: "It's far too ambitious. Really, Noone, you'll have to be realistic. Scale it down to a couple of field teams, and if they get anywhere after a year apply for an increase to the establishment. That's the way to proceed."

"How long is this meeting going to last?" somebody asked, and Richard overheard his being told: "Oh, I expect this thing will be thrown out in about ten minutes."

On the stroke of ten General Templer's door opened and one of his aides appeared. "Gentlemen," he said, "the General is waiting."

As they filed in, straightening ties and pulling down jackets, Templer stood up at his desk and moved across to the conference table. He sat down in the chairman's seat, and the others took their places at the table.

Templer said nothing for a few minutes. He was slowly turning over the pages of Richard's plan on the table before him. On the last page were the conclusions and recommendations. He scanned these and looked up.

He said: "Gentlemen, I have studied this paper and approve it. We will establish the Department of Aborigines on a full Emergency footing, on the lines Mr. Noone has suggested. I would like to add that it has got to work."

Richard caught the eye of the member who had thought it was going to be thrown out in ten minutes. He looked away quickly.

Templer went on: "Further, gentlemen, if there are any obstacles I want you personally to exert your utmost to remove them. The winning over of the aborigines is of the first importance, and I accord these measures the highest priority. Now are there any points you wish to discuss?"

A serious difficulty was pointed out by one of the ante-room critics. This was personnel, Europeans in particular, of whom there was a shortage throughout Malaya. "Where will the eleven assistant protectors and two protectors come from?" he asked.

Templer replied: "I think the simple expedient would be to transfer them from other departments."

A member asked where Asians with the educational qualifications required for a field assistant were going to be found.

Templer looked at Richard, who replied: "I don't want highly-educated men, but men with personality, common sense, experience with aborigines and ability to survive for long periods in the jungle. I think the minimum educational qualifications should be at least Standard V in a Malay school. For that I propose we should offer a monthly salary and cost of living allowance of $222, plus $4 a day jungle allowance. This is certainly higher than the average being offered in other departments for similar qualifications."

"I doubt if you'd ever get the types you require even if you doubled the money," Richard was told. "Indians and Chinese won't risk the vengeance of the C.T.s, and the average Malay is traditionally afraid of the jungle. He believes it's full of ghosts. Experience with Malay police has shown that if you take them into the jungle, after a short while they start agitating to be sent out to a *kampong*."

"What do you intend to do?" Templer asked Richard. "Have you any particular people in mind?"

"Yes, sir—friends of mine from Kampong Perak and others I know in Upper Perak and Kedah. We worked together in the Frontier Patrol and they proved really first-class jungle men."

"How long do you think it will take to get them?" But before Richard could reply Templer had added: "I want these field teams trained and working in the jungle by the first of January."

Two days later Richard and Puteh were on their way to Taiping. They had circularised all the Malays they knew with jungle experience, asking them to come to the Perak Museum during the next two days to discuss the possibility of working in the Department of Aborigines for a very good salary. They thought that maybe twenty would answer the call and then they would have to try at Grik and Kroh for the rest. But forty-five turned up at the museum and Richard was able to report at the next Standing Committee meeting that his establishment of Malay field assistants was complete.

The form of the meetings was always the same. Templer would say: "Right, gentlemen. I now want a progress report on what has been achieved since the last meeting." He would then go round the table and each member would say what he had personally done. If anyone had undertaken something, but had not in fact carried it out, the General would want to know why. Few excuses were accepted.

One great advantage of the Standing Committee was that all Richard's needs were met in the shortest possible time. A couple of days before each meeting, committee members would start telephoning to check with him on what they were supposed to do for him, and to ask if everything was satisfactory. The result was that within a couple of weeks the Department of Aborigines' headquarters had been moved to a spacious office in a converted hospital in the centre of Kuala Lumpur, and the clerical and administrative staff had been expanded to measure up to the new establishment. Most of the European assistant protectors had been posted to their areas and were already recruiting their clerical staffs. Transport, equipment and weapons had been issued and the field assistants were under training.

As General Templer had ordered, the field teams were in position by 1st January 1954.

Richard's anti-C.T. propaganda line was straightforward. His field assistants pointed out that the C.T.s were outlaws who had committed terrible atrocities for their own ends and were now on the run, that the Government intended to punish them, and that there were handsome rewards for helping to bring them to justice.

Richard knew that most of the dominated aborigines would be presented with a difficult choice, a frightening and confusing one. But he hoped that once they could be convinced that the Government was sincere, and that they would be looked after and fed if they deserted, those within the Asal organisations would start to come over. Once he had achieved the disaffection of those who resented the Communists, he felt the pendulum would begin to swing the other way.

With the groups situated close to the forts the problem was a simple one. They were the fence-sitters, not prepared to offend either party and helping both. Soon, as a result of intensified Police patrolling and the initial efforts of the field teams, several hundred of these aborigines were more or less secured firmly for the Government. They had a certain amount of information, but it was of limited value as the C.T.s had generally been scared away from the fort zones.

However, Richard thought that they would be sure to spread the news of how well they were faring with the Government to those who were out of contact, and he was counting too on the goodwill he had personally created with a hundred headmen whom he had recently had flown out to Kuala Lumpur during Operation Valiant. These had been told by the C.T.s that the reason why so many British troops were operating in the jungle was because they had been defeated in Korea and were hiding from the Chinese who were chasing them down the Peninsula. To disprove the story Richard had arranged for them to be shown battalions of infantry and police on parade, and then to be taken to the aerodrome and shown aircraft on the ground. Next they were brought to a hill to watch the Royal Artillery demonstrate their fire power by blasting some huts and jungle on the hill opposite. They were then taken on a trip to the seaside, and after a few days in Kuala Lumpur, during which they were given all they wanted to eat, they were flown back into the jungle.

Richard felt he had countered the Communist lie, but two months passed and still his campaign seemed to be making no impression at all on the out-of-contact groups. Meanwhile General Templer kept continually in touch, asking for the latest news, and the situation got progressively more embarrassing for Richard at Standing Committee meetings. He explained that they could not expect dramatic success right away, that it took time for a field assistant to put himself across, that the Communists had a ten-year start and it was not easy trying to counter their pro-paganda. But the Standing Committee were only interested in results.

Richard began to wonder whether there was anything basically wrong with his approach to the aborigines. He went carefully through all Pat's published work to see if there was any psychological factor he had overlooked, but there was nothing he could put his finger on.

At the same time his newly-expanded department was having teething troubles. There were only thirty field assistants to cover an area of some 30,000 square miles in extent. All these men could not be deployed at once: some had to be held in reserve. Besides, as he soon discovered, some were quite unsuitable for the job and had to be replaced. That could be done without much difficulty where Malay field assistants were concerned, but it was not such a simple matter with unsuitable assistant protectors. Some of these had turned out, perhaps not unexpectedly, to be the most dispensable members of the departments from which they had been transferred. Yet they had contracts which could not easily be terminated on grounds of lack of zeal, the most frequent defect that Richard had to contend with.

Another month passed and Richard had almost given up hope of ever getting anywhere with the groups in categories A and B.

Then one night he was working in the house he had been allotted quite near his old flat, interrogating some headman who had come down from Kelantan, when the telephone rang. It was the duty officer at the 22 S.A.S. Headquarters.

"We've just had an urgent signal," he said. "I can't discuss it over the phone, but the Colonel would like to see you right away."

Richard drove round to the unit to find Colonel Oliver Brooke, the commanding officer, with a number of his officers in their operations room. He handed Richard a signal. It was to the effect that a 'hostile' group of fifty-four aborigines, including ten men who were armed, had sought Government protection near a fort named Telanok which an S.A.S. squadron were establishing near the Cameron Highlands.

"The squadron commander's problem is feeding them," Colonel Brooke said. "They have abandoned their *ladang* and they haven't got a sausage."

"Don't worry, we'll take care of that," Richard said, restraining an impulse to thump the Colonel on the back. Instead Richard went to the telephone and rang Norman Herboldt, his quartermaster officer, to arrange for an emergency air-drop of rations, tobacco and welfare goods for the group.

At ten o'clock next morning Richard telephoned General Templer's military assistant and gave him the news. Within five minutes the military assistant was back on the telephone to say the General was very pleased with this success and hoped it was only the beginning.

Then Barbara Penington, who had flown into Telanok, signalled further details. The hostile group was that of Penghulu Angah from the Ulu Rening, whom Pat had lived with early in 1942. The message continued: "ANGAH HAS TOLD FIELD ASSISTANT NORGEE THAT HE HAS VITAL INFORMATION CONCERNING YOUR BROTHER PAT BUT WILL NOT DISCLOSE TO ANYBODY EXCEPT YOU STOP AM FLYING ANGAH OUT FOR SPECIAL DEBRIEFING STOP PENINGTON."

19 . *Angah's Evidence*

Penghulu Angah was a Semai who had married into his wife's Temiar group some thirty years before, and had succeeded to the headmanship when her father died without male issue. He was a solemn, slow-speaking gentleman who in a western country would have made a sound alderman. But at the moment he was terrified and he looked it.

He was with Richard in the drawing-room of his house in Kuala Lumpur, where he had slept for three nights curled on a rug directly under the ceiling fan. Since he had come out of the jungle he had made no mention of Pat, and Richard, during their evening talks, had discreetly kept off the subject. An aborigine cannot be hurried. If he has information to impart it will come out eventually provided the atmosphere is conducive. Whatever the truth was about Pat, it had certainly been stifled by Krani Hondai and any others who had been asked in the Telom valley. So Richard had to exercise all the self-control he possessed not to appear too anxious or too concerned. Now after three protracted pow-wows about nothing in particular, Pat had at last been mentioned, and Angah was just on the point of saying something when he was interrupted by Ali coming into the room to announce that two aborigines had arrived to see Richard.

"All right, bring them in."

Richard had no alternative: the moment had been lost. And when Angah saw who the aborigines were the blood drained from his cheeks. He said nothing while they were there, gossiping, and when they left he looked so morose that Richard wondered if he would ever talk.

It was now or never, so Richard said, offering the headman a cigarette: "My brother used to say you were his good friend."

Angah nodded abstractedly as Richard gave him a light.

"My brother loved your people. He made your *saka* the first Temiar Reserve. No man can take that land away from you. No man can go there and say, 'I like this land so I will buy it,' because the Government will say, 'That is not possible, for this is Temiar land: the *Tuan* Tata of the aborigines made it their special reserve.' You know that, don't you?"

Angah nodded.

"Why don't you speak, Penghulu Angah?" Richard asked. "You have nothing to be afraid of. When you were working for the C.T.s you had reason to be afraid. But here you are with friends. We do not force you to produce food for us—we give you more food than you can eat. That is why our object is to kill the C.T.s. The C.T.s are wicked. They have committed many atrocities. But we will protect you. On that I give you my word. I, *Tuan* Noone, the blood brother of *Tuan* Tata, make you a promise that no man shall harm you. So do not be frightened. Be at ease. Let us smoke and talk the talk of sundown."

"Yes, *Tuan*."

"My brother loved the Rening river. He used to go up to Dato Along's *ladang*, and live there in a little hut."

"Dato Along is dead. His place was taken by one Ngah, who married his younger sister Berdeuil. Ngah was afraid of Along's ghost, so the group moved down to the Telom," Angah said.

"Was not this the same Ngah with whom my brother stayed on his last journey into Perak?"

"The very same Ngah—he was related to those two bad hats who were with *Tuan* Tata."

"Uda and Busu?"

Angah nodded.

"But my brother trusted Uda. He took him everywhere," Richard said.

"That was *Tuan* Tata's mistake," Angah said. "Uda slept with Anjang when her husband was away."

"But your custom allows a younger brother this privilege. Uda was like a younger brother to him."

"Yet," said Angah, "when *Tuan* Tata learned this he was very

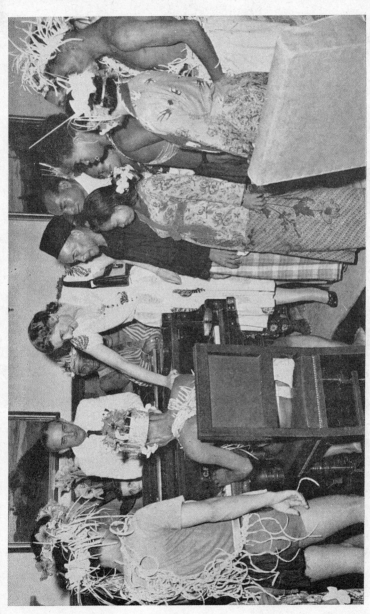

Sir Gerald and Lady Templer with aborigine visitors at King's House. In the jungle they still talk about that party

I, The undersigned, hereby state that I have purchased the bearer's gun for the sum of fifteen dollars; and furthermore, guarantee to replace the gun with another gun in good condition after the war. There is no liability for the bearer to repay the fifteen dollars to me.

H.D.N.

Promissory note given by Pat Noone to Achok, headman of the Kuala Bertam area in Pahang. This is the last intimation of Pat from the jungle angry. He sent Uda away for a while and he was in disgrace. Later Tata forgave him and the three were together, but Uda had no woman to sleep with and he was full of virility. He loved Anjang, and having already tasted her he dreamed of her."

"How do you know these things? His dreams are his dreams, not your dreams," Richard said.

"*Tuan*, the whole of the Telom valley knows of Uda's dreams. He dreamed that Tata would take Anjang away from her people. He dreamed that Tata would make the aborigines fight the Japs and thus get killed. He dreamed that Busu would be given as a hostage to the Chinese."

Richard touched his arm. "Angah," he said reassuringly. "Don't be afraid to tell me anything."

"*Tuan*, it is the terrible secret of the Telom valley."

"I promise no harm shall come to you or your people for divulging it to me."

"*Tuan*, since you give me this assurance I will tell you the truth," Angah said. He looked up into Richard's face. "Your brother was murdered by Uda and Busu."

According to Angah, he had first heard of Pat's death when a runner came up with the news. Angah left immediately for Ngah's settlement, and arrived to find Anjang beside herself with grief. Uda and Busu were there, looking very frightened. They had set out with Pat the day before, but had returned that morning with his revolver, which now with its sinister associations lay in the centre of the long-house floor.

"What had they done?" Richard asked.

"They knocked it out of his hand with staves they had cut," Angah replied. "Then Uda blow-piped your brother."

"Did they admit this?"

"Yes, *Tuan*."

"What did you say to him?"

"I asked him why he had done this terrible thing. He said he dreamed he must. I said, 'Your dreams are false. You killed our Tata because you wanted his wife. You killed him because he has no relatives in the jungle to avenge him. But when the white men come back they will kill you for this deed.'"

"And how did Uda reply?"

"He said that Low Mah had told him the white men were finished in Malaya, and that after the war the Chinese would be masters. But Penghulu Ngah said he did not believe the Chinese, and that we must be careful because if the white men came back we would all be shot since one of our people had killed *Tuan* Tata. He said Tata was dead, but now we must think of our own skins. These were wise words according to our lights, and we agreed that a taboo should be made of the matter."

Richard looked away. Then he said: "What was done with my brother's body?"

"He was buried at Kuala Wi," Angah said. "He was buried according to the Temiar custom. We used to visit the grave and light fires there to keep his spirit warm." Angah thought for a moment, then he shook his head sadly.

"What of Anjang?" Richard asked.

"She pined for her husband. Then after two or three moons she longed to go back to her own people, and Uda took her away into Perak. I heard no more of them."

"She is dead," Richard said, and again Angah shook his head.

20 . *The Honeymoon*

Angah's defection was the stimulus for an intensification of the campaign to win over the aborigines.

Richard had already obtained a further increase to his establishment: a medical section with Indian dressers to handle all the clinical work for the field teams, and two flying doctors to visit the forts and natural outlets and in some cases to attend sick aborigines in the settlements; serious cases and those in need of emergency operations being evacuated by helicopter to a hospital in Kuala Lumpur. And this special medical aid proved possibly the greatest single factor in attracting the aborigines. They began to flock into the forts, and here the field assistants were able to work on them. They were given food and tobacco. They were engaged as casual labour at a wage of two dollars a day to enable them to buy goods at the store. They were encouraged to attend the schools, where lessons and games were organised for children and adults. Further 'civics courses' were laid on in Kuala Lumpur for headmen and senior adults on the lines of the propaganda outing provided for the hundred headmen during Operation Valiant.

Alongside this effort by the Department of Aborigines, Templer stepped up S.A.S. operations in the deep jungle. Field assistants were sent out with patrols to liaise with headmen at the settlements they touched. Supplies of tobacco, medicines and welfare goods were carried as gifts, so that groups which were some distance from the nearest fort and others who were too frightened or too shy to visit it would also receive the Government message at first hand.

These were primarily flag-waving, goodwill patrols, promising security to the aborigines and death to the Communists who lived on them and gave nothing in return. The S.A.S. created a good impression with their self-sufficiency, and the menace and avenging power their presence suggested. The effect was soon apparent from the information that began to come in, some of it valuable information resulting in a number of spectacular kills.

At the Standing Committee meetings, Richard had always contended that once aborigines were convinced of the advantages of siding with Government, success at winning them over would depend on just how safe such a course would look to those contemplating it. The outcome of the deep probing patrols proved he was right, because they were soon followed by a wave of aborigines, sometimes just a few families, sometimes whole groups, leaving their settlements and seeking Government protection at the nearest fort or deep jungle military base. Their usual story was that they were tired of following the terrorists, who devoured the food in their *ladangs* and left practically nothing for them.

Richard saw to it that they were given no cause to regret the step they had taken. They were well looked after. In Richard's view every individual was important, "first on the individual's own account as a human being, second as an ally and third as an ambassador," as he told a group of S.A.S. in a lecture. "Aborigines are exogamous—that is they tend to marry outside the group, with the result that every aborigine has relatives scattered in groups all over the deep jungle. He is in duty bound to see that they are informed of all serious matters likely to affect their welfare."

It was a busy and exciting time for the Department of Aborigines.

From all over the deep jungle came reports of a dramatic

improvement in the aborigines' morale. An indication of this was given from isolated incidents in which single aborigines or groups suddenly turned on C.T.s and killed them.

One of the first occurred at Krani Hondai's settlement, and was motivated probably by the promise of a fat reward Richard had made to the wily old headman. Two C.T.s had been in the habit of calling at his long-house to collect a sack of tapioca every other day, the group's contribution to the local Asal organisation. On this occasion the C.T.s had been given their tapioca, which they had put into the sack, and they were now sitting on the log gangway leading up to the long-house, talking to Hondai and a number of his braves who had gathered round with their blow-pipes. After a few minutes the sound of an approaching aircraft was heard, then suddenly a Valetta appeared flying very low over the *ladang*. Seeing it, the C.T.s took fright and started running towards the edge of the jungle for cover. Krani Hondai made a sign to his men, who immediately let fly at the two fleeing figures with their blow-pipes. One dropped dead in the *ladang*. The other just managed to reach the jungle before he also died.

Hondai immediately sent a runner to inform the S.A.S. at their base in the Cameron Highlands, and the bodies were evacuated by helicopter to Kuala Lipis hospital. Here post mortems were carried out, the first ever on human beings killed by ipoh poison. The reports stated that death had been caused by paralysis of the heart. The man who died first had been hit by several darts, one of which had punctured a vein. The other had received a single flesh wound in the shoulder, so the poison had taken a little longer to have its deadly effect.

Actually Richard never advised blow-piping as a means of killing C.T.s, poison being contrary to the Geneva Convention. Moreover, even the most lethal brew sometimes has a delayed action, and the time-lag makes it too risky for the man at the attacking end of the blow-pipe. During the early part of the Emergency there was an instance in which a group turned on some C.T.s who threatened them. The C.T.s were blow-piped, but before they died they opened fire on the aborigines with their Sten-guns and accounted for quite a number.

Another double killing was reported from the Batang Padang: two Communist couriers were shot-gunned at close range by Abas and his companion, the two young braves whom Richard had briefed at Bidor during Operation Valiant. Every day for four months they had waited near the couriers' route past their *ladang* high up in the mountains near the Pahang border, until finally the C.T.s had walked into the ambush. The aborigines had hidden the bodies and taken the documents they were carrying to Fort Shean. These proved to be high-level dispatches, the loss of which were a serious embarrassment to the M.C.P., as they gave an indication of the poor state of the terrorists' morale. Reference was made in the dispatches to the recent surrender of an entire C.T. section, which had been talked into this action by aborigines who then led them out of the jungle with all their arms and ammunition.

There was even a stranger surrender story in which the principal rôle was played by an aborigine boy named Kabun, whose father and mother had been enslaved by a section of C.T.s soon after the effects of the food denial campaign began to be felt, to find edible plants and roots and game for the party, since they had no other source of food supply. To ensure that the parents did not run away, one of the C.T.s, an armourer who was an expert at repairing weapons of all kinds, took Kabun in his charge as a hostage.

Food was very short, and both parents eventually died of starvation, leaving Kabun an orphan. However, the armourer was a kindly man and the boy became his assistant. They lived together in a little hut filled with weapons of all kinds which the C.T.s brought for repair. Then one day the armourer made up his mind to surrender, but like a large number of C.T.s in the jungle he had been kept in complete ignorance as to exactly where he was. He mentioned his problem to Kabun, who said he knew the path to the trading post, since he had frequently been there with his group. That night they made their escape from the camp, taking away all the arms and ammunition they could carry, and the next day the armourer gave himself up at a police out-post.

For his part in the affair Kabun earned a reward of $13,000. This has been banked for him by the Department of Aborigines, and he is now living with Ché Badrillah, a Malay assistant protector, who has a large family of his own. Kabun is going to school. His reports indicate that he is a brilliant pupil.

Fort Shean had been established on the Jelai river in north-west Pahang to break the grip of the Central Committee of the M.C.P., which at one time was centred in that valley. But it still left quite a large tract of jungle to the south of the Jelai where some eight hundred aborigines were all under pretty effective C.T. domination. This was the territory of Chawog, another aborigine Asal organiser, whose record of murder and brutality was even worse than that of Bah Pelankin already eliminated in Perak.

A fort was contemplated for the area, and two squadrons of S.A.S. went in with field assistants to assess the distribution of the groups so that the best site for the fort could be worked out. Patrols waved the flag along the Betau river, a tributary of the Jelai Kechil, and soon a fair amount of information was volun-teered, confirming reports from Shean regarding Chawog's activities in that and the neighbouring valleys. He appeared to be the terror of the valleys. It was said that he had personally executed several aborigines merely suspected of having given information against the C.T.s, and had tortured dozens of others by various methods he had devised himself. He was hated, but with a C.T. escort and with C.T. backing he strutted about the *ladangs* bullying people with impunity.

Then information was received concerning the location of the house in which Chawog's wife lived, and which he was said to visit unattended by his escort every third or fourth night. A plan to eliminate him was discussed, but again Richard was anxious that the actual killing should be done by aborigines. Chawog's crimes had been commited against his own people.

He visited Fort Shean to ask for volunteers from among those enlisted in the local section of the newly-formed force of Aboriginal Auxiliary Police. Eight men undertook the assignment but stipulated they must be left to act entirely on their own. This was even more than Richard had hoped for, as Chawog had a frightening reputation, and if the expedition were reinforced by Malay police they might somehow contrive to do the killing themselves.

The expedition set off up the Betau river and Richard returned to Kuala Lumpur. He heard no more of them for a week. Then one night a message came through from Fort Shean, that the party had returned from the Betau with the news that Chawog had been killed.

Richard flew into Shean next morning and personally congratulated each of the aborigines concerned in the affair. They told him the story outside the two police lieutenants' mess, while a crowd of aborigines gathered round to cheer their heroes at intervals during the long and graphic narrative.

Briefly, the party had reached a spot a little distance from the house and waited until they were certain Chawog had entered it. They let him have his night's rest, then they surrounded the house in the early hours of the morning. When all were in position, the leader of the party, a headman who knew the Asal organiser, stepped into the clearing and called out to him to come out of the house. Presently Chawog's face appeared at a window. He asked why he had been disturbed at such an unconscionable hour, and the headman replied that he had come to warn him of the approach of an S.A.S. patrol, adding that he hoped this service would not be forgotten.

Chawog reacted immediately. He ran round to the entrance, but was shot as he came down the log ramp leading to the ground. After collecting his arms and ammunition, the party rushed back to the fort, and the fort commander sent out a police patrol to photograph the body for identification.

Richard returned to Kuala Lumpur, where he soon received official confirmation, not only of the death of Chawog, but of his escort as well, the latter having been ambushed by another party of aborigines. Richard had already made arrangements for an announcement of Chawog's death to be recorded in the Semai dialect by a Semai. This was sent out with a voice aircraft which flew up and down the Betau valley giving the aborigines there the news that their oppressor had been killed by his own people fighting on the side of the Government.

Within a day or so odd families began coming into S.A.S. encampments on the Betau. Then the groups started streaming in, and soon it was an exodus in which over 750 aborigines, the entire population of the area, were involved. Emergency food drops were carried out by the R.A.F. Then with twenty field assistants assembling the groups, they were led with an S.A.S.

escort to Fort Shean, where suitable arrangements could be made for their feeding and medical attention. The doctors reported that a high percentage were suffering from the effects of malnutrition, and when asked why they did not have enough food to eat, they invariably replied that most of what they produced had been taken from them by the Asal organisation.

The more important headmen were flown over to Kuala Lumpur for debriefing. This was generally carried out at Richard's house in the evenings. One of the headmen was a particularly jungly-looking Semai from the Ulu Betau, with very long hair hanging down to his shoulders. He was squatting on one of the low, *rotan* chairs in the lounge with his feet up on the cushions, smoking a cigarette, while Richard was questioning him with the aid of a plaster model of the area on the floor. Barbara Penington and Puteh were also in the room.

Like most aborigines, this headman possessed a remarkably specialised memory for the features of the river valley in which he lived. He had been able to describe paths in vivid detail, and when confronted with the plaster model, and orientated by being told the names of the rivers and junctions, he was able to give the exact locations of several C.T. camps. Everything was going well until Richard looked up to see an expression of horror on Barbara's face. Then he noticed what the headman was doing. He had been scratching his head vigorously with his left hand, and had apparently caught hold of something in his hair. He took it out and looked at it between his fingers. Then Richard saw a tiny spurt of blood as he pinched it and popped it into his mouth. He went on doing this throughout the interrogation.

Aborigines are seldom interrogated over long periods; being unused to much mental exertion, they tend to lose interest, and the best results are obtained from several short debriefing sessions. So after an hour or so the Semai was sent back to the departmental Research Station outside Kuala Lumpur where visiting aborigines are usually accommodated. However, when he returned the following evening Richard was surprised to see him in a sarong with his hair cut and Brylcreemed.

"I've had him disinfested," Barbara explained.

Ninety per cent of the success of the deep jungle operations was due to tactical intelligence obtained from aborigines. The C.T.s, limited by the difficulty of collecting food in sufficient quantities, were no longer based in large jungle camps of the kind they had as M.P.A.J.A. guerrillas during the occupation. Instead, they were now scattered in penny packets all over the deep jungle, controlled by tenuous lines of communication from the Politburo in South Siam, where Chin Peng had moved when the Malayan jungles became too hot for him. There were definite courier routes, not single paths any more but zones through the jungle extending down almost the whole length of the Peninsula. The couriers not only varied the actual paths they took through the zones, but became expert at covering up their own tracks so that it was almost impossible for anyone bar an aborigine to follow them. Aborigines are inquisitive people. If a couple of them pick up a set of recent tracks on a hunting trip they must follow them up. If the tracks lead to a camp, then shortly every headman in the *saka* will know about it. In theory, at any rate, every C.T. camp became known to the aborigines in the locality.

Originally the job of extracting this information from them belonged to the Special Branch of the Malayan Police. However, on Richard's recommendation, Templer transferred the responsibility to the Department of Aborigines. Handling aborigines requires a specialised knowledge and a particular technique, and policemen do not usually possess the gentle, patient approach which obtains the best results.

It is the approach that matters with an aborigine. He has to be given a first impression of manifest friendliness without over-familiarity, and a willingness to help. He is a most formal creature, strict in the observance of custom and protocol, so it is important to know what may and may not be done.

It is bad form, for instance, to discuss matters affecting the group as a whole without addressing the headman. It is equally bad form to ask an aborigine his name: the correct procedure is to ask it of someone else, as the belief exists that if a man personally gives another his name, he bestows on him some power or influence over the name and thus over himself. An aborigine should not, if possible, be touched on the head: the head, as a seat of a soul, is taboo to strangers. Aborigine women should be ignored, as one of the quickest ways of alienating a group is to pay undue attention to their womenfolk. A woman should certainly not be offered tobacco, as accepting it from a man has a social significance, almost amounting to a willingness for intimacy among some of the groups. If she has a husband the right form is to give it to him to pass on to her; if not she may take it from the packet or tin, provided the donor is not holding it. The giving of small gifts of tobacco and salt on first contact is a polite demonstration of friendship, but too many gifts may make aborigines suspicious. At the same time rewards and wages must be paid promptly, and promises kept faithfully. An aborigine is true to his word and expects the same sort of treatment as he gives.

Routine interrogations were left to field assistants, whom Richard personally lectured on the vital importance of following the right interviewing procedure, based on Pat's and his own experience. He stressed the necessity of selecting a suitable spot, one that was quiet and secure without being too obvious, of seeing that outsiders weren't present, particularly Chinese, whom the aborigines tended to identify with the C.T.s. He advised picking the best time, which is the evening when the day's work is done and aborigines like to sit down for a chat. He recommended putting the informant completely at ease, and offering him refreshments and tobacco, and he demanded the utmost patience and gentleness. Particularly he warned against overdoing it.

"It is not unusual," he told prospective interrogators, "for an aborigine to adopt a reclining position in the middle of an interview, and then to fall fast asleep.

The main object of these interrogations was to find out where the C.T.s were, and once a field assistant's experience and contacts increased, so did the flow of information coming to him. He passed it in the first instance to the military or police commander with whom he happened to be operating. The commander would perhaps ask for further details, and the field assistant would invite the informant to come up for another interrogation, to try, if possible, to pin-point the location of the camp or hide-out on the map from the description of how to get to it. In many cases the informant concerned would offer to guide the patrol. He would take it to within a short distance of the place, then hide behind a tree while the patrol completed the killing. The system worked smoothly, and a high percentage of deep jungle eliminations were accounted for in this way.

The more involved interrogations were generally carried out by Richard and his headquarters team in Kuala Lumpur. All amenities and aids to interrogation were at hand, and they had the advantage of being able to offer absolute security. But here again only patience paid off. A case to illustrate this is that of a 'hostile' group in Perak who were known to be helping the local Chinese Asal organiser. As more and more information came in, Richard built up a detailed picture of the group. He had a complete list of the names of the individuals, who their relatives were, what arms they had, who were acting as the Asal organiser's bodyguard. They had been with the C.T.s since the start of the Emergency, and he was particularly anxious to win them over as the first step towards breaking up the Asal organisation in the locality.

He was trying to get a message through to them, when he heard from a group near the Cameron Highlands that three members of the 'hostile' group were due there on the following day accompanying their Chinese leader on a food-collecting expedition. Richard contacted the assistant protector on the spot, who laid on a Department of Aborigines' ambush with a police patrol kept well in the background.

They took up positions observing the settlement. In due course the 'hostile' aborigines arrived, two men and a woman, but without the Chinese. They entered the long-house to be followed soon after by a member of the assistant protector's staff. He persuaded them to surrender their arms, as the place was surrounded by police, and to come quietly.

Unfortunately at this stage the police lieutenant in command of the patrol suddenly decided to assert his authority. He pointed out that they were captured enemy personnel and therefore his responsibility. He arrested them, took away their belongings and locked them up, and for the next ten days interrogated them at the police station while Richard did his best to get them transferred to his department. Eventually the Police agreed to hand over their prisoners, and Richard became their temporary custodian. He had never seen such frightened people.

He brought them down to Kuala Lumpur in his car, and quartered them at the back of his house. Shortly afterwards three more from their group were caught in exactly the same way, and they too ended up in Richard's servants' quarters. He then happened to go down with malaria, but when he recovered he was able to start the long, slow process of winning their confidence. He gave them Malay clothes, so that they would not feel conspicuous, he saw they had enough food, and he took them round Kuala Lumpur, showing them the sights. He even took them to the coast to give them their first glimpse of the sea.

Eventually, after three months, Richard began asking them questions about the C.T.s, and once they did start talking it was all he could do to write down what they said. It was an extremely profitable interrogation because they gave detailed information on camps, courier movements, C.T. personalities and morale, as well as confirming what Richard already knew about the rest of their group. Next he got them to record messages to their relatives informing them that they were safe and sound, and these were broadcast by voice aircraft over their *saka*. The result was that soon individuals and families began coming over, some to Fort Brooke, others to the Cameron Highlands, until the count was over eighty people including twelve who were armed.

The difficulty of handling aborigines in Kuala Lumpur was that outside their own natural environment they possess a deep-rooted sense of uncertainty. Perhaps it is the lack of the cover which the jungle affords, or the pace and strangeness of city life, with cars rushing up and down the roads and aircraft landing and taking off at the airport a mile away. At any rate Richard noticed that all those aborigines who stayed with him in Kuala Lumpur were always ready to leave literally at a moment's notice.

One morning he was working in a cold fug of cigarette smoke in his air-conditioned den, when he heard a loud crack like a rifle shot: a branch of his frangipani tree had fallen on high-tension electric wires which pass through his compound. He rushed out to see what had happened and found all his aborigine guests with

their back-baskets on, streaming across his lawn in full flight. He
had to run after them to bring them back.

Still, Kuala Lumpur was not an unhappy place for aborigines.
In Richard's house they could do more or less as they pleased: old
friends of the Noones often compared it to Pat's ménage in
Taiping before the war. The Research Station too was developed
to approximate group conditions in a settlement. Originally on
open ground near Kuala Lumpur, it was moved on Richard's
insistence to a site on a beautiful jungle stream in the mountains
above the town. Here some twenty members of the aborigine
field staff were accommodated in small houses they built themselves in their own group styles. They also constructed a 150-
foot Temiar long-house for ceremonial dances and for housing
any sudden influx of visitors from the jungle. A number of
permanent brick buildings were added, including an office block,
a cottage hospital with clinic and dispensary, a school, and
quarters for a number of field assistants and medical dressers.

That the C.T.s came to regard the Research Station as a major
obstacle to their cause was indicated by captured Communist
documents in which orders were given at a very high level for a
night attack. The guard on the station was heavily reinforced.

As the Department of Aborigines' campaign got under way
further documents were captured indicating the C.T.s' anxiety
about their former aborigine allies. Such references as the
following appeared in documents relating to north-west Pahang:
   "The Sakai are no longer with us."
   ". . . we find spies operating among the masses (aborigines)."
   ". . . concerning X who secretly collaborates with the enemy,
it is undoubtedly true that the enemy tries to make use of him and
his men to establish a base. . . . It is certain that the enemy will
try to destroy our organisation among the Orang Asal (aborigines),

so that we shall have no contact with them. . . . Orang Asal
spies are secretly intimidating and instigating them . . . propaganda is conducted to deceive them. . . ."

Further evidence came from the minutes of an M.C.P. meeting
in south-west Kelantan, at which it was decided that Richard,
Barbara Penington and Puteh, with several other members of the
Department of Aborigines should be eliminated. At the same
meeting it was also agreed that the department was doing more
damage in the neighbouring deep jungle areas than the Security
Forces. The M.C.P. had cause to be worried. By 1st June 1954,
the date General Templer left Malaya, nearly 1,600 dominated
aborigines of categories A and B had deserted the C.T.s and
sought Government protection, and a further 1,300 of category
C had come under Government influence as a result of the
extension of administration to their territories.

A few days before Templer left, Richard laid on a farewell dance
for him at the Research Station, with 300 Temiar and Semai
brought down from the deep jungle to make it a real occasion.
Templer was due to arrive at nine p.m., but a little before eight his
military assistant telephoned to say the General would be late, as
he had only just returned from Bangkok, and that in any case he
wouldn't stay longer than half an hour as an old war wound in
his back was giving him trouble.

It had just gone ten when Templer appeared in the Research
Station long-house, where the dance had started. At ten-thirty
p.m. he showed no sign of moving. At midnight he had joined
the orchestra and was beating out the rhythm with a pair of bamboo stamping tubes. He finally left at two a.m., after inviting
all 300 aborigines to King's House the following afternoon.

They arrived in several bus and truck loads: Barbara Penington
had seen to it that the women at least were fully clad in sarong and
baju (the Malay blouse). Sir Gerald and Lady Templer met them

and took them round the gardens where they had soon stripped the bushes of their blooms. Then into the residence they went, swarming through the rooms, touching and marvelling. They were given cakes, cigarettes and soft drinks, and before they left the Templers shook hands with every one of them.

Next day the 300 were sent back to their settlements. In the *ulu* they still talk about that party.

---

21 . *The Tough Nuts*

After Templer's departure his dual rôle was again divided into two separate functions, and he was succeeded by Sir Donald McGillivray as High Commissioner, and General Sir Geoffrey Bourne as Director of Operations and G.O.C. Malaya. However the general policy governing the conduct of the Emergency remained unchanged, and the Department of Aborigines continued its campaign in the deep jungle.

By the end of 1954 a further 3,200 aborigines had been brought under Government control, including 1,800 of categories A and B, bringing the total of dominated aborigines of all categories up to 6,100.

But in 1955 the line on Richard's graph of monthly successes began to dip alarmingly, and he realised the department, having accounted for all the waverers, fence-sitters, and those within the safety zones of the forts, from now on would have to cope only with groups which were more or less resolutely pro-C.T.

Richard found it particularly difficult to put across the point of view of these tough nuts, as they became known, when he was asked why the Government message appeared not to have reached them, for it seemed unreasonable that they should ignore the material advantages of siding with Government, and continue feeding ravening terrorists from the scanty larder of the jungle.

He assured critics that his propaganda had reached every aborigine on the Main Range, but he explained too that material things have never played an all-important part in the life of the jungle dwellers. They have a code of values entirely of their own, and in their democracy every man has the right to live his own life the way he thinks fit. Nobody can take away a Senoi's sovereignty. The tough nuts had obviously thought about it carefully and they had thrown in their lot with the C.T.s.

To every aborigine in the jungle the Emergency represented an intrusion on his time-honoured way of life. It brought strife into his *saka*, gunfire, bombing, death, hunger and torment. His spirits did not like the Emergency and neither did he, but he was left little choice. He had to make up his mind about which party of intruders he should side with, for he must join one or the other. Logically he looked for the lesser evil.

Puteh once overheard a conversation between two Temiar, who were helping a squadron of S.A.S. to pull up a crop of tapioca their group had planted for some C.T.s.

"I don't know what we're doing," the first Temiar said. "The C.T.s told us to plant this and we spent months clearing this huge *ladang*. Now the white men come and tell us to pull it up. It's not lucky to destroy food. The spirits don't like it."

"Don't worry," the other replied. "As long as we do as we're told by the people in power, we'll be all right."

There was no more to it, save the question of which was in fact the right side. The easiest course, and the one that the majority pursued, was to take the line of least resistance.

193

Aborigines have been accused of cowardice. This is unfair. When sufficiently provoked and when they feel they have been wronged, their vengeance can be swift and terrible. During the early days of the Emergency, a group of lowland Semai living in the marshes at Changkat Pingan, Perak, were attacked suddenly one morning and two of their number were shot and killed. A party of C.T.s were seen running away from the settlement.

Some of the men of the group gave chase, following the C.T.s to a neighbouring Chinese village, where they were seen being met and cheered as heroes by the villagers. This so incensed the Semai, who concluded the villagers were involved in the killing, that they made a reprisal attack on the village. The only arms they had were six shot-guns which they kept for shooting wild pig, but they succeeded in killing every Chinese who appeared. Then they set fire to the houses and scores of people were burnt to death inside.

Such equations are part of the aborigine code, although the underlying purpose is not principally one of revenge. The aborigine is passionately peace-loving, and to his way of thinking just punishment is the only real deterrent against wrongdoing. He believes that the certainty of reprisal is a prerequisite of a harmonious life.

Before the war there was a considerable amount of friction between the Temiar and Chinese who came into the jungle to work tin or jelutong. Trouble nearly always resulted from interference with the aborigine women. The Malays in the *kampongs* along the Nenggiri river used to say: "The Chinese goes into the jungle with a licence for jelutong, then he starts tin-stealing, then woman-stealing, then he leaves in a hurry." That is, if he manages to get away. Scores of Chinese were speared or blow-piped by the aborigines for rape or attempted rape. There was a case in the

Betis valley, in Kelantan, of a jelutong *kongsi* house besieged by a Temiar group after an inmate had raped one of the Temiar girls, having first threatened her with a tapping knife. The Chinese was saved by the timely arrival of the Mikong and some police, who persuaded the Temiar to disperse. The Chinese was arrested and sentenced to a term of imprisonment, but the group was not satisfied. Foolishly he returned to the area on emerging from prison, and was blow-piped soon afterwards.

But there is an exactitude about Senoi justice. A man who has wronged a group never gets more punishment than he deserves, a point which Pat used to illustrate with the story of a European planter in the Cameron Highlands. The planter had employed aborigine labour to clear his estate, but he refused to pay a fair wage. To teach him a lesson they ambushed him on the winding mountain road near his house, having felled a single bamboo across the road so that he would have to get out of the car to remove the obstruction. Then as he bent down to pick it up they let fly with their blow-pipes from the undergrowth. The darts were not poisoned, but about twenty hit him in the seat. At close range a dart can penetrate up to two inches.

It is said that the aborigines came to work as usual next day, and that thereafter the planter paid them the recognised wage.

In the struggle for control of the deep jungle the only loyalties the aborigines recognised were to themselves. They had no political or patriotic interest in the Emergency whatsoever, and except for a few individuals they took sides only because it was the prudent and expedient thing for them to do at the time. Most of those who came over to Government would have switched their allegiance back to the C.T.s overnight without a qualm, had it suited them to do so. Richard had no illusions. He also knew that, in order to ensure their safety, whatever the outcome of the

Emergency, some of the groups already under his control had 'non-aggression pacts' with others still under the C.T.s. Thus, if the C.T.s won, those who had unwisely come over to Government would have advocates to plead their cause with the C.T.s: conversely, in the other event the pro-Government headmen were to act on behalf of the groups which had stayed 'hostile'.

There were groups who ran with the hare and hunted with the hounds, who gave information to the Security Forces that was worthless, and when the C.T.s visited them hid the shot-guns issued them for their own defence. For this reason Asal organisations continued to exist quite near some of the forts, notably Fort Kemar in northern Perak, and the forts in the Cameron Highlands area. There was little excuse for these groups, and it was necessary at times to reprimand them.

But to a group well out of a fort's radius of protection, with only a primitive concept of the issues and little or no information from the world outside, the whole thing was quite bewildering. It was difficult for them to know which side to follow. Those who had been under C.T. domination for a number of years were far from convinced that the Government would win in the end. They had already heard of the defeat of a previous British Government by the Japs, and then the Japanese Army itself had been destroyed, as far as the aborigines knew, by Chinese guerrillas operating from deep jungle bases during the occupation. The Communists assured their aborigine supporters that the same fate awaited the Security Forces, and woe to those headmen who deserted them for Government!

Moreover the Communists had altered their entire aboriginal policy, the Asal approach having been toned down to conform more or less with that of the Department of Aborigines. It became a capital offence for a C.T. to interfere with an aborigine woman. No longer were demands made for food from a *ladang*, unless the C.T.s living near the settlement had actually shared in the work of producing it. And if they had not thus earned themselves an entitlement they had to pay a reasonable price for that which they consumed.

In February 1955 two hostile Semai were captured at Boh Tea Estate in the Cameron Highlands. They had been members of the Asal Protection Corps in the Telom valley, and testified to the gentle treatment aborigines now received from the C.T.s. They disclosed during their interrogation the revised scale of prices for food purchases recently issued by the M.C.P. State Committee for Pahang. The list included such items as six dollars for a fat dog, five dollars for a chicken and two dollars for ten rats. Cucumbers were three cents each, and bananas two dollars for one large stick.

Thus aborigines under C.T. domination were being encouraged to grow more food as a profitable side-line, and now that their security was no longer threatened they could see nothing to be gained by turning their backs on old allies. Some of these 'hostile' groups were under headmen famous throughout the Temiar country—men like Pangoi, Along Sten and Rajah Basor in Kelantan, and Anjang Rajah, Toh Membang, Along Lindong, Kerenching and Pandak in Perak. All these tough nuts had been old friends of Pat. It was realised that special measures were required to crack them.

The answer to Richard's nut-cracking problem was the S.A.S., who had become the greatest exponents of jungle fighting in the world. They had perfected a tree-jumping technique which made them completely independent of an open dropping zone, parachuting straight on to jungle and if they got hung up in the tree-tops letting themselves down with the aid of a roll of webbing. They operated in troops of sixteen to eighteen men, patrolling for periods of up to sixteen weeks, and would emerge pale from the gloom of the jungle, thin from having lived on iron rations supplied by air-drop, with sores, skin disease and festering leech-bites. There were several cases of leeches having entered the glans penis, for which casualty-evacuation by helicopter and surgical attention was necessary.

The S.A.S. specialty was surprise—the surprise attack for instance on a C.T. camp, achieved usually by adopting the most difficult approach. Their secret was moving silently, and they trained by burrowing through bamboo clumps full of crackling dry leaves until a troop could do this without making a sound. On a patrol one man in the troop counted the distance they travelled in paces so that they could always pin-point their position: R.A.F. pilots delivering air-drops could always depend on finding a little yellow balloon floating above the tree-tops to mark the patrol's location on the ground beneath, though frequently an S.A.S. patrol would postpone being supplied for days rather than have its position compromised by the sound of an aircraft. It was hard work killing C.T.s in the deep jungle, but the S.A.S. did it with a sense of dedication.

The S.A.S. and the Department of Aborigines worked together as a nut-cracking team in a series of intensive operations, usually in squadron strength with several field teams assisting. A typical operation was one code-named Gabes North, which began as the result of the surrender of a C.T., Wong Tong Sing, and his aborigine wife. They reported large-scale Asal activity in the upper reaches of the Sengoh river in northern Perak, where the line of the Divide suddenly bulges into Kelantan. Wong Tong Sing knew only of thirty C.T.s and 200 'hostile' aborigines occupying the Bulge, as it was called, but aerial reconnaissance revealed a total of some 400 acres of scattered *ladangs* under cultivation, which was far in excess of the local aborigines' requirements. This suggested the possibility of the Bulge being used as an important transit zone—a belief which was strengthened by the fact that information had also been received of supplies of Benedictine being purchased in Grik and dispatched to the area. Benedictine was the favourite drink of high-level C.T.s. As the senior headman of the Bulge, one Bongsu Helwud, had so far resisted overtures of friendship, it was decided that the heat should be turned on in his *saka*.

B Squadron, under Major John Cooper, was chosen for the task, and the operation opened with his paratroopers converging on the *saka* from east and west. In six days they were in position astride the main paths leading into the Bulge, and they began systematic patrolling of the particularly difficult terrain, most of it above 4,000 feet. They made contact with some of the aborigine groups along the main river, but saw nothing of those forming the Asal Protection Corps.

After a few days a small S.A.S. patrol encountered two C.T.s in a *ladang* in the act of picking brinjals. In the ensuing gun-fight one C.T. was killed and the other wounded. A week later there was another brief battle in a *ladang* with a food-collecting party of five C.T.s, who fled into the jungle leaving a blood trail that the paratroopers followed for two days before losing it. The next battle was on a razor-back ridge between four C.T.s and a party of S.A.S. Both sides blazed away at each other's positions for several minutes. The Communists had the advantage of the ridge, the nature of which did not allow of any flanking movement, and were able to withdraw.

Meanwhile the field teams had been working on the local aborigines, who eventually disclosed that the big C.T. stronghold was on the Klub, a small upper tributary in the Bulge. The Klub was immediately swept from its source to *kuala* in a two-pronged drive, and altogether four C.T. camps and two large aborigine settlements were discovered. But all had been evacuated a short time before the S.A.S. arrived; their protective screen was obviously most efficient, and the indications were that a considerable Asal force of aborigines and C.T.s had got away by an escape route into Kelantan.

They were followed up, however, in a relentless pursuit, and eventually a troop of S.A.S. came across thirty-two weary aborigines who had deserted the main body. A few days later another thirty deserted, and as a result of their interrogation another five C.T.s were killed. That led to a further thirty-five aborigines seeking Government protection, whose headman, Along Serbin, undertook to lead a patrol to capture Helwud, the senior Asal headman. This was successfully carried out, with the result that the whole of his group of eighty came over to Government.

B Squadron was then reinforced by a fifth troop, and they made one of the most significant discoveries of the operation when they came across a hut with a crude water-wheel at the top of a high waterfall. Inside the hut was a wireless set and a water-driven generator, and this, together with the evidence of the C.T. camp and extensive *ladang* acreage, endorsed the original view that the Bulge had formed one of the main C.T. transit centres in northern Malaya.

The S.A.S. continued patrolling the Bulge for the next ten weeks. In that time they destroyed all the C.T. *ladangs*, killed a few more C.T.s, and brought in a further fifteen Asal aborigines who joined their relatives already under Police protection and on Richard's ration strength. Then, after more than four months in the Bulge, B Squadron came out for a rest, while another squadron prepared to turn on the heat in the next *saka* selected for their attention.

That was the nut-cracking pattern. It meant patrolling an area possibly for weeks, until the 'hostile' groups were finally located, or some aborigine could be induced to disclose their presence. Then success would depend on just how swiftly the local C.T.s could be killed and the Asal organisation broken up. This was no easy matter, for the deep jungle terrain entirely favoured the hunted. Here was a vast and highly complex tropical mountain system, with a ramification of countless paths connecting an immense variety of hiding places. Some were flat upper valleys cut off by precipitous ravines from the usual river routes, and protected by towering cliffs and rocky crags. There were few approaches to these secret valleys, so that they could be easily screened by aborigine sentries, and the Communists always provided themselves with alternative escape routes. The moment the alarm was sounded the C.T.s in a camp would split up, and trusted guides would take them to a pre-selected rendezvous. Therefore a successful attack on a camp required both speed and surprise, two elements which were extremely difficult to attain. Pressure had to be applied long and relentlessly on C.T.s before the Asal supporters eventually lost heart and deserted. It was tough, dangerous and frustrating work that required a very high order of skill and endurance. The rewards were undernourished and frightened aborigines, with information leading possibly to a surprise attack on a hide-out, a few kills, more aborigines, and eventually the senior headmen.

Most 'hostile' groups came in sooner or later after the break up of the Asal organisation. Yet there were some who escaped with their Asal organisers, and held out, resisting all attempts to bring them over.

Pangoi was one of these tougher nuts. He was an old man with a deep booming voice, and had been chief of the upper Brok area when Pat was exploring Kelantan. During the war Pat had asked him to help the Communists, and Pangoi had been in association with them ever since. Richard's dossier on him ran to several pages, as he was known to be fiercely hostile, but his record as far as his own people were concerned was clean. He was a good chief, motivated in all his actions by what he thought was best for his *saka*.

He was known to be helping a number of C.T.s, and it was thought that his resistance to the campaign was prompted by his loyalty to a Chinese Asal organiser named Ah Ming, who had originally been a trader on the outskirts of the jungle and had been known to all the groups in Kelantan before he ever joined the M.C.P. From all accounts Ah Ming had the interests of the aborigines at heart, and as far as he could ensure it he saw that they were properly handled by his fellow C.T.s, a number of whom were living off Pangoi's immense *ladang*.

As far as the Department of Aborigines was concerned Pangoi had an infuriating habit of remaining out of touch. He never replied to a message sent to him, and if a Security Force deep-probing patrol was sent to his settlement they invariably found it deserted. Destruction of the *ladang* might have been justified in the circumstances, but Richard would never sanction this for fear that it might result in some of the group dying of starvation.

As Puteh had known Pangoi before the war, Richard sent him up to Fort Brooke, the nearest fort to the *saka*, to make a special effort. Puteh was unsuccessful, although he did hear that one of Pangoi's relatives, the former pro-Jap headman, Menteri Awol, was in touch with him. Discreetly Puteh approached Awol, but he denied any knowledge of Pangoi's whereabouts, so Puteh returned to Kuala Lumpur.

Several months passed, then Richard decided it was time to try again and sent Puteh back to Fort Brooke to renew his efforts.

Puteh, after tactful inquiries, managed to find out roughly where Pangoi's group had moved to open up a new *ladang*, and he sent the old man a message through Awol, asking him to come out and promising protection. Again there was no reply. A few months later Puteh sent him another message, but no reply came to that either.

It was then decided to put an S.A.S. squadron into the area. The S.A.S. went in, but the Asal organisation withdrew and Pangoi and his entire tribe went with them. They disappeared westwards, leaving no trace at all of where they had gone, and after six weeks of fruitless search the squadron was brought out and parachuted a week later on to jungle in the vicinity of Ipoh. This was an operation called Termite, supported by intensive R.A.F. bombing of a series of very large camps.

Before the bombing Richard had flown low over the area and certified that the huts were not of aborigine design or construction, but it so happened that Pangoi and his people were in the jungle near one of the camps during the bombing, and got the fright of their lives. They headed straight back for their own hunting grounds, where they knew all the spirits and could count on some sort of spiritual protection.

As soon as it was reported that they were back in their hereditary territory, Puteh was sent again to Fort Brooke to have yet another try. The group, it seemed, had had enough of working with the terrorists, but Pangoi was not taking any chances. Before committing his whole group he sent four relatives, including his son Alok, to seek Government protection. Alok sent back a favourable report and two weeks later a further twenty-six came into Fort Brooke, to be followed after a few days by another forty-nine. But still Pangoi would not come himself. It is said that he sat brooding in the gloom of his long-house, wizened, white-haired, full of kindly cunning. Fourteen young men stayed guarding him, attending to his needs, for he was much loved by his people.

It was Alok who finally decided matters for Pangoi. The former had suddenly developed an intense hatred for Communists. On their flight into Perak his baby girl had died from exposure to the cold of the heights—they had camped for the night on a pass over the Divide. The morning after the child's death the C.T.s with them saw Alok filling up the grave after he had buried her, and being suspicious made him dig it up again, thus forcing him to desecrate his child's grave. Moreover, since coming to Fort Brooke, Alok had discovered by direct observation and from talking to other aborigines there, that the C.T.s had been filling them with propaganda lies in order to keep his group on their side. Alok was so bitter about this that he undertook to lead a patrol of his relatives to attempt the killing of Ah Ming, and when Pangoi heard of it he and his fourteen companions came out immediately at Fort Brooke.

Alok's patrol spent fourteen days in the area looking for Ah Ming. They failed to locate him, although they did come upon a camp occupied by some thirty terrorists. They thought better of attempting to tackle that number on their own, and reported back to Fort Brooke. An S.A.S. patrol was brought up immediately for the task, and one of the aborigines guided them to the camp. It was attacked and several C.T.s were killed.

Ah Ming, however, still remained at large, and his elimination became the specific assignment of a New Zealand squadron of S.A.S. which had recently arrived in Malaya. Alok was attached to a troop as their guide, and again they set out from Fort Brooke.

After a short time, Alok, who was leading, suddenly stopped and studied the path in front of him. Then he told the troop commander that two or three C.T.s had crossed their path, and he turned off, following the tracks.

For three days Alok led the troop where there appeared to be no path and no sign at all of anybody having previously passed that way. Then, just as it was getting dark on the evening of the third day, he called a halt and informed the troop commander that their quarry were only two hours ahead. He suggested they should camp where they were for the night, and asked that nobody should smoke or light a fire to cook, as smells carry a good distance in the jungle.

Early next morning they continued following the tracks, with Alok in the lead, now moving very cautiously. Suddenly he stopped, and slowly beckoned to the troop commander to come up. Then he pointed through the undergrowth, and the troop commander, looking in the direction he indicated, saw a small hut in a clearing just ahead.

It took the troop an hour to surround the hut, the men edging their way very slowly so as not to make a sound. The two C.T.s in the hut were taken completely by surprise. They came bolting out as the first shot was fired, but were machine-gunned before they had gone a few yards. One of them was Ah Ming, and for his part in the killing Alok collected a reward of $10,000, which was shared by the group. He was also paid $3,000 for bringing out a 'hostile' headman by the name of Ayop, and $700 for finding a big C.T. supply dump of coconut oil, flour, dried fish, sugar and tinned milk.

The success of Alok's patrol strengthened a conviction of Richard's that insufficient use was being made of the aggressive potential of those aborigines who were whole-heartedly on the side of Government. There had been aborigines in the Home Guard for some considerable time, but that was mainly in the low-lying fringe jungle and they had been armed only to defend their own settlements. In the forts, soon after they were established, the

Police had started recruiting A.A.P.s (Aboriginal Auxiliary Police), who were armed and given a certain amount of training, but these were intended more or less to act as guides and porters for the police patrols. Later a modified fighting rôle was introduced for aborigines when the P.A.G.s (Police Aboriginal Guards) were formed. These were based on the forts and were supposed to go out on C.T.-killing patrols, but they had not proved as successful as Richard had hoped. The trouble, he felt, was that they were never really allowed to operate on their own. They were under the orders of the fort commanders who used them for reconnaissance patrols, but the moment they came back with some really hot information, the commander, being a policeman, usually sent his Malay police to do the killing. After a while it was found that the P.A.G.s were being used more as A.A.P.s (porters and guides) than in the rôle for which they were originally intended.

In Richard's opinion this was a waste of specialised manpower, as the jungle was the aborigines' natural habitat, and it was a pity not to make full use of their particular gifts. They had proved keen and courageous in the past, once they really believed in the rightness of the part they were playing in the Emergency, and he felt that if they were given proper military training and allowed to operate entirely on their own they would really prove their worth.

Richard's faith in aborigines was shared by Colonel George Lea, the Officer Commanding 22 S.A.S. Regiment, and he undertook to train three special sections, two Semai and one Temiar, under Bah Pai, late of the Asal Protection Corps, who had been captured in Batang Padang with a tommy-gun but had since become violently anti-C.T.

Then, with the permission of the Director of Operations, Bah Pai and one Semai section were helicoptered to the landing zone at Kuala Misong on the Telom river. Their target was the local Asal organiser, a Chinese named Ah Lu Min.

The aborigines did not get their man, but they did find two large C.T. camps, one of which had been very hurriedly evacuated. In it was a wireless set and a sewing machine with a number of unfinished M.R.L.A. uniforms. In the opinion of Richard and Colonel Lea this rated as a pretty fair first attempt for the aborigine section, since a Gurkha unit had been operating in the area for a month just before the aborigines went in and had found no evidence at all of any C.T. activity.

What Richard really wanted for his aborigine sections was that they should be formed into a special aboriginal unit, with their own crest and cap-badge. This, he felt, would give them some official military standing in the Emergency, and would act as a boost for their morale and self-respect. He mooted the idea to Government, but was turned down and told to make the best he could of the P.A.G.s.

So the campaign continued, with one hostile group after another being subjected to intensive pressure. A few held out, or disappeared, but the majority eventually came over to Government. By October 1956, when Richard left Malaya on home leave, a total of 6,400 aborigines, who had previously been under terrorist domination, were now completely under Government influence. Roughly 600 aborigines still remained on the side of the C.T.s, who were now down to 2,500 or thereabouts.

Richard had managed at one time or another to meet most of the aborigines who came over to Government. His usual practice was to ask how they were, and if there was anything they wanted. Many had known Pat and told Richard so, but a number of them had something on their minds. It concerned his brother's disappearance.

PART FOUR . THE SECRET

*

22 . The Grapevine

Two months before Richard came to England on leave, I had traced his mother to a sedately respectable hotel in Walmer. I had written to say I was particularly interested in the story of her son Pat, and she had replied inviting me to tea.

I found a gentle, soft-voiced little woman, with a deceptively light-hearted manner which was used to cover a considerable reputation as an amateur archæologist.

She asked me when I had first heard of Pat, and I said I could remember before the war listening to a friend describe a visit to Jalong during the excavation of Gua Baik. "Dr. Callenfels was there at the time," I added.

"Oh, I remember him," Mrs. Noone said. "He was so stout he had to be carried to the dig on a cane-chair with bamboos lashed crosswise under it. It took about twenty aborigines to lift him. He had a long beard that came down to his chest, and he would sit there combing it out with his fingers." She smiled. "He and Pat made an oddly assorted pair."

"I would like to try and find out what happened to him," I said.

"Then you simply must get in touch with my younger son, Richard. He has written to say that some astonishing things have recently come out which throw an entirely new light on the mystery."

I learned too at that meeting that H.V. had died in 1955, that

208

Sheelah and her husband were living in the country a few miles from Walmer, and that her younger daughter Doreen was married to a Frenchman and living in Paris.

Before I left, Mrs. Noone said: "Now don't forget to write to Richard. I know he has been preparing a dossier of evidence collected from his private inquiry."

So I wrote to Richard, as his mother had suggested, and two months later we met in Walmer. It was sleeting as we drove from the station to the Royal Hotel in Deal, but we drew chairs up to the blazing log-fire in the lounge, and ordered warming drinks.

He patted his brief-case. "I have got the file in here," he said. "All the evidence is in Malay, but I will translate as we go along."

There were thirteen statements in all. What had happened was that after Penghulu Angah had told Richard his story, a headman named Bah Hitam had sought Government protection in Perak. Bah Hitam had been with the C.T.s since the beginning of the Emergency, and was interrogated by the police at Ipoh. After a couple of days he indicated that he had certain information concerning Pat, and was therefore sent down to Kuala Lumpur and accommodated in one of the servants' quarters behind Richard's house. Richard talked to him for several evenings and eventually got from him the bare facts that Pat had been blow-piped and that this had happened at the River Wi. Bah Hitam was not prepared to say who had committed the murder, although he did add that the body had been buried by Penghulu Ngah. When asked how he had heard this, Bah Hitam replied that a runner had brought the news to his *ladang* on the Penoh river, and that it was his job to see that the information was sent down to the Kinta valley.

Taken by itself the statement was not of much value, but it did confirm two essentials furnished by Angah—first that Pat had been blow-piped, and secondly that the scene of the crime was the Wi.

Then a fortnight after Bah Hitam's defection, a neighbour of his, Tabut, fled with his group to Fort Dixon south-east of the Cameron Highlands. He also wound up in Richard's compound and after a few days of humming and hawing finally admitted that he had been informed through the grapevine that Pat had been killed because of an aborigine woman known as Anjang or Teh. Tabut was more explicit. He cited Uda as the killer, Busu as his associate and Ngah as an accessory after the fact. He also stated that although Pat had been shot with several darts the poison had not been strong enough to kill him and he had apparently run some distance before falling to the ground. Then Uda had come up and killed him presumably with his *parang*.

Next came two statements made to the field assistant Norgee at a *ladang* in the Ulu Telom. The informants were a headman Bah Bintang and an elder, Bah Keraman, who merely said that *Tuan* Tata had been murdered by his guide Uda because of a woman. They too had heard it from a messenger who had brought the news to their *ladang* soon after the killing had occurred.

Then in August 1954 one of Pat's oldest and dearest friends among the Temiar came over to Government with his group and two other groups. He was Long Jim, the famous *saka* chief from the Ulu Plus, and his version of the murder tallied in every respect with those already given by the others. At the same time he gave an indication of how the news of Pat's death had spread, for it had come to him not only from Pahang, but from Kelantan. Several runners had brought it travelling by different routes. Long Jim added that several other *penghulus*, namely Gubnor, Ladang, To Ulu, and Penagor, would bear him out.

These in fact had not yet done so, but others had, and their individual versions, all recorded separately and at different times, differed in none of the substantial facts. Most of them told of the sadness that the news had brought to the groups, and the shame they had felt because their Tata had died by the hand of one of his own 'children'.

Sooner or later, what had happened was known across the length and breadth of the land of the Temiar; that it reached the groups in the north is shown by the testimony of Ngah Toris, a headman of the Jemheng, an upper tributary of the Temengor river.

Richard had known Toris for some time. He was a young man who had lost all his teeth as a result of a gum infection. Richard had got him a set of false teeth through the government dental officer in Kuala Lumpur, and in return Toris had told him what he knew about Pat. The interview was recorded on tape, and here is an edited transcript:

TORIS: "I never actually knew your brother because when he came to my *saka* before the war I was very young. However my father knew him well, and so did Raja Dalem who used to be our *saka* chief, a very old man indeed. Raja Dalem used to tell me about your brother, and when we heard how he had been murdered we were all wretched . . ." Toris then gave details of the murder and the motive as described by the others who had testified, but omitted to mention the names of the killers.

RICHARD: "Did Raja Dalem tell you the names of these two treacherous followers of my brother?"

TORIS: "They were Semai."

RICHARD: "Actually they were Temiar."

TORIS: "No, *Tuan*, Temiar would never do a thing like that. You can't trust the Semai—they are quick to use their blow-pipes without thinking. My father often told me to be careful of the Semai."

RICHARD: "What were their names?"

TORIS: "I was told they are with the Communists somewhere in Kelantan. They must have changed their names."

RICHARD: "What names did they have originally?"

TORIS: "They were Semai names——"

RICHARD: "No, they were Temiar names."

TORIS: "But they had Semai blood in them. I am sure of that. My father used to say you could never depend on the Semai."

RICHARD: "I have heard exactly the same story of my brother's death told me by headmen and others from all over the Temiar and Semai territory. Each account gives the same two names, so I already know who the killers are. But the more people who tell me this story the better, then I know that without doubt it must be true. Don't be afraid to tell me. I assure you no man shall touch a hair of your head for what you have disclosed to me. But I would appreciate it very much if you also trusted me with their names."

TORIS: "All right then, the first is Uda, and the second is his cousin Busu. They have a lot of Semai blood in them."

RICHARD: "Thank you for this evidence. Tell me, if a member of your group murdered another person, what would happen to him according to your custom?"

TORIS: "He would be killed. If we knew definitely who had committed the murder we would kill the murderer."

RICHARD: "Who would kill him?"

TORIS: "The man who was told to do it. But no one would know."

RICHARD: "How do you mean, no one would know?"

TORIS: "Well the headman of the group would tell one of his people to kill him when he was far away from the *ladang* in the jungle—hunting, maybe, or catching fish. No one else would know how the murderer died, and no one would ever speak of him again. It is our law that a murderer's name shall be taboo, and that of his executioner shall be told to no one."

RICHARD: "Does this often happen?"

TORIS: "No, *Tuan*, hardly ever. It is our custom, but Raja Dalem told me he had only heard of one case in his life. The murderer knows what to expect and usually runs away from his group and is never seen again. That is exactly what these two did. The whole trouble was of course that they were Semai. Had they been Temiar it would never have happened. That is what my father said."

Except for the evidence of Angah, who had actually gone to Ngah's *ladang* and seen both Uda and Busu after they had returned with Pat's revolver, the rest of the evidence was hearsay. Richard was prepared to accept it for the purpose of his inquiry. As he pointed out, if Pat had died through sickness or accident, it would have been unthinkable for a story to have been put out by people actually related to both Uda and Busu that they had murdered him. Those who had supplied the evidence had first heard it, not as rumour, but through the reliable and efficient news broadcasting system of the deep jungle.

"It is still hearsay," I observed. "But what you really want is the testimony of somebody closely involved—somebody like Ngah."

"Well," said Richard, "why don't you come out to stay with me in Malaya and help me to continue the investigation?"

23 . The Spiv Contact

I went out to Malaya in April 1957. Richard, who had already returned after his leave, met me in Singapore, and we toured the Federation in his Jaguar. We went to Taiping and visited the small white-distempered museum. In the aboriginal section were display cases full of exhibits Pat had brought back from his expeditions, still exactly as he had arranged them. In the office was a huge steel safe which nobody, not even the Japanese, had been able to open because Pat had taken away the key. It had still been unopened in 1946 when the search was instituted for his research material, and for a while there had been great hopes of what it might contain: the feeling was that Pat's only reason for committing his valuable records and documents to the missing filing cabinet had probably been that the safe was already full of more vital papers. H.V. had been sent a cable to this effect, and had written enthusiastically to Richard suggesting that the papers in the safe might include some clue to Pat's years of research work, even possibly a draft of the thesis which he had never had the opportunity to complete.

Eventually, a European expert on safes was located in Singapore and brought up to Taiping. He worked on the door, which was over five feet high, and after several hours the safe was opened. All it contained was Pat's collection of French recipes, a few sheets of music—his repertoire of songs—and his book of Müller's exercises with his muscle measurements on the fly-sheet.

As H.V. wrote in a letter to Richard: "If only he had committed these personal relics to the filing cabinet and his research to the safe, think of what a legacy he would have left!" In

Taiping we also visited the New Club, where we picked up one of the many stories still circulating about Pat. It concerned one of the journeys he made to Gua Musang in the Golden Blow-pipe, the Singapore–Kota Bharu express which tunnels through some 400 miles of jungle with wayside halts every few miles. It was somewhere about twenty miles short of Gua Musang that the communication cord was pulled and the train came to a stop. It was discovered that the emergency signal had been given from Pat's compartment, but he had disappeared. A week later he turned up at Gua Musang. His explanation was that he had been reading in the train when he happened to look out of the window and see two Temiar near the track. As the spot was outside the Temiar tribal limits, he had stopped the train and gone out to investigate.

We carried on northwards through Grik and up the road to Kroh that Pat's platoon had been sent to defend. At Kroh we stopped at the rest-house which had served as a Kempeitai head-quarters since Richard had last stayed in it during the Frontier Patrol period. We bathed in Berkeley's sulphur spring, and drove up past the overgrown Kedah Positions, where the Bren-gun carrier Richard had brought out from Siam still lies at the side of the road, on to Baling, then down to Ipoh where we heard another of the legendary if somewhat dubious stories about Pat—how he introduced soccer to a tribe of recently reformed head-hunters in Celebes, and got them really interested in the game by saying the ball was an enemy's head.

The Protector of Aborigines at Ipoh, Richard Corfield, took us out to the Kinta Intake where a group of ex-'hostile' Temiar had been resettled. They had to be given a gentle reprimand. Instead of drawing water from the river, they had found it more convenient to broach the pipe-line to the town.

We motored up to the Cameron Highlands. A squadron of S.A.S. were operating in the area, and we climbed up to the H.Q. troop to see Major John Slim, the squadron commander, who had a section of Senoi Praak (Fighting Senoi) operating under his command: this was part of the aboriginal military unit Richard had eventually received permission to raise.

No. 1 Section, under Sergeant Bah Hussein, had in the last few days broken up a party of four C.T.s and three 'hostile' families, the remnants of Bah Panjang's group from the Jor valley area. The Senoi Praak had attacked their camp and killed an aborigine and a C.T. who decided to shoot it out. A second C.T. had been wounded with an F.N. rifle and had now been on the run for three days, but seven aborigines had surrendered and were now in a Department of Aborigines' long-house at Tapah.

We visited them—seven terror-stricken people half-expecting their heads to be cut off any minute. One was a boy of about fourteen. A Malay field assistant with us borrowed a *parang* to sharpen his pencil and the boy screamed.

The operation in the Cameron Highlands was part of a big drive throughout Malaya to destroy as many C.T.s as possible before Independence on 31st August. Food denial was being intensified, and lines of cars and lorries were being searched at barriers outside every town we passed through: a special Emergency ordinance made it a serious offence to carry food without a licence.

In Kuala Lumpur the R.A.F. airfield was a scene of bustling activity, with planes taking off and landing every few minutes. A helicopter had come down near an ambulance, and a soldier with a chest wound was being transferred into it. A squadron of paratroopers were lined up waiting to take off, to descend later like avenging angels near some jungle hide-out.

In the operations room a crowd of pilots and navigators had come in for briefing. These included three voice-aircraft crews. One plane had a message for the 5th Independent Platoon of the M.R.L.A.:

"HULLO 5TH INDEPENDENT PLATOON.

YOUR OPERATIONAL COMMANDER LAU FATT HAS SELF-RENEWED.[1]

LAU FATT KNEW THE ARMED STRUGGLE IS USE-LESS.

HE CHOSE WISELY.

MEMBERS OF 5TH INDEPENDENT PLATOON, YOU FOLLOWED YOUR LEADER IN BATTLE.

NOW FOLLOW HIM TO A NEW LIFE.

COME OUT AND SELF-RENEW AT ONCE."

It had been recorded in Mandarin Chinese on a continuous tape, and it was to be played back through a bank of sixteen loud-speakers powered by a Diesel generator while the voice Dakota flew at just above stalling speed over the sector of jungle where the independent platoon was thought to be hiding.

The second plane had a message directed at one man, a suspected waverer:

"LI MUK. LI MUK. LI MUK.

WE KNOW YOU WOULD LIKE TO SELF-RENEW.

WHY DON'T YOU?

YOUR LEADER MISUSES YOU.

HE FORGETS YOUR YEARS OF LOYAL SERVICE.

LEAVE HIM.

COME OUT AND JOIN YOUR FRIENDS.

GOVERNMENT PROMISES YOU GOOD TREAT-MENT."

[1] A euphemism for 'surrender'.

The third message was for a C.T. section who at the moment were being hotly pursued by the S.A.S. in the Cameron Highlands area:

"HULLO NG TUNG, PA KU, CHI CHUNG.
HULLO CHUN LUEN, SIU SAN, NAM WA.
COUNT YOUR MISERIES.
FOOD CONTROL STARVES YOU.
MASSES TURN AWAY FROM YOU.
RAIN CHILLS YOU.
ORANG ASAL HAVE DESERTED YOU.
LEAVE THE WRETCHED JUNGLE."

Later, to study the C.T.-eliminating machinery at first-hand, I flew in the different types of aircraft on a variety of operations, and I visited the jungle forts. As a gauge of its efficiency, the Department of Information quoted me the total number of C.T. casualties as about 12,000, with another 2,000 still to be accounted for.

Richard's establishment had now increased to 110 field assistants, and over a hundred field staff, with fifteen assistant protectors, three protectors (one for each of the deep jungle states—Perak, Kelantan and Pahang), a quartermaster and headquarters clerical staff of sixty, and a medical and welfare section consisting of two doctors, a nurse, and twenty-seven dressers. The annual expenditure vote of the department was now $1,500,000.

Puteh, now a father of six, held a special appointment: that of senior field officer, functioning more or less as Richard's adjutant and personal contact man. He had been awarded the M.B.E. in 1955 for his services to the campaign.

Having won over to Government all but 300 'hostile' men,

women and children, the department was now rather more involved with the administration, protection and welfare of those under its control than the pursuit of those who were not, although of course the latter had top priority.

However, the first essential for the good administration of primitive peoples is a sound knowledge of them, and this, as Richard admitted, was still sadly lacking. When the department was first put on its Emergency footing all he had to go on, as a basis for his deep jungle strategy, were a few articles Pat had written, several reports he had submitted to Government, an account of his work in some early letters home, and a monograph he had published in 1936. Luckily the monograph was a thorough job. Not only did it provide all the requisite information on the breed and culture of the Ple-Temiar Senoi, but a demographic study of the population, in which most of the settlements were plotted on his map with the names of the senior headmen. Although Pat's census of the population was eighteen years old, he had given vital statistics concerning age distribution, sex ratio, marital indices, average size of family, fertility rates, differential survival values, and other factors bearing on fertility and elimination, which enabled Richard to arrive at a pretty fair approximation of the number of 'hostile' Temiar he had to contend with.

But he was far less fortunate with regard to the Semai Senoi, their ethnic cousins in the south. Although Semai culture followed the general Senoi pattern, comparatively little was known of their tribal personality. Their population was thought to be about 13,000, but details of its distribution were very sketchy.

A considerable amount of work had been done on the other aboriginal races of Malaya, yet for Richard's purposes at the time it was of little value. None of the observers appeared to have worried very much about such necessary administrative information as the correct name of the tribe, its exact location and the extent of its hereditary territory. Considerable confusion prevailed as a result of different writers using systems of nomenclature to suit themselves, and sometimes from deliberate falsification. For example, in one standard work a tribe is mentioned as "the Pago people of the south". Richard spent a lot of time, energy and money trying to locate this group only to discover in the end that it was nothing but a figment of the writer's imagination.

Richard's first job then was to start mapping the distribution of the aboriginal tribes of Malaya on huge maps made up of inch-to-the-mile topographical sheets joined together. There is very little jungle in the whole country that is not regarded as being owned by somebody, and so far he has more or less completed the jigsaw of tribal territories except for blanks in South Pahang, East Trengganu and South Kelantan. These blanks he is gradually filling by going into the areas himself and trying to meet the Negritos who inhabit them.

It was Pat who first upheld the right of the aborigines to the jungles they have inhabited for thousands of years: they were the original Malayans at the time when jungle stretched from coast to coast right across the entire Peninsula. Then came the Malays followed by the Chinese, Europeans and Indians, and more jungle has been alienated for rice and rubber and tin mines which leave ugly sterile gashes across the green pattern of the landscape. With each new wave of development and civilisation the aborigines have been driven farther back, and their jungles have been getting steadily smaller. There is no immediate danger, but if the encroachment continues the time will eventually come when there will not be sufficient jungle in Malaya to support its aborigine population.

It may be arguable that the aborigines could well be accommodated on open ground and fitted more productively into the national economy than they are at the moment. Yet, as Pat pointed out, this would not only constitute a violation of their individual and collective rights, but result almost certainly in their de-tribalisation or extinction.

Recent experience has shown how relatively easy it is to destroy a primitive group. It was found after resettlement, in which thousands of aborigines were moved from their hereditary jungles to other jungles often similar in practically every respect, that they were never really able to adapt themselves to their new environment, and many became homesick, or just lost heart and died.

The aborigine is a specialist at survival in terrain which holds terrors for most people from the outside. In the jungle he has the respect of these people: he is the equal of any man. But in the town his innocence and naïveté make him an object of ridicule, and for the first time in his life he knows what it is to feel inferior. Individual reactions vary, but usually if an aborigine is subjected for too long to this psychological disturbance, it leads in the end to an almost complete breakdown of his tribal personality, the process known as de-tribalisation. Twenty years ago, Pat recorded this corrosive effect on both the individual and the group. He had encountered cases of abortion and infanticide among groups exposed to the contact of alien cultures.

As he wrote: "Infanticide is not, to my knowledge, *normally* practised; the Temiar love their children and I should say it was unknown among the interior groups. . . . Among other primitive peoples the effects of infanticide are often explained away by reference to 'black magic', and it is remarkable that in Jalong, for instance, a very high proportion of deaths in infancy are attributed to *bajang*. *Bajang*, according to the Malays, is a form of sorcery practised by certain people, for which some Siamese know the antidote. It is described at Jalong as an evil influence conveyed by an insect like a grasshopper, with a red body and black teeth, which appears at night: its buzzing is greatly feared. The symptoms, as described by the people at Jalong, follow a certain course. The tongue becomes white and then yellow-brown, then it falls back into the throat, and the child becomes red in the face and dies of suffocation. I have not yet had a chance of seeing a case of *bajang*, so whether this forms a clinical picture which is familiar to a doctor remains to be seen. *Bajang* is definitely localised, since it was never quoted to me outside Jalong."[1]

Since then Richard has had ample opportunity to study the problem, for as he put it: "The spiv contact constitutes one of my major headaches."

One difficulty lies in the fact that the average aborigine is intelligent. Those who are sent to the fort schools are quick to learn, just as those who go to the towns after resettlement are quick to acquire a veneer of sophistication. They are to be seen occasionally in some big towns like Ipoh, either dressed as Malays, or exploiting themselves more or less as a tourist attraction, in full ceremonial dance regalia, some of the women being prepared, it is said, to expose their breasts to be photo- graphed—for a dollar. The pimps have been quick enough to recruit a number of pretty young girls as prostitutes to work in the brothels: the men also get a taste for the bright lights, and there have been instances where every adult in a group has become infected with V.D. within a short time.

There are other side effects of the amenities of civilisation. In the jungle the aborigine man has never been used to wearing

[1] *Report on the Settlements and Welfare of the Ple-Temiar Senoi of the Perak-Kelantan Watershed.*

anything more than a loin-cloth and the woman a sarong, both garments being made out of cloth obtained by barter from the trading post, or from the inner bark of the ipoh or the terap tree. (Fungus skirts are hardly used any longer.) They have no other protection, so that when it is cold at night on the high *ladang* the families sleep huddled together round their fires. When the deep jungle forts were put in, Barbara Penington encouraged the aborigine girls to wear brassières "because of the policemen", and the braves took to wearing shorts and singlets. The result was a spread of skin disease, because the brassières, shorts and singlets were communal property, and there were many cases of pneumonia, as it never occurred to the aborigines to take off their newly-acquired garments when they got wet.

But in Kilton Stewart's view—and he has visited several Temiar groups recently—the most disastrous impact on the aborigines has come from the political discord of the outside world. As he said: "First Pat Noone went round telling the groups the Japanese were bastards. Then the Communists went round saying the British were bastards. And now Dick Noone and his boys are going round contradicting them and saying, no, the Communists are bastards. It is hard to know yet but the result of all this may have proved psychologically disruptive. A few of the deep jungle groups who reaped rich rewards for services rendered have certainly been influenced by all the Western gimcracks they have been able to buy. One boy of twenty had a radio set—his group had been living on the dole for eight months because they had been very useful to Government, and it was now too unhealthy for them back in their own *saka*. I do not know where it will all end, but I think it is vital to preserve this culture. These Temiar are the only people in the world who have found the secret of harmonious co-existence."

Every effort is being made to preserve all the primitive cultures by the Department of Aborigines, but Richard has an enormous sociological task on his hands. Every 'hostile' group seeking Government protection has had to leave their *ladang*, and they have arrived at a fort, base-camp or natural outlet carrying all they possess and generally in need of food, medical attention and protection.

Feeding them presented no difficulty—the ration scale, mostly rice, costs only twenty-five cents per day per head. There was seldom any difficulty about shelter, as aborigines can build themselves a long-house in a matter of a few days. But from the outset something positive had to be done about their future.

Richard found that the worst thing was to allow them to become too dependent. Their morale would then go down, they would start worrying about ghosts and there was often trouble about women. Moreover if their state of dependence was extended over too long a period they usually stopped breeding.

The first step was to get them to settle and clear a *ladang* in some place well away from the vengeance of the terrorists whom they had deserted and informed against. To get them to agree to such a course often required heroic patience on the part of the field assistants.

The aborigine, unused to taking orders in his own total democracy, cannot be expected to do exactly what he is told or go just where he is directed. The wisdom of any decision affecting him has to be explained, or, better still, he must be made to think the original idea came from him. Richard's most successful field assistants were those who by skilful auto-suggestion could get an aborigine to dream the very action he was required to take.

At last a group would agree to move. A safe *saka* would be selected for them and the local groups consulted. But snags would invariably be found, not by the hosts, but by the refugees, who would either not care for a certain headman or not know any of the local spirits or think that so-and-so might cause trouble.

One important reason for getting an ex-'hostile' group into a safe area was to begin its brain-washing. It had to prove itself thoroughly on the side of Government before Richard would think of rearming the braves to undertake their own defence. His policy has always been to disturb the distribution of the groups as little as possible, but the ideal solution, that of putting rearmed groups back where they belong, has not always been possible. The C.T.s are still strong in some areas of deep jungle, moving out when the S.A.S. invade, but coming back again the moment the paratroopers are withdrawn. These C.T.s are gunning for the groups who betrayed them, and Richard is not prepared to risk a massacre.

Only rarely has he allowed a group to be evacuated to Kuala Lumpur. It has been necessary at times, but as soon as possible the group has been taken back into the jungle. Aborigines, he says, are never entirely happy away from it, never really secure outside the spiritual umbrella of a well-fortified group soul. Pat, who understood this psychological need, never kept Anjang out of the jungle and apart from her people for very long.

However, Richard has had to think of some way round the difficulty where his field staff are concerned. He began by waiving Government regulations stipulating only a fortnight's leave every year, so if a member of the field staff wanted to stay away longer for any reason of his own no attempt was made to dissuade him. Furthermore, he has formed all the field staff and their families at the Research Station into a group of their own, and engaged for them a well-known Temiar shaman, possibly the most powerful now that Dato Bintang is dead.

We visited the Research Station. From a flagstaff fluttered the regimental colours of the Senoi Praak:[1] crossed blow-pipes and quivers surmounted by the head of a seladang on a green background. Two Senoi were on guard, in jungle greens with red berets and armed with carbines, covering the approaches to the station on the river-side.

That night the Research Station group danced a dance called the Jinjang, led by Angah Sideh their new shaman. A number of dancers fell on the heaving floor in a trance, and, in the disassociated state following it Angah Sideh and a few of the men picked up burning pieces of wood and popped them into their mouths.

Later, Richard and I talked to Angah Sideh about Pat, whom he had known very well: indeed, the shaman's wife and Anjang were sisters, and what he has disclosed has filled in the gaps in her story.

She had stayed with her sister for a while after Uda had brought her back from the Telom valley and its bitter memories. But Anjang had changed. No longer was she the happy, if serious-minded girl her relatives had once known. She was sleeping with Uda, but, as she told her sister, he had threatened to kill her if she did not. He was having nightmares, and one night had got up suddenly and attempted to strangle her; fortunately some of the men of the group had run into their cubicle in the long-house and pulled him away from her. On another occasion he had attacked her while in a trance: his trances had become steadily more and more violent, and he had been asked by the group to desist from taking part in the dances.

He did not let her stay very long with her relatives, but took her with him from one group to another, until eventually they wound

---

[1] The Government of Malaya has since authorised Richard to raise three squadrons of sixty men each.

up at Legap. She was now suffering from her bronchial complaint, and from what is known she was too ill to move on any farther. There followed the cataclysm of resettlement, and she came down with the Legap group by raft to near Lasah. She died a couple of months later.

Richard had sent for Penghulu Ngah, whom we considered to be the most important witness in the inquiry, apart of course from the two who were actually present with Pat when he died. To our intense disappointment a message came back from Ngah's *ladang* that he was ill and could not come out to Kuala Lumpur.

"I know he's perfectly fit," Richard said. "But he just doesn't want to see me, and there's nothing we can do about it."

Then a few days later a message came from Toris, the young headman with the false teeth, that one of his relatives had actually been living with Ngah's group at the time that Pat had disappeared. The relative, who was now in the Ulu Jemheng, had told him the whole story of the killing, and was apparently prepared to repeat it to Richard.

Toris's message included an invitation to his settlement, and Richard sent the messenger back with the reply that we would come as soon as possible.

---

24 . Akob's Blow-pipe

Part of Richard's tour programme included his visiting the deep jungle groups either to establish or renew personal contact with the aborigines, so it was a simple matter to arrange an expedition to Toris's *ladang*.

The R.A.F. offered to fly us, with Raman, Richard's Javanese bodyguard, to Fort Kemar, in northern Perak, the nearest fort, but our escort of ten armed aborigines had to march in from the road-head at Grik, and they set out three days ahead of us. In that period I was fitted out with jungle greens, and issued with a carbine, sixty rounds of ammunition and a complete set of equipment. The C.T.s were reported fairly active where we were going, and the whole expedition was being conducted on the lines of a military operation.

The flight in an R.A.F. Pioneer took about an hour, and we came down through a funnel of cloud to land on a plateau just above the Temengor river. The plane taxied up to the entrance in the barbed wire enclosure, where the fort Police guard had turned out and were standing stiffly to attention with a mass of un-disciplined aborigines swarming round them.

We were met by the two European lieutenants: Bob Berry, the fort commander, and John Illingsworth, the platoon commander.

"I'm afraid your escort hasn't turned up," Berry said.

Kemar was very much like the other forts I had visited: a fortified locality with hutted accommodation for its garrison of thirty-five Field Force, and an aborigine clinic, school, club-hut and store. Articles on sale included sarongs, *parangs*, trinkets, lip-sticks, brassières, tooth-paste, tooth-brushes, razors and hair cream: but no food, candles, medicines, cotton-wool, bandages, footwear or articles of uniform, or anything else that would be of particular use to the C.T.s.

There was still no sign of our escort when Toris arrived at three o'clock in the afternoon with some of his kinsmen. They had come from their settlement expecting to meet us on the way.

Toris was worried. He pointed out that if we waited much longer we wouldn't be able to reach his place before nightfall. He added that the mountain trail was steep and slippery, and that swift-running rivers had to be forded, or crossed by felled tree-trunks, all of which was dangerous in the dark. He advised leaving right away, without the escort, and this we did: with our own carbines and two of the aborigines carrying shot-guns, Richard considered we had sufficient fire power to make the encounter hot enough for any C.T.s who thought of taking us on.

The track fell away steeply from the plateau on which the air-strip had been cut. Down we went, and immediately the jungle closed over us. We were in a dim twilight reeking of decayed vegetation and noisy with the metallic, clicking diapason of countless insects. Creepers trailed overhead, some like cords with sticky aerial roots, others fine threads that reached down and stroked your face with a slimy touch. Illingsworth had warned us the area was bad for leeches. They were on the track like strips of brown boot-lace an inch long, waving their wet, sightless sucking ends.

Toris led the way with one of the shot-guns, followed by Richard, Raman, myself, and a second armed aborigine whom Toris had appointed my temporary bodyguard. The remainder came straggling behind. Whenever I turned I looked into the grinning face of my bodyguard and the muzzle of the shot-gun he was carrying pointed at the small of my back. My repeated impulse was to put up my hands.

We climbed down to the Temengor river and followed it to where the Jemheng tumbled into it under the massive white trunk of a jungle giant that provided a bridge of some six feet in diameter near the base. We turned up the Jemheng, along a fairly wide path that crossed and re-crossed the river to pick the less difficult bank. We climbed a thousand feet, touching at two small settlements on the way, and just as it was getting dark we reached the *kuala* of a small stream called the Kabut.

The clicking insects were so near and clamorous they overruled the rough insistent roar of the river that had followed us all the way. Toris had taken us up a spur, and as we climbed near the top dim light began to appear in the oppressive canopy above us. Then, as we went up a little higher, we stepped at last into an oasis of late evening light and free unoppressed air—Toris's *ladang*, with the settlement to one side, a dim outline of untidy, flimsy structures full of flickering firelight and the shadows of crouching figures seen through the split-bamboo walls.

As we walked up towards the settlement, stepping over recumbent tree-trunks, a dog began barking. Then the group knew we had arrived and people were streaming out to find out what had kept us.

Toris had built a little guest-house for us, and here we put down our packs and carbines, and stripped to remove the leeches which were on our legs and shoulders and in the groin. I had always heard that the correct way to get a leech off was to touch it with a pinch of salt or the glowing tip of a cigarette; otherwise it left its teeth in the skin, causing the wound to fester. But my bodyguard began pulling them off and flicking each one neatly through the open window, over a bunch of eager faces filling the lower half. I left it entirely to him. He, if anyone, ought to know what to do about leeches.

Richard and I changed into vests and sarongs, had a couple of whiskies, and ate some fragrant hill rice which Toris's wife had cooked for us in bamboo, with a tin of stewed steak, and cheese, biscuits and coffee. Then, after we had eaten, our hosts crowded into the house for smokes and pow-pow, and that went on till the early hours of the morning, when the rumble of voices moved to the house next door, and they seemed to rumble on and on, and they could still be heard rumbling and muttering and hawking when the pale green dawn came in through the split-bamboo walls.

The Jemheng was red and swollen from the night's rain. I had bathed where a tree had crashed across and branches and other debris had dammed up the stream to form a pool among the rocks, and was walking back in my swimming trunks, with my towel and toilet bag. A few scrawny chickens were scratching among maize plants growing behind a hut. Under a thatched shelter, a couple of young girls were pounding rice in mortars hollowed out of a section of tree-trunk. A party of women, with back-baskets holding several sections of bamboo filled with water, were coming up from a clear little stream by the side of the *ladang*; like most aborigine women they affected a curious stiff-legged walk. Toris's eight-year-old son Da-ang was making faces at a baby.

At the guest-house Richard was making a list of Toris's require-ments: two goats, some ducks, some *changkols*, sickles, ground-nut and long bean seeds, tobacco plants, and a gong for the orchestra.

Then Awok, my bodyguard of the day before, appeared with his shot-gun. He was out of breath, and he spoke quickly to Toris, whose pleasant, cheery face suddenly became taut.

"He has just picked up the tracks of three or four C.T.s," Richard said. "The tracks were so fresh rain-water was still seeping into them. He says he could even smell the C.T.s."

A somewhat tense discussion ensued, the upshot of which was that six P.A.G.s would patrol the approaches to the *ladang*, as well as the high ground on the opposite bank of the river, from where any would-be sniper could get a commanding view of the guest-house. Richard also ruled that no one on the expedition was to go anywhere, even behind a tree, without a weapon.

Toris's chief anxiety was Kerenching. As he pointed out, every group for miles around would soon know that Richard was in the area, but only Kerenching's group were ever likely to inform the C.T.s.

I asked why, and Richard explained that Kerenching was unfortunately a case of gross mishandling by the Police. He had been a prominent Asal personality in the Ringat river area. But the first time he sought Government protection at Grik he was disarmed and locked up (he later escaped), and when in 1955 he again tried to come over to Government, and went up to Fort Kemar, the fort commander shouted at him and he ran away. Now Kerenching was firmly on the side of the C.T.s, and for two years he had resisted all Richard's attempts to win him over.

Our escort arrived that afternoon. One of them had hurt his leg, which was why they had been delayed. But as it was now too late to go up the Jemheng to see Toris's relative, we spent the rest of the day making a study of the settlement.

The *ladang* was about five acres in extent: a chaos of charred tree-trunks lying where they had fallen away from their stumps, with a rebirth of airy green tapioca coming up between. It supported the forty-four men, women and children of the settlement, which was in fact the largest in the Temengor area: there was a tendency here towards small splinter groups of three to four families breaking off from the parent group and opening up small plantations of their own, though they return every week or so to attend the principal ceremonial dances.

Another distinction of these northern Temiar lies in their architecture. Instead of one long-house, there were several houses in Toris's settlement, small ones occupied by single families, others a little larger for two or three families, and a fairly large T-shaped house in which seven families lived in cubicles and on platforms at different levels reached by log gangways. The walls were of vertical strips of split bamboo, though we did find some houses in the area with substantial anti-tiger walls of lengths of whole bamboo lashed horizontally to upright poles. Yet the most distinctive feature of all the local dwellings was not so much their shape as the fact that they were built flat on the ground instead of being raised up on stilts, as bamboo huts and houses are almost everywhere else in Malaya. Richard thought this might be due to the influence of the neighbouring Negritos to the north, as the admixture was fairly apparent.

One effect of a solid earth floor was that the group dancing that night induced none of the active audience participation which I had noticed in the Research Station long-house, where the springy floor conveyed the rhythm most forcibly to everybody. Here the crowding, solemn-faced spectators encroached on the dancing circle and pushed it rather out of shape. In a dim corner sat the orchestra of little doll-like creatures, their cheeks and foreheads painted with the lipsticks they had bought at the fort, some wearing brassières in deference to the occasion and Richard. Their music was pure bamboo melody: the gong, a Malay instrument, hadn't yet reached the settlement. But Toris had heard one in Kuala Lumpur, and soon another true Temiar orchestra would be violated.

The shaman (Uda) sat on his hunkers near the orchestra, improvising round the rhythm. It wasn't a religious occasion, merely a party to welcome us, and he sang of how the girls had spent the entire day making garlands and chains by cutting strips of palm leaf with razor blades. How they had collected aromatic wild mint and put it in their hair and above their ears. How some had put blue *chakah* flowers in their hair, others red *tanjong*, others white *sayoh*, others *sepaku*, others *gapeh*, and they had done all this because the *Tuan* Adviser had come to stay in their *ladang*, and four *penghulus* from other *ladangs* and many of their people had also come to see him. Then Uda sang of the rivers and the mountains they knew, and how good it was to live here in this *ulu*, how cool at nights, how gay the birds were in the trees, how few the mosquitoes. Though there were many flowers blooming in the tree-tops, so the bees were being a bit of a nuisance. Uda sang too of the rivers and spirits, and of the twin peaks, Relai and Kayoh, that were formed when two ancestors went fishing, and stuck their rods into the river bank, and fell asleep, and slept so long that their rods were petrified into limestone. Uda was still singing and the dancers were still dancing at four in the morning.

Next day we set out in full force up the Jemheng river. Toris led the way with Awok, followed by five of the escort, Khamis (Mah Meri), Aweh (Temiar), Giau (Jahai Negrito), Abdul (Temiar) and Mat Topo (Temiar), then Richard, Raman, and myself, and behind me the rest of the escort. Sireh (Kensieu Negrito), Jai (Jahai Negrito), Bah Nanuk (Semai) and Mat Jelebu (Aboriginal Malay). We climbed up a twisting track that ascended high above the river until its roar faded and the sound was eventually lost in a dark gorge tangled with trailing vegetation. Then the track too went down into the gorge till it touched the wet rocks, and crossed the river and re-crossed it.

Presently the Minchar came crashing in with water it had drained from Gunong Besar. Here the main track turned off up the Minchar: the route Pat and his entourage had taken on their terrible march south to escape the Japanese. But we continued up the Jemheng, going on another three miles to a clearing that suddenly raped the cool virgin gloom of the jungle with hot blinding sunlight.

Here was a stocky, anti-tiger house, half on the ground and half on stilts, with thick *bertam* thatch, and a door with a threshold. Nearby stood a sort of summer-house on stilts, and sitting cross-legged inside it were four young maidens with wild mint in their hair on either side of their faces. They were making mat baskets.

A man in a loin-cloth came out to meet us. He was Akob, whose statement we had come to get. He must have been about thirty, judging from his narrative: it was a strange and remarkable story, and here are extracts from the statement Richard prepared. It was read back to Akob and endorsed with his thumb imprint.

"When I was a young man and my virility was great, I dreamed I must go up over Gunong Besar and seek the longest piece of blow-pipe bamboo growing in the jungle to make for myself the most wonderful blow-pipe of all the Temiar. The best bamboo is *buloh seworr*, which is only found on the upper slopes of certain high mountains in the Ulu Perak and in the direction of the setting sun—it comes to us here along the ancient trade routes our ancestors used. But even this *buloh seworr*, was not long enough for me—for I had dreamed that my blow-pipe should be four times the length of my right arm.[1] So I went forth alone. I was afraid, for there were many tigers in the forest and I knew none of the spirits. But I needs must follow the *gunig* of my many dreams . . ."

He then described his adventures in search of the record *buloh seworr*. He went up over Gunong Besar and reached the Plus river, which he followed to its headwaters on the Kelantan Divide, crossing over and coming down the Ber river. On the

---

[1] The average length between internodes of good *buloh seworr* is seven feet: Akob wanted a barrel of roughly eight feet.

Ber he heard of very long *buloh seworr* on Bukit Senjort: he climbed Senjort, but although he found plenty of good blow-pipe barrels on it, none were four times the length of his arm. He went down into Pangoi's settlement which was then at Kuala Blatop, and the people there told him that Bukit Tajam was the place to try. Bukit Tajam lay high above a haunted pass leading over into Pahang, and with terror in his heart Akob went up and spent a night in the spectral moss forest believed to be the dwelling-place of the ghosts of dead Blatop chiefs who are buried there.

But Akob was not satisfied, so he followed the divide west-wards and tried on Gunong Swettenham, over 6,400 feet. Again the *buloh seworr* here was not quite long enough, so he came down into the Telom valley and reached Ngah's *ladang* where he decided he would stay for a time. Here he met a beautiful girl named Amoi and his search for his blow-pipe was forgotten while he courted her, and married her, paying the bride-price in many good lengths of *buloh seworr* he had cut on his adventure. Soon after his marriage Akob met Pat, who had just returned from Pulai with Anjang, Uda and Busu.

"They stayed in a little house near Ngah's *ladang*, and one day *Tuan* Tata asked me to help him repair the roof of the house, which was leaking. He spoke Temiar very well, and when I told him this he replied that he had become a Temiar, and would live for all time among the Temiar.

"He had no baggage with him, and wore only a pair of shorts and rubber-soled shoes. Attached to his belt was a revolver in a leather holster, and on the other side, wrapped in cloth, were some papers which I took to be writing of some kind. He always smoked a pipe, using the hill tobacco we grow in our *ladangs*.

"When I had repaired the roof he asked me if I would help Anjang to kill a chicken which they were going to eat. This I did. It seemed that the *tuan* was sick at the time.

"Next day Penghulu Ngah asked me to collect maize seed for planting in the *ladang*, and I therefore went to Kuala Ta-nai where there was some to be had. A week later I returned to Ngah's *ladang* and found that Tata was not there, although both Anjang and Uda were there. I asked where Tata was, but no one would tell me.

"After a few days I saw Busu in the jungle near the long-house. He was hiding in a little hut. He appeared to be very frightened and ran away when he saw me. So I went straight to Penghulu Ngah and asked him what had happened to Busu. I demanded to know the truth about Tata. I told him I was determined to find out, so he told me that Tata was dead—murdered by Uda and Busu, as Uda had had a dream that the *tuan* was going to make the Temiar fight the Japs and thus get us all killed. I asked him how the murder was done, and Penghulu Ngah said that the three men had set out together, leaving Anjang behind. When the party reached the Wi river they stopped for a rest, but, instead of sitting down as Tata did, both Uda and Busu cut staves for themselves out of *rokap* wood, which as you know is very hard and thorny.

"*Tuan* Tata asked what they were doing, but Uda, it seems, approached him with a menacing expression. Seeing him thus about to attack, Tata drew out his revolver and held him at bay, whereupon Busu by throwing his staff knocked the revolver out of Tata's hand. Then Uda quickly took a dart from his quiver and put it into his blow-pipe, and, realising what he intended to do, Tata fled in the direction from which they had come, with Uda running after him. Busu, it appears, called out to Uda to desist from his purpose, but Uda did not listen to him. Busu hung back, but when he heard a loud cry from Tata he ran up to find that one of Uda's darts had struck him in the eye. Two other darts were in his right thigh, and he was vomiting. He knew he was dying, for he cried out that his people would avenge what they had done. Uda then killed him with a stroke of his *parang*.

"Having told me all this, Penghulu Ngah warned me that I must never tell anyone about the murder, as although the information had been passed on, the whole thing was now taboo. Shortly after this, a Semai named Apung, who lived near the Cameron Highlands road and who I believe is still there, stone deaf, told the One-Eyed Along of Kuala Kerla,[1] that *Tuan* Noone was still alive. The story was that he had walked out of his grave and was somewhere in the upper Telom area. When this news reached Uda he became very frightened, and going straight to the grave, dug it up, only to find the body still there. Nevertheless, he was being pursued by Tata's ghost, who entered his dreams and whom he could not conquer. So to try and escape he went away into Perak. I believe he took the unfortunate Anjang with him, but I had already left the Telom valley by that time, taking Amoi with me."

Akob had finished his story, and Richard, who had been writing it down in Malay, handed the book and pencil to Raman, and went out into the sunlit *ladang* where he sat on a tree-trunk and smoked a cigarette.

I turned to Akob and asked him through Raman: "Did you ever find that single blow-pipe bamboo four times the length of your arm?"

"Yes, I found it," Akob said.

He went on to explain how he had told Pat of his quest, who replied that he once knew another youth in the Ulu Brok, a youth very like him, who was also seeking the longest blow-pipe in the jungle.

Akob had asked if he had ever found it, and Pat said yes, he had

[1] Shot by the C.T.s in 1955.

met the youth again some time later, and examined the blow-pipe. It was certainly the longest he had ever seen.

"It was not just two bamboos joined together?"

"No," Pat had said. "It was one single bamboo at least four times the length of your right arm."

"Where did the youth seek it?" Akob had asked.

"He had gone up the Blatop river to the mountain on which it finds its source (Swettenham)."

"But, *Tuan*, I have already tried there."

"Try again," Pat had advised.

So, when Akob was taking his young bride back to his family *ladang* in the north, they went up and searched on Swettenham, and here at last he found the blow-pipe of his dreams.

---

25 . *Ngah Comes Across*

We stayed two weeks in the area, based at Toris's settlement, from where we made trips to the outlying groups, staying a day or two with each. We went to Penghulu Asoh's *ladang* on the Lanweng river, to Penghulu Ngah Gading's, a little above Akob's place, to Penghulu Pandak's in the Ulu Temengor, to Penghulu Anjang's just below Fort Kemar.

We met the people and filmed them going about their daily work. We photographed the different racial types. We recorded their music and songs. We drew plans of their houses. We measured their blow-pipes and made imprints of the decorative patterns on the blow-pipe handles and on the quivers. We made word lists and notes on magico-religious beliefs, and bought various objects for the museums under Richard's control.

Actually, Richard said, our research was not being conducted in accordance with the approved anthropological method: he should have selected one group for intensive study by a departmental team of anthropologists, so that other groups could then be compared against it and a picture built up of the entire race. That he hopes will be possible when times are normal again. Meanwhile he has to content himself with a general survey of the culture and dialects.

At last the time came for us to leave the Jemheng. As Richard wanted to visit some groups lower down the Temengor river, we were going to travel out by raft to Grik, a journey Pat had made on several occasions. The five headmen of the area, with some eighty men, women and children from their groups were coming too. They had cut hundreds of nine-foot lengths of *rotan* to trade in at Grik: the lot could have been taken down-river by a dozen men; the others had jumped on the band wagon.

On 29th April we set out from below Kuala Jemheng where, in a large, dark pool, some thirty-five bamboo rafts had been constructed: small up-river rafts each of twelve to fourteen bamboos twenty-five-feet long, with a low platform in the middle for two or three passengers or an equivalent weight of cargo, and steered by two raftsmen with poles, one at either end.

In view of the possibility of an ambush, and our vulnerability while sitting on rafts out on the open river, Richard thought it advisable that he and I should travel on separate rafts, with all the rafts forty to fifty yards apart. Our party led the way, with four of the escort on the first two rafts, then Richard with Raman and Aweh on the third raft, myself with Khamis on the fourth, the remaining four escort aborigines on the fifth and sixth, and our three baggage rafts behind them. Following in the rear came our support party, determined, it appeared, to make this the junket of the season.

The journey took five days. We begin at a fairly good pace, with spurts of speed as we darted through rapids and shallows, the steersmen prodding the rocks and boulders with their poles to head the rafts through negotiable channels, and muttering quietly to the local spirits for help.

We float down luxuriant green canyons, so narrow at first that in places we have to part aside curtains of trailing vegetation in order to pass through. Acres of bamboo cover the precipitous banks, the young fast-growing shoots thrusting upwards for seventy to eighty feet before the points taper off to bend like obedient fishing rods on a seaside pier. Later the leaves will come out, and the bamboos dip lower and lower with the increasing weight of foliage, until finally they crack and fall over, trailing their pointed finger-tips in the stream.

There is a wonderful variety in the pattern and animation of the scene round every bend in the river. New vistas keep unfolding, endless permutations of trees, palms, lianas, flowers and the insistent and ubiquitous bamboo, with galleries of enormous ferns and lusty maidenhair occurring here and there, and patches of water lilies, red, blue, white and fleshy pink inhabiting the flatter banks. There is *tepus* (wild ginger) with its sexy scarlet and black flowers and its sword-shaped leaves, and *serinden*, with its creamy pineapple-shaped flowers and tall graceful leaves used in Siti Minang's Chinchem dance.

There are trees struggling in the coils of *rotan*, trees with smooth white trunks garbed in oddly fashionable creations of trailing parasitic growths, high solitary trees rising from cliff faces draped with creepers of massed flame- and orange-coloured flowers, trees canopied with scarlet waxy bells, *jambu* trees covered in white flowers like burst powder-puffs with red hearts.

The river too is full of surprises. Little sandy islands suddenly appear out of rippling stretches of water alight with the sun, landscaped with boulders and beeches and willow-like bushes and sometimes ornamental trees, with shallows rattling and swirling over smooth pebbles, and occasionally the leap of a fish.

Then there are quiet, still stretches when sounds die on the water and you drift very slowly, aware of the occasional plop of a raftsman's pole in the stream, aware that your seat is wet because the raft has often been submerged and that the sitting platform is particularly hard.

The wet bamboos have dried quickly, for the sun is blistering hot, and the carbine you are holding at the ready is almost untouchable. You curse the C.T.s for stealing this beauty, for your eyes should be focused past the wall of the jungle, searching the gloom for the ugly nostrils of shot-guns or the muzzles of the Sten-guns and Bren-guns the bastards never returned.

A bird screeches somewhere in the forest and you look up to see a hornbill helicopting awkwardly from one of the slopes across to the other. Swiftlets with retractable undercarriage are darting about in an orgy of flight. Again the plop of the raftsman's pole. A bright blue dragonfly has settled on the upper tip of it, and you notice the man's knotted calf muscles, the naked brown buttocks, and the *parang* stuck through his loin-cloth at his waist. He is Penghulu Asoh, who guided Pat on the terrible march, taking him on from the Jemheng right as far as Lasah.

Ahead of us Richard's raftsmen are poling frantically, and now faintly at first, then getting louder, we hear the roar of the next rapids. An island approaches, an island with a *jambu* tree—a *jambu* tree leaning over an odd little patch of water, where, by a freak of currents, the surface is undisturbed, and *jambu* petals are floating on it as still as in a Chinese painting. Butterflies swarm round a fallen fruit. High up against the grey wall of a cliff a solitary tree is shedding leaves: it is a moment of autumn for that tree, a very personal autumn for there is only one perpetual season in a tropical jungle.

Then we swing through the rapids at a good ten knots over a number of low-pouring shelves. We have descended thirty feet, and the river is a little slower and wider and steadier below it.

A little farther downstream we passed under a length of *rotan* stretched across the river, then along the bank by a series of levers to a little hut. A man was sitting in the hut, waiting for a tug on the *rotan* which was connected at the other end to a fish trap. When a fish entered the trap he would shut it by giving the *rotan* a hard pull.

Next an abandoned *ladang* appeared round the bend, thick with secondary jungle already up to the high stumps, and presently we came upon the current plantation with a settlement of neat thatched houses. Already the people were running down the bank to meet us.

The main house was an architectural gem, partly in full contact with the ground and partly on stilts at three different levels, so that at each elevation it seemed an entirely different house. The walls, constructed variously of split and slit bamboo, palm matting and even whole bamboo, either vertically or horizontally, with a subtle placing of square or oblong windows, completed the baffling effect. Inside the house, the families were living on seven different levels, so contrived that no cubicle was immediately above anybody else's living space, and the impression was of a poetic, almost surrealistic use of bamboo. There were mechanical inventions everywhere: ingenious fish-traps and pig-traps, exquisite bird cages made out of a single length of bamboo, slit and ribbed, the parts being held together with neat *rotan* lashings, and decorations, puzzles and fetishes, all dream-inspired. Oddly, however, these gadget-conscious people had not yet discovered the ladder, for all the family flats in their main apartment house were approached by ramps or gangways.

Three miles farther on we reached the settlement of Penghulu Ulu Balang. He had built us a charming little guest-house, as it had been planned that we should all spend the night at his settlement. But Ulu Balang himself was not there to receive us: he had left for Grik, we were told, the day before. This seemed very strange, since he knew we were coming, and Richard and Toris drew their own conclusions.

Richard pointed to the *ladang*: it was about thirty acres, though the group itself numbered no more than forty people. We walked over it picking our way between the fallen tree-trunks and the naked stumps. Richard found the evidence he was looking for: tree-stumps that had been sawn across instead of chopped.

"C.T.s have been helping to clear this *ladang*," he said. "Aborigines never use a saw."

He thought better of staying with people who were obviously playing a double game, and we went on past the mouth of the Krim river to a site where we camped for two days while bigger rafts were constructed for the wide deeper reaches of the next part of our journey.

Each big raft was twenty-four bamboos wide and about fifty feet long, with a second deck of twenty-four bamboos pushed under and lashed to cross-pieces for added buoyancy. Amidships was a fairly elaborate sitting platform with a railing and thatch canopy to keep off the sun, and the raft was navigated by four men operating giant sweeps made of long bamboos with slit bamboo blades. They were lashed to high rowlocks, in pairs fore and aft.

At five that evening we came out into the wide-open Perak river, bathed in dazzling sunlight. Just north of the *kuala* was the village where Pat had buried his thirteen boxes of research material.

We camped on a sandy beach opposite the entrance of the Temengor. We had acquired twenty-seven chickens on the way, and these formed the basis of a feast we all had that night, with piles of rice, tapioca, bananas and fern tips.

Next day we went across to the village: it was derelict and overgrown, as the inhabitants had been resettled elsewhere. We had come to see if the Japs had possibly overlooked any of Pat's boxes. Puteh had given us a rough idea of where they had been buried, and we spent the entire day digging and probing about, but without any luck.

Then the following morning we began the final leg of the river trip, on which we were to have what was listed as an 'incident—minor' in the Emergency situation report.

The Perak river here was a considerable volume of water which suddenly began a speedy descent over a wide bed of black igneous rock, splitting up and rushing through a multitude of noisy channels. Success in negotiating the river depended on knowing the right channel, and all the way down we saw evidence of the fact that aborigine navigators were not always infallible: wrecks of old rafts were piled up on the rocks, their yellow, dried-out bamboos tangled, like heaps of match-sticks tipped out of a box. Here and there a huge trunk of valuable timber lay high up on the rocks, left there in some past flood. We passed noisy sucking whirlpools, and spouts where water came up bubbling and drumming out of holes in the rock beneath.

The light was good, because the jungle fell back before wide banks of tall tiger-grass, and Richard, who had got on to my raft at Kuala Temengor, began filming. It slowed us up considerably because he would go up on to the bank to select a vantage point from which to 'shoot' the procession of rafts drifting past. But we had all day to cover only thirteen miles to Kendrong, where we would be met by departmental transport to take us on to Grik.

At about noon we were nearing Kuala Ringat. Soon after that we drifted into an extended rapid, and the raftsmen were rowing energetically to guide us into a channel near to the left bank. We made it just as we were rounding a bend under a high rock outcrop, and now the raftsmen were rowing the opposite way to correct our position somewhat. I remember as we cleared the rock we were touched by a light up-river breeze which began fluttering the leaves in our platform canopy.

I think it was just then that I heard the shooting. It came from up the bank, and a moment later I was deafened by the sound of firing near my left ear as the aborigine sitting on guard on the port side of the raft opened up with his carbine. Almost immediately other members of the escort also opened fire, and I noticed that the raftsmen in front had let go of their sweeps and were crouching, holding their heads.

I stood up on deck as I could not see from under the canopy, and I began firing at a clump of boulders a little way up the bank.

There was a sudden shuddering jolt, with the sound of cracking bamboos, as our prow rode up over a rock against the bank. The deck lurched and I fell backwards into the water. I had a glimpse, as I was being taken along, of the raft lifted high on the rock and the escort scrambling on to it.

I got into an eddy in the lee of the rocks, touched ground under my feet, and splashed up to the bank, where I crouched panting behind some long grass. One of the raftsmen came out of the water next to me. There was a lot of firing farther up along the bank, and after a few minutes it dawned on me that no reply seemed to be coming from our attackers' position. Then I saw three of the escort running forward, bent double, and I went out following them.

The C.T.s had gone after we got to their position after firing a long burst into it: their empty cartridge cases were left scattered about. We ran on into a dip where the tiger-grass closed over our heads, and we milled about, blindly at first, unable at times to move, cut and scratched by the tough sharp blades.

Then I saw Aweh going past me. He was clearing a wide path by throwing himself on the grass with his carbine held above his head with both hands, and as the grass went down beneath his weight he would leap on to the next lot in front of him. I followed behind him, and we emerged at the bottom of a slope that rose out of the grass into thick bamboo. We went up, firing into each clump or cover before we reached it. There were no tracks at all.

Presently Richard arrived with Raman: both were barefooted as they hadn't put on their boots that morning. We went on up in two sections, and reached a ridge some 300 feet above the river. Here after a time Aweh picked up the tracks of about four men: two or three wearing rubber-soled shoes, and one barefooted and therefore presumably an aborigine.

We pursued the tracks along the ridge for a couple of miles, then straight down hill to a stream where we lost them. We continued splashing up the stream, with the scouts searching the banks for an indication of where the C.T.s might have left it, but we drew a blank, and finally Richard called off the chase. As he said, even assuming we did pick up the trail again, we did not have the necessary food for a determined follow-up which might take even weeks without necessarily resulting in a kill.

We returned to where all the rafts were moored, near our wrecked one, with the aborigines aboard them stupefied with horror. The raft was repaired and we continued to a sandy island, a few miles farther on, where we camped for the night.

We discussed the attack by flickering firelight. Richard was inclined to think that some C.T.s, possibly on their way to Siam, had seen what they took to be a police patrol as they were about to cross the river, and just could not resist such a defenceless target as a raft being taken along through a rapid, having been on the run themselves for so long in the jungle war. However, by the fortunate accident of our running up on the rocks, we had been able to counter-attack quickly, and the C.T.s finding themselves in danger of being outflanked had hurriedly withdrawn. We were fortunate, he added, that the C.T.s were notoriously such bad shots, having neither the spare ammunition nor the opportunity for target practice: as far as we could make out only two bullets had hit the raft and their range could not have been more than fifty yards.

Only the bare facts appeared in the Combined Police/Military Daily Situation Report, Serial Number 3109, dated 6th May 1957:

"GRIK. 3 May (VE 122671). A party of Department of Aborigine personnel while rafting down Sungei Perak were fired on by three/four C.T.s using Sten-guns and carbines. The party returned the fire and followed up, but later lost track of the C.T.s who made good their escape. No known casualties."

When we got back to Kuala Lumpur, Ali was standing in the porch of Richard's house. He touched his forehead in greeting and spoke to Richard in Malay.

"You'll never guess who's waiting to see me," Richard said excitedly. "Our prime witness Penghulu Ngah."

"So he's feeling better."

"He probably knows I know everything at this stage. He's thought it over and decided he'd better come across or else he might be involved himself in the murder. He's a wily old scrounger."

Ngah and one of his relatives were smoking cigarettes and drinking orange squash in Richard's study. The headman was about sixty, and he wore a khaki shirt and a pair of shorts, with a cloth band tied round his forehead. His grey hair was closely cropped and he had an untidy grey moustache. He could barely speak at first he was so taut and strung up with fear, and the first ten minutes or so he spent describing the stomach disorder, fever and chest trouble that had kept him from coming to see Richard when first summoned. If he had arrived with any doubts about telling Richard the whole truth, these were dispelled the moment he heard how we had been up into the Ulu Jemheng and obtained Akob's statement.

That evening Ngah too made a statement, adding his right thumb-print at the bottom of the document. It reads:

"I followed your brother for many years before the war. He took me on journeys and looked after me very well in those days. Then came the Japanese and your brother fell upon difficult times. I gave him a lot of things—shoes, a shaving mirror, a pair of sun-glasses and a comb. He gave me a gun and I went hunting for him so that he could have food . . . I gave him wild pig, fish from the rivers which I caught myself, and my own chickens; sometimes he would go away but he always returned to my house. I loved him. I was then living near Kuala Rening on the Telom river. Then one day your brother disappeared. He disappeared from my territory, *Tuan*. He disappeared from my house, *Tuan*.

He was not in anyone else's area but mine, *Tuan*. I ask your forgiveness, for he was in my area when he disappeared, and I was headman when it happened, a terrible fault to admit. Please forgive me, *Tuan*. Now I will tell you everything. It was Uda . . ."

He then repeated the story of the killing as he had told Akob.

"When Uda returned to my house I asked him where Tata was. He replied, 'Don't ask me. Your heart and my heart are not the same.' I forced Uda to take me to the spot and there I found the body. 'Why did you kill him?' I said. 'What harm did he ever do to you?' But the killer ran away, and I fell to the ground and wept. I was so ashamed to think that one of my own people should have committed this horrible crime against the only man who had ever helped us, and who was father to us all. . . Yes, your brother had a pistol, but Uda threw it into the river. After some months he took Anjang away into Perak, and from that day to this he has never returned to us."

Ngah and his relative went and Richard and I sat up discussing the evidence. The headman had promised to provide several other witnesses from the group, who had actually seen the body stuck with two darts in the thigh (Pat had pulled out the one in his eye), and the *parang* wound.

There was more than enough evidence now to convict Uda, but as Richard pointed out there are worse punishments for an aborigine who has committed such a crime than any the law provides. Particularly in the case of a Temiar, since violence and disloyalty are so much against his nature. He can never quite escape from his conscience no matter how long he lives, nor free himself from the memory and horror of the act as he has no means at all of expiating it and staying alive. He cannot count on the spirits for help. No *gunig* will ever enter his dreams, and his trances remain the violent trances of one whom only malevolent spirits succeed in possessing. Thus he cannot participate in the spiritual life of a group or hope to obtain benefit from the occult guidance on which the Temiar depend. All his life he must contend alone against nature and against the forces impelling him towards his nemesis, which is a particularly horrible death by bamboo.

A length of bamboo can only be cut with an oblique stroke which leaves a sharp stump sticking out of the ground. The Temiar nemesis is to fall upon one of these stumps in such a way that the bamboo enters the anus and the victim is impaled. Pat had once told Richard that he had heard of rare cases where men had been found thus impaled, suggesting the possibility of an act of expiatory suicide committed by falling on to a stump from an overhanging branch of a tree. Pat had found it difficult to imagine how the angle of penetration imposed by the nemesis could otherwise be attained.

Uda's whereabouts are not known. If he is alive it is more than likely that he has changed his name and identity, and is living with one of the 'hostile' groups or the C.T.s. But his impulse must be to keep on the move, seeking some place where the spirits will not know what he has done, and perhaps where some local *gunig* may be prepared to haunt his dreams. At the back of his mind too will be the fear of what he probably believes will eventually be his lot, for Pat cried out as he died that his people would avenge him, and to Uda's way of thinking, by *his* people Pat undoubtedly meant the Temiar.

The dying acquire prophetic powers, according to the Temiar belief. Many of their epic stories have as their theme the necessity for fulfilling a last wish and the inevitability of a man's last words. At the moment of delivering the final *parang* stroke, Uda would have been aware that Pat had already sentenced him to death.

Richard closed the file. "As far as I'm concerned the mystery of my brother's disappearance is solved to my complete satisfaction," he said.

"And Uda?"

He thought for a while. Then he said: "You know, something tells me that justice has been done, but whether through the spirits or by the Temiar we shall never know. Remember Toris's words when he quoted the Temiar law: 'The killer's name shall be taboo, and that of his executioner shall be told to no one.' "

One further document was added to the file. It came from Achok, the headman at Kuala Bertam on the Telom river. He was invited to Kuala Lumpur along with five hundred other aborigines for the Independence celebrations in August. He approached Richard on the night of the big feast and dance held at the Research Station.

"*Tuan*," he said, "do you remember when we last met?"

"Wasn't it at Kuala Misong during Operation Valiant?"

"Yes, *Tuan*," Achok replied. "You asked me then about your brother, but I am ashamed to say I lied to you then. I lied, *Tuan*, because I was afraid. That is the only reason, because I loved your brother very much. He took me with him to Pulai and he stayed at my *ladang*."

"I understand, Penghulu Achok. I know how things were. There was a taboo on the matter and you could not speak."

"But now I can give you something which your brother told me to keep. He said that even if he should die his family would honour the promise. I have kept this thing all these years in my loin-cloth."

"What is it, Penghulu Achok?"

"It is a letter, *Tuan*," Achok said, producing a scrap of paper from the folds of his loin-cloth. He carefully opened the paper and handed it to Richard, who looked at it in the flickering light of a hearth fire. It was tattered and slightly charred, but the writing though faded was quite clear. The letter read:

"I, the undersigned, hereby state that I have purchased the bearer's gun for the sum of fifteen dollars; and furthermore, guarantee to replace the gun with another gun in good condition after the war. There is no liability for the bearer to repay the fifteen dollars to me.

"H.D.N."

Achok explained that he had offered his shot-gun to Pat, who had insisted on paying a fair price. But since he had only fifteen dollars he had given Achok the promissory note.

Richard asked Achok to come to see him at his house so that they could discuss the matter further, and the headman turned up the following evening.

"Penghulu Achok," Richard said, "my brother has promised that you should be given a good gun. I will give you one, unless you prefer to have the money instead."

Achok opted for the money, and Richard gave him seventy dollars, the price of a new shot-gun.

Richard kept the scrap of paper. It was typical of Pat that the last intimation of him from the jungle should come in the form of an account outstanding. It was just like old times paying Pat's debts.